Give him
for Dick Frederick

Give him, if you will,
the sanctuary he gave to nesting swans,
their snow-stormed plumage to rest in
alongside their tucked heads, their span
of flight, two by loyal two, their breath.
He needs the white arch of their necks
over his new life of death.

Give him epitaphs,
reed-edged, of moorhens
as they dip their nibs into the murky pond;
and ruffled manuscripts composed
by webbed feet through water,
that pin to banks bygone bonds.

Give him no palaver;
just a goose-wing to sweep away
grief, the antlers of that forest stag

hung from a hangar one day –
needed now to hang memories upon.
His bench from which he steadied vistas
will prove he has not gone.

Give him coppices, the trees
he felled. He will resurrect their crowns
for oaks, ash and beech to stand
to attention, like they did for him,
sentinels reinstated where shock
has ploughed up the land.

Give him the stretched horizon
to pull taut, that he might herd into its pen
the clouds scattering like sheep,
every dog of his brought to heel again.
He will manage the downs, the sky,
push aside the wind to shift cliffs of sea
from chalk cliffs, star-high.

Give him the heavy horse and hoe:
no machine, and the world to shoulder.
He is still that ram, shield, boulder
axe of a man, gentling all in his care.
His footprints carpet his rooms.
His stillness and silence fill the air.

Give him fireside tellers
for his stories, and leg-pullers who twist
his teases, then tease the twists,
getting their own back on him at last
where he is suddenly missed.
Lay him a place at table and in his gap
he will rattle a tin plate of grist.

Give him back the fields he worked
so he can be worked into them differently
with no respect for boundaries.
He will give them back to us
when we lean over five-bar gates,
drawn to him in his great infinity.

Patricia McCarthy

The Ropery
for Kathleen McCarthy

It was always there: the ropery.
Her grandfather had plaited the river
into a rescue-rope for his progeny –
twisting ivy in the trees at Waterside
into hammocks for the wind, her guide.

With the best corders, she paced
the walk before barges in full sail –
through old wives' tales of wastes
in hemp, discounting the unvaried miles
of lines hung from a stiff wheel.

And the river grew with her into a sea –
laying itself, a cable, beneath ropes
that thrashed and coiled for her delivery,
taking on the strength of eighty men
so that she could make a voyage alone

to the Orient on the Blue Star Line,
Marseille, Penang, Colombo, Hongkong
and ropes of an Empire doused in wine.
Natural then that a sailor should come
with a fishing net like those at home

to where, a mermaid not, she nursed
cholera, smallpox, all dressed in white,
and he, a different spinner, hackled
soft yarns for the arch of the swords
under which she went, proud, his bride.

Then the escape through Indo-China seas
from internment that proved no relief.
The last blacked-out ship and enemies;
the miscarriage in the typhoon – while
her river, serene as the protesting Nile,

showed a zigzag route through Curaçao,
cutting its own straits before Panama:
jute, flax and horsehair in the bows.
Steeping bundles of her experience
in unconsciously-resumed local accents –

from the mill-site, waist thickened,
she walks backwards, a corder again,
marking her tides on banks that bend
away now from sepias of pastoral scenes,
importing pollution, not locust-beans.

And under the trees pared by a knife
to t-shaped gallows, she winds up
the main threads of a lived-in life.
A grandfather's girl's: the river –
bound to continue after binding her.

Patricia McCarthy

This poem is from *A Second Skin*, printed here by kind permission of
Harry Chambers, Peterloo Poets

AGENDA

CONTENTS

TRANSLATIONS OF ESSAYS IN FRENCH ON RILKE

REVIEWS

Front cover:

Wood-cut by **Caroline Trant**, an artist, formerly a painter, now making Artists' Books under the Parvenu Press. Over the last ten years she has worked with poets such as David Harsent, Peter Abbs, Judith Kazantzis, James Simpson sand Nicki Jakowska, in books where words and images form parallel texts. She has also produced a book of Lorca's Sonnets of Dark Love with texts and images cut in wood. She also uses her own texts in more theatrical and sculptural book installations. http://carolyntrantparvenu.blogspot.com shows images of her work and details of where she is exhibiting. Or contact mail to:parvenu.c@ukonline.co.uk

Editorial

Welcome to this special double issue of *Agenda* on Rainer Maria Rilke which appreciates Rilke in English through new translations/versions of Rilke's own poems; through translations from the French of essays on Rilke; through poems written to, on and for Rilke; through essays, reviews, and through the work of two chosen young **Broadsheet** poets and the usual **Notes for Broadsheet Poets,** this time focusing on extracts from Stephen Cohn's translation of Rilke's manual for young poets: his insufficiently known *Letters to a Young Poet,* and on Don Paterson's 'Fourteen Notes' on his recently published *Orpheus, A Version of Rainer Maria Rilke* (Faber).

In a letter written to Ernst Schellenberg from Paris on 2 September, 1907, almost one hundred years ago, Rilke demonstrates that he himself did not like criticism, not particularly for personal reasons, but because he felt that the 'just and unjust remarks' made by any critic would insert themselves 'like foreign bodies' between him and his work, getting rid of 'the unconscious elements in this inward and intimate relationship which binds the workman in so recondite and enigmatic a manner to his work to its past and to the future that awaits it'. He felt strongly that the universal unconsciousness in what the artist is undertaking is imperilled by criticism and therefore he regarded criticism with suspicion 'as a letter to the public which the author ... ought not to open and read'.

The 'critics' in this issue can more aptly be called 'celebrants' who pay reverence to and illuminate for those less initiated than themselves the extraordinarily powerful work of this poet. Hence I am sure Rilke would approve!

Thanks to the above contributors, and also to all readers and subscribers who of course contribute silently and humbly with their own voices and selves. According to Rilke, the task of all humankind is to be translators, singing, praising and unifying transformation. Karen Leeder of New College, Oxford, endorses this by stressing, in her Introduction to Martyn Crucefix's recently published translations of the *Duino Elegies* (see introductory essay for the review), 'Rilke in fact insists that all human beings share the ability to translate the world'. Indeed, we are all translators of a sort.

Thanks also to the Arts Council of England, and to the Po-shing Woo Foundation for making this double special issue possible.

*   *   *

Up to you all, then, to perform multiple works of translations of translations within this issue and to be inspired to delve further into the fascination that Rilke will always exert. Readers might be interested to take on the interesting exercise of comparing some of the translations/versions in this issue, and of comparing translations/versions published here with the corresponding works already published in book form. This is an illuminating task in the process of translation.

Marcus Frederick   Patricia McCarthy

Introduction

Why is it that the fascination for Rilke never seems to diminish? Why has he had such a profound influence on European poetry, and on poetry written in English in particular? Born in 1875, ten years after W.B. Yeats and ten years before Ezra Pound, why, outside German-speaking Europe, has he such a name? Why is *Agenda* now dedicating an issue to him?

Several possible reasons come to mind. Modernism had made its mark in Britain and America with Eliot and Pound, but it could be said that the movement was basically French and, when 'filtered through scraps of Provençal' made Dante more important than Shakespeare; hence the French influence was not liked by everyone. When the J.B. Leishman and Stephen Spender translations were published by the Hogarth Press in the 1930s, they made a great impact and delivered something completely new and serious in poetry, different from Pound and Eliot, even though parallels can be drawn between Eliot's *Four Quartets* and Rilke's *Duino Elegies* in terms of the way the images develop and symbolically intensify the spiritual transcendence or redemption of man. In his essay in this issue, Manfred Engel makes further interesting connections between the two poets.

Rilke, with what Patrick Bridgwater calls his 'incurably poetic personality', certainly managed to produce a fresh language which expressed the inseparability of intellect and emotion, and of the interior and the exterior, offering great insights into our own mortality and what it means to be human. William H. Gass noted this: that with Rilke 'everything (life and death, for instance) lies on a continuum as colours do'.

In Stephen Cohn's words, it was 'as if the Singing God had handed him a key', with the rhythmical force of his work an intrinsic part of the meaning, and the texture of his language pushing, almost, beyond language. Marjorie Perloff endorses Rilke's popularity: 'It is Rilke's invention of a language abstract, detached, meditative – and also profoundly erotic. No English or American contemporary of Rilke's has produced anything quite like it'. The German poet, Durs Grünbein, in an unpublished essay translated for me by Luke Fischer and Lutz Näfelt, 'Ein kleines blaues Mädchen: 'Das Karussell'. Ein Rilke-Manuskript im Marbacher Literaturarchiv', also praises Rilke's great discovery, learned presumably from Rodin and painters such as Cézanne, that the plasticity of the imagined could be achieved by refining images of movement, with 'the conscious running direction of the line, and the proper torque of a verse that enables the poet to circle around his object and to record it from various angles'. Durs praises the way Rilke can jump from Cubism to Impressionism in a line.

Sean O'Brien, himself a considerable poet and translator of Rilke, suggests that a reason for some very gifted poets being drawn to tackle Rilke translations/versions 'lies in Rilke's insistence that poetry is not something other than poetry'.

Rilke made a considerable impact on English poetry and influenced, on both sides of the Atlantic, among others, W.H. Auden (who first of all said that 'the things bless him', and Rilke's *Sonnets to Orpheus* inspired Auden's 'Journey to a War'. However, he later rejected him because he considered him too far on the side of death rather than of life, and damned him in a one-liner, calling him 'the greatest lesbian poet since Sappho'), Sidney Keyes, Alun Lewis, Edith Sitwell, Robert Lowell, Stephen Spender, C. Day Lewis, Hugh MacDiarmid, Randall Jarrell, James Merrill, Adrienne Rich, the novelist J.D. Salinger, and Louise Glück. French, Chilean and Iranian poets have also been influenced by Rilke, as have Woody Allen films, and various composers such as the British Oliver Knussen with his unaccompanied 'Rilke Songs' and 'Requiem: Songs for Sue', Shostakovich in his Symphony no. 14, Paul Hindemith who set Rilke's 'Six Chansons' to music. American, Danish and Norwegian composers have been inspired to set his poems to music too.

Another reason for his impact: Rilke gives himself to the reader in such an intimate way that many readers feel an almost exclusive kinship with him and look to him for solace, advice in bereavement or a failed relationship, or for affirmation in times of stress and anxiety, for example. He addresses the reader familiarly as 'you' or else identifies complicitly with the reader as 'we', and he makes the reader feel privileged to be a confidante because he deals in the big, daunting issues of life and death, and with questions regarding our mortal existence here on earth. The poet Jo Shapcott has talked of reading Rilke as 'more like writing – or, at least, some connected experience like conversing, touching, praying'.

Yet the reassurance and security many English-speaking readers feel personally in Rilke's hands is ironic in many ways. Michael Hamburger tells us that Rilke had 'a bizarre aversion to English poetry and the English language', although Rilke himself wrote that 'Art can only proceed from a purely anonymous centre', demonstrating the legacy of 'negative capability' handed down to him from Keats. It is precisely this need, like Keats, to let, as Michael Hamburger points out, 'the mind be a thoroughfare for all thought, no fixed opinions' that accounts for his linguistic innovations, especially his 'dynamization and neologization of verbs and their prepositions' which make for a musical fluidity and interpenetration and make nonsense of those who try to fit Rilke into any neat cosmology, ontology or theology that some think Rilke enunciated in the Elegies and the Sonnets. For example, Erich Heller, in *The Disinherited Mind* (London,

1957), cites Heidegger as having remarked that his philosophy was an unfolding in thought of what Rilke had expressed in poetry. Michael Hamburger is emphatic against such readings, which not only miss that Rilke's poetry is 'profoundly committed to the real', but miss also, as Hamburger stresses, the fact that any 'pseudo-philosophical superstructure raised by Rilke' in the Elegies, for example, 'is a poetic statement valid only within the confines and context of the poetry itself' and has 'no other foundation than that of poetic process'.

Ironic too when the reader feels, at the same time as this kinship, a tantalising sense of mystery, a sense of something more being pointed to than the given, something that can never quite be grasped and is purveyed often through linguistic innovations with their complex syntax and word coinage. Even the intimacy between poem and reader is suspect when one considers that Auden called Rilke the 'Santa Claus of loneliness'. Indeed, Rilke chose to live his life in isolation, opting for solitude deep within himself. When he chose finally not to undergo psychoanalysis, he saw it as a choice between 'becoming a little human' and 'ceasing to write'. The ingredients in his psyche which isolated him were those that were vital to his creativity as a poet even though the personal crisis which dominated his poems from 1912–15 was provoked by the very solitude and human unrelatedness he assumed in the service of his art.

In *An Unofficial Rilke, Poems 1912–1926* (Anvil Press Poetry, 1981), Michael Hamburger sensitively chooses to translate the different styles of strong poems often discounted by Rilke, including the more playful poems as he was emerging from this crisis in the early twenties, before sinking into the final crisis of his diagnosis of leukaemia. Rilke himself was not very adept at 'living' his own personal life; in fact, he seemed to put most of his human attributes on hold in order to be fully dedicated to his art. Michael Hamburger proposes that Rilke's unquestioned faith was not 'in art for art's sake, but rather in art for life's sake and – as far as Rilke's person was concerned – in life for art's sake'. For example, despite the corpus of his work that Marjorie Perloff says 'can only be described as the ontology of sexual love' to which the realities of everyday life, even life in the war years take a back seat, and his acknowledgement of the erotic alongside the transcendent, it seems that he could not reconcile the bestial side of his male nature with love, and conflict came from this dichotomy. He went through a multitude of mistresses, and he admitted to Princess Marie von Thurn und Taxis in a letter from Paris, 21 March, 1913: 'I am no lover at all; it touches me only from the outside, perhaps because no one has ever really shaken me to the depths, perhaps because I do not love my mother... All love is an effort for me, an outlay'...
He certainly avoided commitment of any sort – whether with a woman,

his own daughter, or an animal. Nothing was allowed to come between him and his total dedication to his art. Friends he felt safe with, but often dealt with them through the distant medium of letters. Indeed, his letters serve as commentaries on, notes for and illuminations of his poetry and of his prose.

Why, then, are we focusing upon this 'jerk', as John Berryman called him in one of his *Dream Songs*, upon this privileged, narcissistic, egotistical sycophant who could not sustain any full relationship, who had a string of aristocratic patrons and patronesses off whom he sponged, who was quite up himself about his art, was a dropout from economic realities and from the domestic realities of marriage and fatherhood, freeing himself from ties of any permanent residence and nationality, and saw the outbreak of war as little more than a disruption of his work? How ironic it was, however, considering Rilke's lack of involvement in the war, that his book which he dismissed as 'an intolerable mixture of verse and prose', *The Lay of the Love and Death of Cornet Christopher Rilke*, was a best seller on the front, having sold over 180,000 copies by the end of World War I. A copy of this little cult poem was found in a German dugout in the Sarre in 1939, together with a revolver, telephone and table of logarithms.

David Young, translator of the *Duino Elegies* (Norton, 1978) summarises: 'He has been worshipped and he has been reviled'.

Onto the worship, then. Marilyn Monroe, one of the first camera-induced iconic fatalities of the media age, was reported by a friend of Arthur Miller to have loved the *Duino Elegies* in particular, and Rilke's *Letters to a Young Poet* and to have referred to his poetry as her 'city of refuge'. There is no doubt that, in requiems, elegies and sonnets, he proffers comfort, and consolation, pointing always to another dimension – not to a Christian heaven, though he did flirt with Christian piety as a lapsed Catholic in an early work *The Book of Hours* (a version of which, by Christine McNeill and Patricia McCarthy, is being published by **Agenda Editions** to coincide with this issue), and in a later sequence in 1912 *The Life of the Virgin Mary*. There remained, perhaps, a residue of Catholicism in his subtle inclination towards mysticism, harking back to the thirteenth century Meister Eckhart even in his insistence on the unity of life and death and how in love and death we surrender ourselves completely and become all beings, entering the general life akin to Jung's universal consciousness, and evidenced in his interest in Swedenborg. Rilke's main influence, however, was not any orthodox God but Nietzsche. Rilke's pagan angels are totally unrelated to Milton's cosmos, and his three-layered world of angels, humans and animals has no hierarchy. Erich Heller, in his essay 'On the Modern German Mind', claims: 'Name almost any poet, man of letters, philosopher who wrote in German during the twentieth century and attained to stature and influence; name Rilke, George, Kafka, Thomas Mann, Ernst Jünger, Musil, Benn, Heidegger or Jaspers – and you name at the same time Friedrich Nietzsche. He is to them what Thomas Aquinas was to Dante: the categorical interpreter of a world which they contemplate poetically or philosophically without even upsetting its Nietzschean structure'. Rilke also belonged to the German tradition of extreme exposure and alienation going back to Goethe's Werther, and Hölderlin's poetry, recognising the seedy quarters of Paris, where he strolled, from Baudelaire's verses. Though influenced by the existentialists, he avoided their nihilism, and while he made no extensive studies of Eastern philosophies and religions as Yeats and Eliot did (although Manfred Engel, in his essay in this issue points out Rilke's knowledge of Egyptology), his attitude to death resembles that of Buddhists or Hindus: that death should be folded into life, and life into death, thereby making our brief existence on this earth in the here and now all the more precious, and graced by the praising of it with the saying, 'Oh, for such saying as never the things themselves/hoped so intensely to be'.

We are focusing on him because as Gass says of the *Duino Elegies*: 'These are not poems ... These are miracles'. And Michael Hofmann, in his book *Rilke in English*, due out in the next couple of years from Penguin Classics, is setting Rilke alongside such writers of founding importance in European Literature as Virgil, Horace and Dante, as well as showing his influence on twentieth century poetry.

Most of all perhaps we are focusing upon him because of the extraordinary invocatory power of his poetry, already mentioned, that becomes personalised for all those who immerse themselves in it. Jo Shapcott, whose *Tender Taxes* (Faber) are her responses to some of Rilke's poems that he wrote in French, also commented: 'The relationship of the reader to these poems is unlike any other I can think of' and I am sure that most readers of Rilke, albeit at one remove through translation or versions, would agree.

Perhaps my experience is a typical example of how Rilke becomes a person's own poet: as if he exists just for you and for nobody else. I discovered Rilke quite by accident – or was it fate? – in a secondhand bookshop in Washington D.C. where I had just arrived, from England, to live with my first husband in my early twenties, having had the devastating news on arrival there that my father had been knocked down by a car and killed while crossing a road. The *Duino Elegies* (the Leishman/Spender version) seemed to find its way into my hand as though meant for me, even though it was scribbled over by an American student, with notes in the margin, and alternative vocabulary in looped handwriting in smudged ink half-obscuring some of the printed words. In my grief, I read and read the poems, comforted and strengthened and helped out of my own traumatised helplessness by this 'Rilke' whom I immediately claimed as my one true friend in that alien land. I had the odd feeling that no one else could possibly know Rilke, except this random student who seemed to have struggled too technically with the sense and had probably missed the essence of the poetry. How strange, now, then – or apt, maybe – that at another time of great bereavement, having lost my mother just a few weeks ago, I should, decades later, be working on a special issue of *Agenda* on Rilke, and find myself strengthened once more by his words.

* * *

There is no doubt that in translation we always know a poet by proxy; there is always a compromise of sorts involved. Translation can enhance or detract from the original and it is up to the reader to use his/her own judgment, according to the criteria to hand. However, Durs Grünbein claims that Rilke belongs to a rare group of poets who, through the veil of translation, gain a certain clarity. His poems, he says, are akin to sculptures covered for reasons of transportation, their contours thereby coming all the more clearly into relief. And indeed, every time a new translation of Rilke comes out, Peter Porter speaks of 'a new Rilke' being 'reborn in English dress, one not always recognised by German-speakers'. It is interesting that Luke Fischer who appears in this issue comments that he is repeatedly surprised by the relative lack of familiarity with Rilke amongst many educated Germans; 'he is certainly more highly regarded in the non-Germanic world at the present time'. Marjorie Perloff, in her essay 'Reading Gass Reading Rilke' (originally published in *Parnassus*), makes a fair point that if English-speaking poets were 'as ambitious as the poet they revere, they would try to read Rilke's poetry in German' so that they could have a sense of Rilke's sound and rhythm, and lyrical flexibility. They (we) should, in other words, follow the example of Rilke who, when interested in Kierkegaard, took the trouble to learn Danish in 1904 so that he could translate Kierkegaard's letters to his fiancée. True, the letters were more straightforward to translate than the complexities of Rilke's poetry, difficult even for Germans in German; nevertheless Rilke's proficiency in Danish after a very short time of study was an exemplary achievement. Peter Porter describes Rilke's German as being 'as rich and involved as a tropical jungle' – all the greater the achievement therefore of translators who, as Peter Porter suggests they should, feel for what in poetry is not determined by a particular language and manage 'to seek the underlying structure of Rilke's thought-and-feeling, and only then to cope with its clothing in words'.

This brings us to what our criteria are for successful translations as opposed to versions. Translators who publish bi-lingual editions without doubt take more risks than those who omit the original German, and for the reader with even only a smattering of German, it is helpful and rewarding to be able to cast an eye across the page to at least peek at the original. Stephen Spender, who often featured in *Agenda*, stressed the importance of the English 'flowing', no matter how 'exact' the translations are. He was fully aware of the challenge of translation, and pointed out the dangers of translations, 'exact' or not, being both idiomatically and rhythmically wrong, not what is meant in English at all. He spoke prophetically, however, when he declared that the 'effort' to translate Rilke is one that should be continued from decade to decade. For this is indeed what has been undertaken, mainly by poets, only a few of them bi-lingual.

In his introduction to his very fine translation of the *Duino Elegies* (Menard Press, 1999), Patrick Bridgwater modestly states his aim: 'The proof of my translation is of course in the reading, but the present one aims to produce a version which is both as close as possible to the original and poetically plausible. It is an aim that is more easily described than realised'. Peter Porter, introducing Stephen Cohn's equally fine translations of the *Duino Elegies* (Carcanet, 1989) defines the challenge of the Elegies: 'Conjuring it down on the page becomes the job of a shaman. One thing you cannot do is to find a loosely colloquial Procrustean form ... and pour all the protean poetry of the Elegies into these containers like a confectioner making sweets'. He offers his guidance, including, among other suggestions: 'Your translation must have grandeur, essential size in its component parts, and speed to catch the marvellous twists of Rilke's imagination... The English should not diminish or over-elaborate'. He praises the translations of Cohn, whose first tongue is German, for matching all the requirements he sets out and for adding 'a natural eloquence of his own' to make the Elegies 'the most flowing and organic' of those he has read. This goes a long way to countering Erich Heller's negative approach: 'I am convinced that we shall have to be content with adequate paraphrases of the Elegies' meaning: a poetic rendering of them seems to me unattainable. And, indeed, how could Rilke's unique attempt to re-interpret the whole of human experience (an 'anthropological enterprise') in lyrical language be reproduced in another idiom?'

Thank goodness, then, for the persistence of some talented translators and version-makers. **Martyn Crucefix's *Duino Elegies***, described as 'vivid, new translations' by Karen Leeder in her Introduction, has come out recently from Enitharmon (£9.95). Crucefix braves the Elegies with style and his translations flow, cohere, clarify and musically articulate this difficult body of work. He acknowledges his indebtedness to the rhythmical translations of Rilke by the American, Stephen Mitchell. Any minor, slightly clumsy lapses into the prosaic are more than compensated by the electrical charge of the whole which transcends translation. Assessment is difficult by any reviewer who has had the Leishman/Spender versions ringing in his/her ears over the years, since automatic comparisons are unavoidable and the temptation, unfair as it may be, is to peer into the new translations to detect where they diverge from the original standard set in one's head. For example, in the Ninth Elegy, Crucefix's line 'Here is the time for what can be said' compares with the Leishman/Spender proximation: 'Here is the time for the sayable'. This leads to a niggling concern that translators after Leishman/Spender at times bust their guts to differ from the latter at all costs, although is 'what can be said' a more contemporary idiom than 'the sayable'? 'The sayable' certainly has a more musical ring to it than the clause 'what can be said'. That apart, the impetus is sustained, as is the way Rilke often invites meanings behind the meanings; the challenge is lived up to and I believe Spender would have approved of this as a much more than competent translation for the first decade of our century.

A commentary on each Elegy is appended to this book and this is helpful for those not initiated in Rilke. There are some interesting, well-put, even original points that illuminate the translations, but in general the commentary seems to tend towards paraphrase or textbook notes for examinations and, while this might well be the aim, the comments, as such, seem on the whole too pedestrian to do the finely achieved translations proper justice.

Don Paterson, in his taut *Orpheus, A Version of Rainer Maria Rilke*, recently published by Faber (£12.99 hardback) makes many highly interesting, intellectual points in both his 'Afterword' and 'Appendix: Fourteen Notes on the Version', analysing man's attitude to death and the consequential quest for meaning in life, and human 'singing'. (See quotations from these – and from Rilke's *Letters to a Young Poet* translated by Stephen Cohn – in **Notes for Broadsheet Poets** at the end of this issue and online: www.agendapoetry.co.uk). He takes great pains to distinguish between translations and versions and points out that to read a translation as a version, or a version as a translation, leads to disappointment and confusion. Translations, he claims, date more than free versions – he criticises Leishman's rhymed translations of the Sonnets for being 'uncomfortably aureate', i.e. dated – and points out the concomitant danger in both translations and versions: that they can be translated 'not just into the language but into the culture of the age' (unlike the poem in the source language fixed forever in time and diction). Thus translations could end up being 'more central to a culture than that of the language in which they were first conceived'.

It is interesting to note that, having been accused of obscurity in both the *Duino Elegies* and the *Sonnets to Orpheus*, Rilke himself wrote what he thought were explanatory notes for them, but his commentaries came out like difficult prose-poems and made the poetry seem even more inaccessible than before!

Paterson skilfully states his case for deviating from the original, in his free, beautifully honed sonnets. 'If the content tries to stay fixed', he explains, 'the rhymes will merely be inflicted and will be a disaster'. End-rhyme needs to be 'naturalised by everything that precedes it', and implies a 'fluidity of sense'. This 'fluidity has to be carefully negotiated. If rhymes are to be used – especially in a rhyme-poor target language – then some aspect of the content must change'. Of course this is opening the floodgates to the age-old arguments about translation, faithful renderings and exactness, and there is no doubt that translators who offer bi-lingual texts will disagree with wide divergences from the original. Not prefaced by 'unless in expert hands', Paterson insists that to imitate both form and content leads to the disaster of 'translationese' which 'buckles under the pressure'. Rilke, it seems, would have agreed with him, for in his translations of Valéry, executed in the last part of his life, he kept the outer structure or corset of the poem, but deviated vastly with the contents and images so that, like the Don Paterson sonnets, Valéry's poems became Rilke poems more than anything.

Paterson's versions of Rilke's Orpheus sonnets have a decided ring to them in English, are admiringly unadorned, moving and fluid, wedding the lyric to the music to offer meaning in the utterance. For example in Sonnet XXV, Part Two, named by Paterson as 'Cycles', the wonderful third line of the sestet 'The winds exchange a word in their own tongue' can be compared to Stephen Cohn's delicately translated line: 'Sometimes one breeze sends another a sign'. While most lines of Cohn and Paterson diverge, as Paterson takes far more liberty with distilling the original through him to reproduce versions he calls 'selfish', to memorise for his own use, which have 'just a little of the self-sufficiency of the German' – there are some overlappings. Unlike Cohn, Paterson is no native speaker and acknowledges his indebtedness to other translations such as Stephen Mitchell's and Cohn's, and Cohn's notes, in inspiring his versions. For the best appraisal in English of Rilke's *Sonnets to Orpheus*, it is interesting to read Cohn and Paterson, for both are impressive in their different ways and with their different aims, though this statement remains unqualified regarding the German sonnets which Rilke 'took on the run' and referred to as 'the freest and most transfigured verse that might be understood as belonging to this form'. Of course, it has to be acknowledged that Rilke did not always succeed. Heller, in an unpublished letter, asks if there is another great poetic design in literary history that contains as many subjunctives, 'perhaps's and 'maybe's which are 'testimony to the precariousness and occasional inner insecurity of this adventure'.

Fitting to end, then, as we began, with Rilke's impact on English-speaking people in the language of, as John Bayley calls it, 'Rilke-in-English'. Peter Porter puts it down to the fact that 'Rilke's mind has got into our minds and thence into our sensibility and language'. If all the translations/versions could invent Rilke in English as John Bayley, longstanding former trustee of *Agenda*, says Stephen Cohn achieves: 'in something of the same way that Rilke himself had reinvented in German the pure and pellucid language of the great Romantic poet, Hölderlin', and with the feeling that 'something new has been added to English poetry itself', we would all sing to the heartbeat of the Orpheus sonnets – which is that of the Earth itself.

Patricia McCarthy

Five translations of Rilke: Michael Hamburger

Michael Hamburger is perhaps the most highly acclaimed translator of German poetry. Among his many works of translation are the poetry of Rilke and Hölderlin. He has also written several critical books on translation and poetry. He has won acclaim for his own poetry and is devoting the remainder of his years to his own work. He lives in Suffolk with his wife, the poet Anne Beresford.

Solemn Hour

He who now is weeping anywhere in the world,
without reason weeping in the world,
is weeping for me.

He who now is laughing anywhere in the night,
without reason laughing in the night,
is laughing at me.

He who now is walking anywhere in the world,
without reason walking in the world,
is walking to me.

He who now is dying anywhere in the world,
without reason dying in the world,
is looking at me.

Love Song

How should I hold my spirit back, how weigh
it lest it graze your own? How should I raise
it high above your head to other things?
Oh gladly I would simply relegate
my soul to something lost that darkly clings
to a strange silent place, a place that stays
quite still when your own inmost depths vibrate.

But all that grazes us, yourself and me,
is like a bow to us and joins two strings
together, so that one voice only sings.
To what stringed instrument have we been bound?
And in what player's hands do we resound?
Sweet melody.

People by Night

Nights are not made for the crowd.
Night separates you from your neighbour,
but even so you should not look for him,
and if you light up your room at night,
to look into human eyes,
you must consider whose.

Men are terribly distorted by the light
that trickles from their faces,
and if at night they are assembled,
you will see a tottering world
confusedly heaped together.
On their brows the yellow shine
has chased away all thought,
in their glances flickers wine,
and on their hands
hangs the heavy gesture which they use in their talk
to make themselves understood;
all the while they are saying: I and I
and mean: Anyone.

Prayer

Night, silent Night, into whom are woven
objects quite white, red, brightly tinted things,
scattered colours which are raised
to one darkness, to one stillness – bring
me also to communion with the manifold
creations whom you convince and make your own. Is it
that still my senses play too much with light?
Would even now my face

22

contrast discordantly
with lifeless things? Judge by my hands:
do they not lie like tools, inanimate?
Is not the ring itself
smooth on my hand, and does the light
not lie upon them, full of trust
as upon paths which, sun-lit,
branch out as in the dark? . . .

Spanish Dancer

As in your hand a sulphur matchhead, white,
this way and that before it can ignite
sends twitching, flickering tongues within the round
of near spectators, hasty, hot and bright,
in jerks her circular motions are unwound.

And suddenly, all flame, it blazes there.
with one more glance she sets alight her hair
and all at once with daring art she lays
her gown's whole length right into that same blaze
from which, like serpents, startled by your tread,
awake and rattling, her bare arms are spread.

And then: as though her fire were running low
she gathers it, discards it with one throw,
imperious now, disdainful, and looks down:
and still it flames, refusing to submit –
But sure in victory with a smile that's sweet
and welcoming, she lifts her face from it
and stamps it out with small and sturdy feet.

Dolphins

Those, the real, who everywhere would give
to any like them that by which to grow
and, more, provide them with a place to live,
by little signs of kinship came to know
these peers within the fluid realms the god
drenches, with dripping tritons, leaves below:

for then the mammal in their kind would show
quite other than the dumb insensitive kind
of fishes, but related by their blood
and from afar to human things inclined.

Now a school of them came tumbling by,
blithe, as though they felt the waters gleam:
warm and friendly ones whose tireless ply
with hope entwined the voyage, it would seem,
when lightly wound about the rounded bow
as round a vase's curve above the base:
blissful, without a care, safe in that place,
erect in air rushed with the weather's force
or dived and let the rushing waves replace
their ripple for the trireme's happy course.

And the sailor took his new admission
into the lonely dangers of the crew,
for his friend, companion, gratefully
thought up a world, believing it was true
he could love a garden, god, musician
and the stellar year's tranquillity.

Note: Michael Hamburger says he found the above in a folder of very old translations, some of them of Rilke, unpublished, going back to his adolescence.

Six translations of Rilke: Stephen Cohn

Stephen Cohn was born in Frankfurt-am-Main in 1931. In 1933 he came to England with his parents, early refugees from Nazi Germany. On leaving school he served in the Royal Artillery and then studied sculpture at Hammersmith School of Art and later at the Royal College of Art. His working life has been divided between sculpture, painting, printmaking and lecturing and writing of various kinds.

Cohn's three books of Rilke translations are published in the UK by Carcanet (*Duino Elegies*, 1989; *New Poems*, 1992; *Sonnets to Orpheus* with *Letters to a Young Poet*, 2000). Recently he has given talks on his Rilke translations at Boston and New York Universities, and at New College, Oxford.

On a Spring Day in Paris

O April and O, all the deaths it bears
and the black dead-carts of the hauliers
progressing through the light and its excess,
as if again a sullen heaviness
had gathered to weigh down on every thing
the spring has made grow lighter... Now the young,
their children's smocks so recently outgrown,
are on their way to be confirmed – amazed.
Their whites, exalted as before God's throne,
grow quieter beneath the elms' first shade.

Aus einem Frühling, Paris, RMR, Paris, April 1913

Horn of Plenty

What could be more generously shaped
than this vessel shouldered by the goddess?
reaching far beyond our human compass,
hugely magnified by what we crave.

In the horn's capacious spiral every
attribute of ripeness is held ready,
and the pure hearts of the innocent are
the moulds awaiting all that it will pour.

Up above, the airy gift of flowers
still cool from their early morning's freshness,
scarcely palpable, as is invention,
but as near-at-hand as our experience.

Does the goddess mean to scatter bounty
over hearts unable to contain it,
over World's unnumerable houses,
every creature who might walk her highways?

No, for standing tall and over-life-size
she withholds her crammed horn of abundance
while beneath her rivers flow – prepared to
sail her gifts into the woods, the meadows.

Das Füllhorn, RMR, Muzot, February1924
(dedicated to Hugo von Hofmannsthal for his 50th birthday)

The Magus

He summons it. It shrinks back, then it stands.
What stands? The Other, now conjured to presence.
All that is *not he* all at once creates
a face which turns to show itself the greater.

O Magus! now you must endure, endure!
Place irresistibly upon the scales
your self, your dwelling, every thing that weighs,
to counterweigh and match against the Other.

The die is cast. The contract has been drawn.
Refusal cannot hold against the summons.
But his own face, dark behind masking hands,
shows midnight. For the Binder too is bound.

Der Magier, RMR, Muzot. Dated 12.2.1924 (at midnight)

Before the Spring

Harshness relents. Now, all at once, some kindness
comes to dress the grey and naked grassland.
Rivulets restore the tones, the colours.
Tender, clumsy gestures

grope towards the earth from distant Space.
Footpaths penetrate the land, display it.
And, in wonder, you can now perceive
life-force rising in each leafless tree.

Vorfrühling. RMR, Muzot, February 1924

Going for a Walk

My eyes already graze the sun-bathed hill
beyond my journey, scarcely yet begun...
just as some object not yet graspable
holds up its far-off vision to draw us on

even before we've touched transforming us
into that scarce-known other: whom we are.
We send a sign. The wind sends back an answer,
but only counter-winds blow through to us.

Spaziergang, RMR, Muzot, March 1924

Untitled

Where the sun lives, in this street in which
the halved and hollowed tree-trunk has long been
a drinking trough that soundlessly renews
its water's level surface, I relieve
my thirst, letting my wrists alone experience
the water's joyfulness and provenance.
Simply to drink might seem too much, too obvious,
whereas the temporising gesture serves
to quench my consciousness in liquid brightness.

And if you came to me, all I would need
to quieten and calm myself might be
gently to lay two hands to rest upon
the tender curve of your young shoulders, or
perhaps upon the ripeness of your breasts.

An der sonngewohnten Straße
RMR, Muzot, June 1924

Four translations of Rilke's *Sonnets to Orpheus*: Martyn Crucefix

Martyn Crucefix has won numerous prizes for his poetry, including a major Eric Gregory Award and a Hawthornden Fellowship. His collections include *Beneath Tremendous Rain* (Enitharmon, 1990), *At the Mountjoy Hotel* (Enitharmon, 1993, *On Whistler Mountain* (Sinclair-Stevenson, 1994), *A Madder Ghost* (Enitharmon, 1997) and *An English Nazareth* (Enitharmon, 2004). He is a founder member of the group ShadoWork, specialising in performing and writing collaboratively. His new translations of the *Duino Elegies* (Enitharmon) are reviewed in the Introductory essay of this issue. (For information on his work, visit www.writersartists.net).

I ix

Only to one who can raise
the lyre – in shadow even –
may the skill be given
for unending praise.

Only he who has eaten
poppies with the dead,
will he never again
lack the least sound.

Reflections in water
may for us grow blurred:
Know what is there.

Only in that double-world
are voices altered –
eternal and mild.

I xiv

With flower, vine leaf, fruit we journey.
It's more than the language of years they speak.
A bright revelation rises from the dark
which has perhaps a gleam of jealousy –

in fact from the dead who feed the earth.
Of their part in this, what do we know?
It has been their role for so many years
to lard the clay with their free marrow.

Only now we ask – do they gladly do this?
Do they thrust it up, this concentrated fruit,
heavy work of slaves, for their masters?

Or are *they* masters, laid asleep at the root,
yet granting us, from their excess, this inter-
mediate thing between brute force and kiss?

I xv

Wait ... that taste ... it has already flown.
... Only a little music, a stamp, a hum –
you girls, in your heat, girls, your silence,
dance the taste of your fruit experience!

Dance the orange. Who can forget it,
how it will drown in its own sweetness
and struggle against it. You possess it.
Its transforming into you is precious.

Dance the orange. The warmer landscape,
throw it from you until its ripeness
shines in our native air! Revealed, brightness,

fragrance on fragrance. Forge what kinship
you're able with the pure, off-putting rind,
with the juice brimming the lucky mind!

I xxi

Spring has come back. And the earth is
as a child who has learned poems by heart;
many, so many ... and for all her hard
and lengthy study she wins the prize.

Her teacher was strict. We loved the snow-
white hue of the old man's beard.
Now we can ask what the green is called,
what is the blue: she knows, she knows!

Now you are lucky, earth, free to play
with the children. We want you to stay.
Happy earth! The happiest wins out.

What teacher taught her – oh, so many things –
all imprinted there in each root,
in long tangled stems: she sings, she sings!

Translations of Rilke: Sean O'Brien

Sean O'Brien's sixth collection of poems, *The Drowned Book*, is to be published by Picador in autumn, 2007. His verse translation of Dante's *Inferno* appeared in 2006, and *Cousin Coat: Selected Poems 1976–2001* in 2002. He is the winner of the 2007 Northern Rock Foundation Writer's Award and is a Professor of Creative Writing at Newcastle University.

'O Rose, o pure contrariness, delight'

O Rose, o pure contrariness, delight
That underneath so many eyelids
Nobody is sleeping you.

'Komm du, der letzter, den ich enerkenne'

So now, you are the last thing I shall learn,
Pure pain that has become my flesh.
Where once it was my mind that burned, so now
I burn in you. This kindling had long withheld
Submission to the flame you breathed on me,
But now I feed you, now I burn.
Inside your fury, all my gentleness must likewise
Turn to fury – not this world's, but Hell's.
Without a future or a second thought, at liberty
I climbed the knotted pyre of suffering,
Convinced that for this heart there was
No future to be had, the storehouse silent now.
Am I what burns, so utterly transformed? Am I?
I bear no memories into this blaze.
Oh, but to live. To live: to be outside.
But no one knows me, and I burn.

'O Night, dispersed into the deep'

O Night, dispersed into the deep,
Your face against my face,
Night-face, that so exceeds
My own astonished look.

O Night, a tremor in my gaze
But steadfast in yourself,
You are the unborn genesis
That will outlive the things of Earth –

Night, full of youthful bodies hurling
Fire from their roaring skins
Across the soundless
Interplanetary spaces.

O Night, O over-reacher, see,
Since you exist, I shrink away,
And yet am one with this dark Earth
And dare to be inside you now.

Two of the ten Duino Elegies: Alison Croggon

Born in 1962, Alison Croggon is one of a new generation of Australian poets which emerged in the 1990s (see her work and a review of it in the Australian issue of *Agenda*, Vol. 41, Nos 1–2). She keeps a respected blog of theatre criticism, Theatre Notes (theatrenotes.blogspot.com) and edits Masthead Literary Arts Ezine (masthead.net.au). She is also the author of the popular young adult fiction series, *Pellinor* (Walker Books). Her most recent poetry collections are *Attempts at Being* (Salt) and *The Common Flesh* (Arc). A new collection, *Translations from Nowhere*, is forthcoming from Salt in 2008.

The Second Elegy

Every angel is terrible. And yet, alas,
I desire you, almost fatal birds of the soul,
hearing of you. Where are the days of Tobias,
when one of the radiant stood at the plain front door,
slightly disguised for the journey, no longer alarming
(a young man to the young man looking curiously out).
If the archangel, perilous behind the stars, trod now
only one step down here: our own hearts
beating so high would kill us. Who are you?

Early blessings, you coddle creation's
mountain ranges, the red dawning edges
of all making. – Pollen of blossoming godliness,
hinges of light, corridors, stairs, thrones,
expanses of being, shields of rapture, tumults
of stormily joyous feelings and suddenly, singly,
mirrors: which draw up again their own flowing beauty
into their own faces.

For we, when we feel, evaporate; ah,we
breathe ourselves out and away; from ember to ember
giving a fainter smell. Here perhaps someone might say
yes, you enter my blood, this room, the spring
feels itself with you ... it's no use, he can't hold us,

we dwindle in and around him. And those who are beautiful,
o who holds them back? Appearance continuously
enters and leaves their gaze. As dew on the early grass
what is ours rises from us, as the heat of a
steaming dish. O smile, where do you go? O upturned glance:
new, warm, vanishing wave of hearts –;
alas, that's what we *are*. Does the universe
in which we dissolve, taste of us? Do angels capture
only their realness, streaming to them,
or sometimes, in error, a little
of our being? Are we only diffused
in their features, like a vagueness in the gaze
of pregnant women? Unremarked in the vortex
of their recoil to themselves. (How should they remark it.)

Lovers might, if they understood, talk
amazedly in the night air. For it seems that everything
hides us. See, the trees *are*; the houses
we inhabit still persist. Only we
pass everything by like an exchange of air.
And everything unites to conceal us, half in
shame perhaps and half in unsayable hope.

Lovers, you, who fulfil yourselves in each other,
I ask about us. You seize yourselves. Have you proofs?
See, what happens to me is that my hands
move within one another, or my used
expression considers itself in them. That gives me a little
sensation. Yet who would gamble existence on that?
But you, who swell each other in rapture, until overcome you
implore: no more –; you who under each other's hands
grow ample as vintage grapes;
vanishing sometimes, only because the other
wholly seizes the upper hand: I ask you about us. I know
you touch so blessedly because the caress persists,
because the place doesn't fade, that you, fondlings,
conceal; because beneath it you feel
pure duration. So your embrace almost
promises eternity. And yet, when you endure
the first frightened glance, the yearning at the window,
and the first walk together, once through the garden:
lovers, do you yet exist? When you join your mouths

one to the other –: drink on drink:
o how oddly the drinkers elude their action.

Weren't you amazed by the prudence of human gesture
on attic steles? weren't love and departure placed
so lightly on shoulders, that they seemed to be made
from stuff other than us? Think of the hands,
how they rest without weight, despite the strength of the torso.
Those masters knew this: we are so big
we encompass this, and may touch it so; the gods lean
hard against us. But this is the business of gods.
Could we but find our own strip of orchard,
contained, pure, narrow, human,
between river and rock. Then would our heart overstep us
even as theirs. And we can no longer
gaze after it into those soothing figures, nor in
those godly bodies, where it more modestly expands.

The Seventh Elegy

Woo no more, no wooing, outgrowing voice,
be your natural cry; your cry pure as the bird
when the heightening seasons lift him up, almost forgetting
that he is a pitiable animal and not just a single heart
they fling into brightness, into the ardent sky. You plead
as wholly as he does, no less – for the yet invisible
friend to arrive within you, in whose silence an answer
slowly awakes and warms itself over listening, –
your venturing touch which kindles feeling.
O and spring comprehends –, there is no place
which doesn't carry the note of prophecy. First each little
inquiring sound, which with the gathering stillness
expansively hushes a purely assenting day.
Then the steps upward, the call-steps up to the dreamt
temple of futurity –; then to the trill, the fountain
whose urgent jet already grasps its collapse
in a play of promise ... And before this, the summer.
Not only all of the summer mornings – not only
how they change themselves into day and shine of beginning.
Not only the days, so soft around flowers, and above

so strong and forceful about the forming trees.
Not only the prayer of these unfolding powers,
not only the paths, not only the fields of evening,
not only, after late storm, the breathing clarities,
not only approaching sleep, and a prescience, evening . . .
but the nights! But the high
summer nights, but the stars, the stars of the earth.
O once to be dead and endlessly know them,
all the stars: for how, how, how to forget them!

See, there I called for the lover. But not only
she came . . . Out of their fragile graves
girls came and stood . . . How then could I confine,
how, this continually calling call? The sunken still
constantly want the earth. – You children, here it means as much
to wholly feel one thing, as a thousand.
Don't think that fate is more than the package of childhood;
how often you overtake the beloved, panting,
panting, after the blissful flow, to nothing, to free air.
Being here is magnificent. You knew it, girls, you also,
sunk in your seeming lack – in evil
city alleys suppurating with open rubbish.
For each there was an hour, maybe not
even an hour, one measure of time barely
measurable between two whiles: there she had
being. All. The vein-full being.
But we forget so easily what the laughing neighbour
neither confirms nor envies. We want to possess
the visible, although the most visible joy
first gave itself to perception when we transformed it within.

Beloved, world can be nowhere but within. Our lives,
changing, arrive there. And always the outward
meanly contracts. Where once was a durable house,
an abstract structure, wholly imagined,
stamps itself in the brain.
The zeitgeist forges huge silos of power, extracted
out of everything, formless as the excited throng.
It knows the temple no more. Of all the heart's extravagance
secretly we spare this one. Yes, where only one endures,
one once petitioned thing, once served, once knelt before –
holding itself, just as it is, already there in invisibility . . .

Many see it no more, missing their chance
of building it now within, with pillars and statues, greater!

Each dulled return of the world has such disinherited,
neither the dawns nor the nights belong to them.
For nearness is also far from mankind. This must not
confuse us; the proof within us is strong
of this yet perceptible form. It once stood beneath us,
in the midst of destiny, in annihilation, it stood
in not-knowing-where, as it was, and bent
stars to itself out of the steady sky. Angel,
I'll show you, there! In your aspect
it stands, rescued at last, now finally upright.
Columns, pylons, the Sphinx, the shoring buttresses
of domes, grey in the strange, vanishing city.
Wasn't it miraculous? O Angel, be amazed, because we *are*,
o great one, tell how we desired so much, my breath
cannot encompass such praise. So after all we haven't
neglected the spaces, these vouchsafed, these,
our spaces. (How terrifyingly vast they must be
if they're not swamped by millennia of feelings).
But a tower was great, surely? O Angel, it was, –
great, even next to you? Chartres was great – and music
reached still further and overstepped us. But even only
a lover, o alone at the nightly window...
didn't she reach to your knee –?

                                        Don't believe that I beg.
Angel, I even beseech you! You don't come. For my call
is always full of away; against so strong
a current you cannot advance. Like an outstretched
arm is my call. And its hand opening
to the grasp above remains against you
open, as defence and warning,
Ungraspable, further on.

Two versions of Rilke: Peter Abbs

Peter Abbs is Professor of Creative Writing at the University of Sussex. He is the author of seven volumes of poetry, including most recently *Viva la Vida*, published by Salt in 2005. His polemic against Post Modernism, *Against the Flow*, was published by RoutledgeFalmer in 2003. Peter Abbs says of his work below: 'These poems are more transformations than literal translations. What I have tried to do is to express the spirit of poetry, to find a contemporary idiom for their voice.'

Haus, Brücke, Brunnen, Tor

(from the Ninth Elegy)

What traveller comes back with a handful of dust
from the place he loves? Rather, he brings back a word
he has found. A word that glows in his mouth,
a gentian. It blossoms blue and yellow on his tongue.

So are we here merely to say: *house, bridge, stream,*
gate, tree, window or even the words: *pillar, tower*?
But say them, remember, to say them with such power
that the saying sublates the things themselves ...

Now is the time for telling and this is the place. Speak
and testify. Let us begin with the hour we were born.
Huge machines are gouging the earth. Let our words
flower in the dust. Even grief seeks its redemptive form.

Sonnet to Orpheus

(Sonnet v)

Raise no commemorative stone. Roses
shall blossom all summer for his sake.
For this is Orpheus. His metamorphoses
are magical. And constant. It's fatuous to rake
the world for reasons. Once and for all,
where there's singing there's Orpheus. His words
are transformative as music. His oracular call
outlasts the plastic wreaths and slogans.
It's hard for us to grasp transcendence.
For even Orpheus dreads that wrenching moment,
when he travels swiftly beyond us.
Yet when his hand slips from the lyre,
there's no subterfuge. And nothing's superfluous.
Angelic imagination vaults to its freedom.

Four translations of Rilke: Patrick McGuinness

Patrick McGuinness's first book, *The Canals of Mars*, appeared from Carcanet in 2004, and his translation of Mallarmé's *For Anatole's Tomb* in 2003. A pamphlet, *19th Century Blues*, was a winner in the 2006 Poetry Business competition and is published in May 2007 by Smith Doorstep.

Le Grand Pardon

(after notes by Rilke)

We talk, but what do we know?
Somewhere the Angel of Oblivion,
radiant, leans his face into the wind
that turns our pages.

Farfalettina

All in a flurry she reaches the lamp, and her vertigo gives her one last teetering respite before she is burned. She hits the green baize carpet of the table and against this advantageous background she spreads herself out for an instant (a duration of her own which we can never measure) in the full luxury of her inconceivable splendour. You'd think she was, in miniature, a lady having a *malaise* at the theatre. She'll never make it. And besides what sort of theatre caters for such frail spectators? ... Her wings: tiny golden wands fluttering like a double fan in front of nobody's face; and between them that thin body, a cup and ball where two emerald eyes have dropped. My beautiful one, God exhausted himself in creating you. Now he throws you to the flames so he can regain a little of his strength – like a child breaking into his piggybank.

[Untitled]

We have read the tulips; we have read
two stanzas of daffodils:
we are moved, a little distracted,
we read them the way young girls might read.

The terraces are making up a sonnet
from their retreating tiers;
then the arrival of a goldfinch
lays down a comma.

[Untitled]

(after notes by Rilke)

As Venetian glass
from the moment it is born
knows this shade of grey
the uncertain light that catches it

so your gentle hands
knew in advance
they were the scales that weighed
the fullest of our hours.

Translation of Rilke: Charlie Louth

The Fishmonger's Display

(Naples)

On a slightly sloping marble slab they lie in groups, some on the damp stone itself with just a bit of blackish moss under them, others in shallow baskets, the strips of wood soaked through and dark.

With their silvery scales – one of them bent upward in a smooth curve like an arm bearing a sword on an escutcheon, the silver of it shiny and taut. With their silvery scales, lying in a jumble, made of old silver, tarnished black, and, on top, one that seems to be coming back mouth-first from the heap behind.

Once this mouth has caught your eye you notice others, twisted towards you, as if to complain, to lament. And then (prompted by a thought perhaps), the eyes. All these flat, horizontal eyes that seem to have glass over them like watches, which when they still looked everything they saw washed up against, dissolved in water. They were no different then, just as unseeing and passionless (because the water would not carry their looking); as shallow and cold and empty as headlamps by day. But borne along by the resistance and compliance of that heavier world, they silently and surely cast tracing after tracing, hint after hint, movement after movement inwards, into a broad, light consciousness; silently and surely they proceeded, on the point of a decision they did not betray; silently and surely stood for days against the current, sheathed in it, sometimes crossed by the dark of a drifting shadow.

But now they have been extricated from the strands of their looking and laid out flat, though they are no less inscrutable for that. This pupil here is as if covered with black fabric, and the gold circle round it has been applied like very thin gold leaf. With the kind of shock you get when you bite on something hard, suddenly you come to know the full impenetrability of these eyes and have the impression as you survey the table of being confronted with nothing but metal and stone.

Each twist is hard to the touch, like a curved horn, all the white is silver or platinum or lead, the red is like the undercoat on iron, and the heap of steely-glinting awl-shaped fish lies there cold and heavy like a heap of tools which have been used to cut others, of stone.

For look, next to them: big round smooth agates shot through with brown and pale and golden veins, bits of rose quartz and pieces of jade with a slow coursing within; smooth chrysolites and rock-crystal going over into amethyst; and jelly-fish opals. And a very thin film of water is still clinging to them all, they seem too heavy for the light of this world and too tightly sealed. Containers one has given up trying to get open.

Three translations of Rilke: Terese Coe

Terese Coe's poems, translations and book reviews have appeared in many poetry magazines including *Poetry* in the US, and in the UK in *Orbis* and *Poetry Nottingham*. Her first collection of poems, *The Everyday Uncommon*, won a Word Press publication prize and was published in February, 2005. She has received several grants from Giorno Poetry Systems, was recently awarded a residence at the Vermont Studio Center in the US, holds an M.A. in Dramatic Literature, and lives in New York.

Evening in Skane

The park is high. I walk out of its dusk
like walking out of doors, to open ground
and evening. In wind, the same wind the clouds
and rivers feel, the windmills
slowly grind and wheel at the edge of the sky.
Now I too am a thing in its hand,
the slightest under heaven. Look:

Is that a sky?
              Blessedly light blue,

Where, ever more clear, cloudbanks fly
and deck themselves in every white on white,
and over that, a grand and grayish pallor,
thin but radiant, as if vermilion had bled
through a warm backdrop of colour.
And over everything, this silent radiance
of sinking sun.

              Incredible creation,
stirring inside, borne up by itself unheard,
forming shapes, great wings and folds and mountains,
all before the first stars, and suddenly there:
a gate at such a distance, only a bird,
perhaps, could know how far it is, or fair.

Late Autumn in Venice

The city no longer drifts like a piece of bait,
catching all the days that come to the top.
The palaces of glass have a brittle ring,
and summer hangs from the gardens like a mop
of marionettes, head over heels, and murdered.
But out of the ground, out of the skeleton where
the old forest stood, a purpose rises,
as if overnight the general of the sea

had doubled the fleet in his arsenal, and the clear
dawn air had drowned,
already tarred with the fleet whose oars were beating,
urging itself forward, yes, the meeting
of flags, and then the wind was wildly ripping,
deadly in its radiance, its whipping.

The Halo of the Buddha

Centre of all centres, seed of seeds,
nested almond self-enclosed and sweetening—
toward all stars your kernel flesh proceeds;
you are the universe: Receive my greeting.

Now you feel that nothing else constrains you;
in the neverending dwells your husk,
and there the pure juice presses in and through,
moved by light emblazoning the dusk

while high above, your suns come out,
full and fiery, turned about.
Yet what already has begun
in you will outlast every sun.

Note: Dr Claudia Grinnell acted as consultant on these translations.

Three translations of Rilke: Will Stone

Will Stone, born 1966, is a poet and translator living in Suffolk. His published translations include *To the Silenced – Selected Poems of George Trakl* (Arc Publications, 2005) and *Les Chimères* by Gerard de Nerval (Menard Press, 1999). He also contributed essays, translations and photographs to *Bruges-la-Morte* by Georges Rodenbach, (Dedalus Ltd., 2005). A chapbook collection of his poetry *The Late Time* was published by Taw Press in 2006. His critical work has appeared in *Poetry Review*, *Modern Poetry in Translation*, *PN Review*, *The Guardian*, *The TLS* and *The London Magazine*.

The Parks

From *New Poems* (the other part) 1908, Paris

i

Irresistibly the parks rise up
from the gently mouldering decline;
glutted with skies, over fortified
customs, which endure

so upon the clear grassy lawns
they broaden out and withdraw,
always at the same sovereign
cost, as if in its patronage,

through the unceasing assemblage
of profit that stamps royal greatness,
rising from themselves, they appear
beneficient, grandiose, purple, resplendent.

Tenderly held by avenues
left and right,
following the advance
of some intimation,

you step all at once
into the gathering
of a shadowed water basin
enclosed by seats of stone;

in a time divided
that dies out alone.
On moist pedestals
where nothing more will stand,

you draw a deep
expectant breath;
while the silver trickling
from the dark prow

already counts you among
its own now and murmurs on.
And sensing yourself under stones
that listen, do not stir.

iii

The lakes and calmly enclosed ponds
are not yet informed of the questioning
of kings. They linger beneath veils,
for at any time his grace

might pass this way; and then they wish
to soothe the king's ill-temper or sorrow
and from their marble edges revive
tapestries with time-worn reflections

to hang down, as if around a square;
on green ground, with silver, grey, rose,

a gift of white and stirring of blue
flowers in the border's wave
and a king and a woman too.

iv

And nature, venerable, as if wounded
only by the offence of that unresolved,
looks to kings for such laws,
herself blessed, that she might raise

her trees' dreams and elaborations
upon a tapis-vert of billowing green
and paint evening from the image
lovers in the avenues had given,

with that smooth brush
which seemed to radiantly enclose
a smile, varnish-clear, resolved:

A beloved of nature, not her most noted
but one, that she herself conferred,
and nurtured to grander ambition
on a rose-sated isle of love.

v

Gods of the avenues and balconies,
gods scarcely divine, who
grow old on neatly trimmed pathways,
Dianas who were smiled upon
when the royal hunt stormed past

Like a wind carving the high of morning,
urgent, surging –;
at most smiled-upon, but never

beseeched gods. Elegant
pseudonym, beneath which one
took refuge and flourished or burned, –

willingly inclined, smilingly engaged
gods, who still sometimes now and then

grant that which they once granted,
when the blossoming of blissful gardens
bears away their cold composure;
when they quake from the first shadows
and give promise upon promise,
all undetermined, boundless.

vi

Do you sense how none of these
pathways stands nor falters;
from calm stairways falling,
down through a void of incline
gently lured on over terraces,
pathways, between raised banks
steered, slowed down
out to the broadening ponds,
where (as if to an equal)
the plentiful park gives them

to the rich expanse: the one
which with light and its reflections
permeates its possession,
and from all sides
intimates the far off distances
when from the dusking ponds
the cloudy evening revelry
vaults heavenward.

vii

But there are basins in which the Naiads'
reflections no longer seek to bathe
and lie drowned, contorted,
the avenues in the far distance
barred by balustrades.

Always a damp leaf fall descends
in steps, down through the air;
each bird call doubtful,
as if poisoned every nightingale.

Even spring grants little here,
these shrubs have lost belief;
Grudgeful, enduring
the aged jasmine's sickly perfume

mingles with decay.
A cloud of gnats shadows your progress,
as though behind your back
all is instantly blurred, extinguished.

Nightingale

Nightingale ... whose heart
Shines past the others,
Priest of love, whose cult
Is a cult of passion,

O sweet troubadour
Of the night that haunts you,
You embroider a ringing ladder
Upon its velvet abyss.

You are the voice of saps
That in trees stays silent;
But to us, your students, Nightingale,
You consign the same secret.

*French original from 'Suites Breves' – 'Le Petit cahier' 1922

Autumn Day

Lord it is time. The great summer has now passed
Lay your shadows on the sundials
And on the meadows free the winds at last.

Command the lingering fruits to fill themselves;
Grant them just two more southern days,
Urge them on to completion and chase
The final sweetness into the heavy wine.

Whoever has no house now, will never have one.
Whoever is alone now, will remain alone,
Will stay awake, read, write long letters
And will roam the avenues, up and down
Restlessly, when the leaves are driven.

Two translations from Rilke: Anna Martin

Anna Martin has lived in Germany and later became the Head of Modern Languages at a comprehensive school in South London. She is the foreign editor for the Hippotamus Press and an occasional reviewer of French and German poetry and translations.

From *Frühe Gedichte*

I was a dreamy child of tender years
when a fiddler passed our garden plot,
I looked up uneasily and said,
'Oh mother let me go...'
then at the sound of his first note
something broke within.

I knew before his song began
that this would be my life,
so do not sing, you stranger man,
or this will become my life.

You are singing of my joy,
my pain, you sing my song and then
you sing my fate far too soon–
for when I become a man
I can never live it so.

He sang and walked on his way,
he had to travel on,
singing the pain I never felt,
singing my happiness away–
he took me with, he took me off
to that place no one knows.

From *Groszstadtpoesie*

For, Lord, the great cities are lost and dying things,
the greatest of them taking flight from flames;
there's no succour that could comfort them,
their brief time is coming to an end.
There people exist, living badly and hard
in mean rooms, uneasy of bearing,
more wary than a herd of newly-born;
outside the earth watches and breathes,
yet they are, but no longer know it.

There children grow up on window ledges
always in shadow,
never to know that outside there are flowers
calling to an airy day full of happiness and wind;
they remain children and sadly so.

There young girls blossom into the unknown,
longing for their childhood peace;
the thing for which they burned has gone,
thus trembling they close in on themselves.
And lead days of disappointed motherhood
in darkened backrooms, beaten and whimpering
through the long nights and cold years, listless and weak,
and in the dark await their deathbeds;
their yearning has slowly led them there
to die little by little, die in chains,
departing like a beggar woman.

There worn-out, pallid people live
and die astonished at the harsh world;
none seeing the gaping grimace
through which the smile of a tender race
is deformed in nameless nights.

They wander about degraded by toil
serving senseless things without feeling,
their garments fade on them,
their fine hands soon age.

The unthinking crowd hurries by ignoring them
though they are tentative and weak,
only timid homeless dogs
follow them in silence for a while.

They are subject to a hundred torments
crying out with every strike of the clock,
as all alone they circle the poorhouse
waiting fearfully for the day of admission.

Out there is death. Not the sort whose greetings
were wondrous in childhood
but a mean death as perceived there;
it hangs green and bitter
like a fruit within them that never ripens.

Luke Fischer and Lutz Näfelt

Luke Fischer is a poet, philosopher and translator. He was born in Sydney in 1978. He is completing a doctoral dissertation on a philosophical (phenomenological) interpretation of Rilke's *Neue Gedichte* with Lutz Nafelt. For the last two years he has been living and conducting research in Tübingen, Germany.

Lutz Näfelt was born in 1980 in Ludwigsburg, Germany. He is studying German Literature, Music Theory, and Philosophy in Tübingen.

Early Apollo

As sometimes through the branches still void
of foliage a morning looks which already
is wholly in spring: so is there nothing
in his head's bearing that could prevent the lustre

of all poems striking us almost fatally;
for in his gaze there is still no shadow,
his temples are still too cool for the laurel
and only later from the eyebrows

will the rose-garden raise itself, high-stemmed,
from which singular petals, released
will float upon the trembling of his mouth

that now is still silent, never-used and gleaming
and drinking something only with his smile
as though his singing were infused in him.

The Blind Man

Paris

See, he moves and interrupts the city,
which does not exist in his dark place,
like a dark crack moving through a bright
cup. And as on a sheet of paper
the reflections of things are painted

on him; he doesn't take it in.
Only his feeling is astir, as if
capturing the world in small waves:

a silence, a resistance –
and then he seems waiting whom to choose:
consigned he raises his hand,
almost solemnly, as if to marry.

The Pavilion

But even now through the arched doors
with their green rain-clouded glass
is a reflection of smiling preciosities
and a gleam of that fortune to be felt
which, once there where they no longer lead,
was hidden, transfigured, and forgot.

But even now in the stone-festoons
above the door no longer in use
an inclination to covertness remains
and a quiet sympathy for it –

and they sometimes tremble, as though reflected,
when a wind casts shadows over them;
also the emblem, as upon a letter
much too happily, hastily sealed,

still speaks. How little was displaced:
everything still knows, still weeps, still aches.
And while departing through the tear-damp
solitary avenue

one feels for a time on the roof's rim
those urns standing, cold, cloven:
though determined, to hold together still
around the ashes of old sighs.

Two poems after Rilke: Lotte Kramer

Lotte Kramer was born in Germany with German her mother tongue, and she came to England as a refugee with the Kindertransport in 1939. She is a widely published poet, with ten collections to her credit, the latest being *Black Over Red* (Rockingham Press, 2005). A bi-lingual selection of her poetry was published in Germany.

It is a Castle

It is a castle. The fading
coat of arms above the gate.
Treetops glow like fleeing
hands higher in front.

A gleaming blue flower
rose in the slowly sinking
window for show.

Not a weeping woman –
she is the last one waving
in the broken building.

Palm

Inside of the hand. Sole that only walks on
feeling now, nothing more: opening up
to a mirror
conceiving heavenly streets, they too are
moving ones.
That has learnt to walk on the water
it gathers,
that walks on the well's rim,
transforming every road and lane.
that appears inside other hands
creating with them
the same landscape:
moving and arriving in them,
fullness of arrival.

Translations of Rilke and a commentary: W.D. Jackson

W.D. Jackson lives in Munich. His two books of poetry and translation, *Then and Now – Words in the Dark* (2002) and *From Now to Then* (2005) are published by the Menard Press.

A Post-Romantic Portrait (On Poetry And Death)

'O sage, Dichter, was du tust'

i

Early Apollo

As sometimes, when the woods are dry and leafless,
A dawn looks through them that's already bright
With Spring: so there is nothing in this griefless
Face which could shade the almost fatal light

To which all Poetry might here expose us.
For there's no shadow yet in how he sees,
His head's too cool for bay-leaves, and the roses
Will only later grow as tall as trees

And form a garden out of his old brows
Whose single, fallen leaves, when song or hymn
Bursts from his lips, will move where his mouth blows,

Which is still silent – pristine and still gleaming –
And, smiling, drinks in something which comes streaming
As if all song were entering him.

The Unicorn

The saint looked up. And prayer slipped from his mind
As a helmet falls from the head – distracted
By the silent, unbelieved-in, never-expected
Animal drawing near like an abducted,
Helplessly pleading, all-white, wide-eyed hind.

The creature's long, stiff legs of ivory-white
Moved forward with an easy, balanced tread;
A blessed gleam went gliding through its coat,
And on its lucid, peaceful, beast's forehead
Its horn shone like a tower in bright moon-light,
And rose as each step forward raised its head.

The mouth, beflecked with rosy, greyish foam,
Was puckered, and the white teeth, shining through –
Whiter than all – gleamed in the glade's pale glow.
The slightly panting nostrils noticed who
Was there, whereas its looks, which no
Object restricts, cast visions on the gloom,
Weaving a saga cycle in deep blue.

Self-Portrait from the Year 1906

An ancient, aristocratic ancestry,
Whose eyebrows' arches brook no compromise.
The fears of childhood still in his blue eyes,
And here and there a deep humility. –
A servant's. Or a woman's. No stable-boy's.
The mouth formed as a mouth, large and precise –
Not to persuade but state what's just, what's free.
The forehead without guile, contentedly
Shadowed and bowed in spiritual exercise.

These scattered features time will make or mar,
Which have not yet been fully concentrated
By suffering or success, or penetrated
To lasting goals. Yet a real face seems fated
To come together here, as if from far.

Corrida

(In memoriam Montez, 1830)

Since he lightly burst from the toril,
Almost small, with startled eyes and ears,
Taking on the stubborn picadors
And the banderillas – look, the bull

Like a storm-cloud has increased
To a massive, black, accumulated
Hatred, as of all he's hated –
Clenched his head into a fist,

Taking nothing now from any man
Lightly: now, with bloody banners showing
Over lowered horns, obscurely knowing –
Having always been against the one

Who, in his embroidered, pink silk-suit
Quickly turns and, like a black bee-swarm,
Lets the deeply consternated brute
Pass beneath his mauve and golden arm –

Raising easily misdirected, hot
Eyes again towards the still ungored
Man who, forming lightly on the spot
Chiaroscuro circles without thinking,
Quicker than his eyelids' blinking,

Now prepares – serene, unhurried, calm,
Cool, and leaning forward on his arm
Over that on-coming, great
Wave with all its thrust of wasted hate –
Almost gently to insert his sword.

Turning Point

*'The way from deep feeling to greatness is
through sacrifice.'* – Kassner

Looking had long been his glory.
Stars would drop to their knees,
Wrestled there by his gazing.
Or, if he knelt to look,
Even the gods grew weary
Breathing his powerful incense;
Smiled at him in their sleep.

Towers he would look at until –
Frightened – they shook;
Building them up again, quickly, in one!
Yet how often the landscape,
Heavy laden with day,
Rested at last in his peaceful awareness, evenings.

Animals, trustful, moved
Into his open gaze,
Grazing. The captive lions
Stared, as at inconceivable freedom.
Birds went flying through him –
Straight through his soul; and flowers
Looked again in his eyes, as
Large as in children.

And rumours that someone was *looking*
Moved all the less, the
Questionably visible,
Moved the women.

How long looking?
How long inwardly lacking –
Pleading from deep in his eyes?

While he sat waiting, away from home; a hotel's
Distracted, averted bed-room
Sullen around him, and in the evaded mirror
Again the hotel-room
And, later, from the miserable bed
Again:

Consultations held in air,
Incomprehensible consultations –
Over his feeling heart,
Over his heart which in spite of his pain-racked
Body still made itself felt –
Were taking place and deciding:
That it had no love.

(And denied him greater glory.)

For there's a limit, you see, to looking.
And the well-looked-at world
Wishes to flourish in love.

Work of the face is done,
Now do heart-work
On the images captured within you; for you
Overpowered them: but now you don't know them.
Look, inner Man, at your young inner Woman,
At the one you have won from
A thousand natures, at
The creature you've still only won, the
Never yet loved one.

Sonnet to Orpheus

A tree ascends! O unimpaired transcendence!
O Orpheus sings! O high tree in the ear!
And all grew silent. Yet in that deep silence
New bearings, and new clues, and change were there.

Creatures of stillness crowded from the clear,
Relaxing wood – from nest and hiding place;
Till soon it seemed their inner quiet, their grace
Of movement came from neither greed nor fear

But from their listening. There in that bright clearing,
The howls, shrieks, roaring in their hearts felt small.
And so, with scarcely shelter to receive it –

A burrow or den, as dark desires conceive it,
With quivering door-posts and an earthen wall –
Your song created temples in their hearing.

Translator's Commentary

Most of the above translations are from *Neue Gedichter* (1907–8). 'Turning Point' is a later work, and 'Sonnet to Orpheus' is the first poem in *Die Sonette an Orpheus* (1922). Rilke composed his own epitaph – about a year before he died in 1926 at the age of 51.

Of another poem in *Neue Gedichter,* Joseph Brodsky wrote in 'Ninety Years Later', 'Written in 1904, "Orpheus. Eurydice. Hermes" by Rainer Maria Rilke makes one wonder whether the greatest work of the century wasn't done ninety years ago.' Beginning in the 1930s and '40s, Rilke's appeal (one might almost speak of popularity) in English-speaking countries has continued to increase as time goes on – such that, as Brodsky says, 'translating Rilke has become practically a fad'. Other readers (and translators) will have other explanations but I can think of three reasons for this – two good and one not so good – which 'A Post-Romantic Portrait' incidentally illustrates while building up its admittedly selective (and perhaps still unfinished) picture of the poems' original author ... Walter Benjamin once claimed that one of his ambitions was to produce a work made up entirely of quotations. One species of quotation can consist, fairly obviously, of various sorts of translation and adaptation, and in this sense the 'Portrait' is in fact a short example of a work made up entirely of quotations. For anyone unfamiliar with the originals, the translations in this case try to get as close as possible to the forms as well as the sense of Rilke's words, the significance of his forms in *Neue Gedichter* being the same as or very similar to their English equivalents. Again, other translators (and readers) will have other preferences. But if any of our translations are valid as poetry, the main reason, as Brodsky insisted, 'is, in the first place, of course, Rilke himself'.

The first and most obvious reason, then, for Rilke's appeal is the strikingly high proportion – even for a poet of his acknowledged status – of what Eliot called 'genuine poetry' in his work. In spite of the compression and difficulties of some of his syntax and much of his thought, Rilke validates over and over again Eliot's claim 'that genuine poetry can communicate before it is understood'. As in the case of Dante, whom Eliot was writing about, Rilke's poetry can do this in spite of a reader's poor grasp of the language of the original or poor translations. In *Neue Gedichter,* in particular, this 'direct shock of poetic intensity', as Eliot describes it, has much to do with Rilke's virtuoso handling of metre and rhyme and also with the play of his syntax within and across his lines and stanzas, as I have tried to show in the translations. The striking physicality of the poems' images, their extraordinary condensation (*'Dichten = condensare'*, as Pound famously if inaccurately condensed it) and the mature Rilke's genius for selecting *le mot juste* are other elements involved. At any rate, the original poems are frequently 'breathtaking' (Brodsky's epithet), and every *aficionado* of Rilke will remember which lines or which poem grabbed him first – and, once grabbed, as Eliot says, 'nothing but laziness can deaden the desire for fuller knowledge'.

The second reason I can think of for Rilke's appeal may be that once one has actually got down to understanding – or trying to understand – what the poetry is more specifically about, one finds, again, a remarkably high proportion of emotional and spiritual truth or wisdom. The spiritual sort, in particular, is so unusual in Anglophone poetry that once the reader has been 'exposed' (see 'Early Apollo') to the light of poems like 'L'Ange du Meridien', 'The Unicorn' or 'Archaic Torso of Apollo' – to mention three favourites of my own – Eliot's 'desire for fuller knowledge' is frequently excited all the more. Like a lot of exciting or shocking or otherwise memorable experiences ('Poetry isn't, as people imagine, merely feelings,' Rilke wrote in *Malte Laurids Brigge*, 'it is experiences'), this sort of poem often feels new but also familiar. One reason for this may be that, although he can be looked on as the consummation, or ultimate apotheosis, of European Romanticism (after which it could only decline

65

– and has, with one or two exceptions), Rilke also went *beyond* Romanticism in that he pursued the subjective into what are virtually objective regions of emotional and spiritual observation. Of course, there is no observation without an observer, but let's say he arrived at and operated on a level of consciousness whereby he was able to see and write of emotional and spiritual realities which we really do seem to have in common. Patrick Bridgwater in the introduction to his excellent translation of *Duino Elegies* (1999) quotes Rilke as having written in 1920, 'Art can proceed only from a purely anonymous centre.' In theory, Rilke is an elitist, of course, but in practice virtually anyone can recognize his meanings in themselves. This is, for me, the very heart of 'Post-Romanticism' – the realization or (as Rilke would have it) *experience* of the fact that the innermost self is not a personal identity but a nameless and even numinous impulse which we have in common. 'Namenlos bin ich dir entschlossen' – 'Namelessly I am committed to you' – he wrote in *Duino Elegies* IX, and the life-blood of this commitment, for Rilke but also for anyone, is the existential freedom which we have in common – not merely to react but to decide, not merely to be formed but to transform, not to evade but to subsume, not to blame but to praise.

The third and more dubious – if understandable – reason for Rilke's popularity is also related to his Romanticism. Rilke, like everyone else, was a man of his age, and it is perhaps not very surprising, given the general cast of his mind, that the characteristic withdrawals and self-assertions of the Romantic reaction to the 'Dual Revolution', as Eric Hobsbawm called it, of the late 18th and 19th centuries are also easy to find in or read into his writing, which can easily be taken, in other words, as bearing gifts to the escapist or even solipsist in all of us – as Auden presumably meant by describing him (ambivalently) in his *New Year's Letter* (1940) as 'the Santa Claus of loneliness'. Of course, Auden and Rilke, for all the former's admiration of the latter's artistry), were very different sorts of poet, and the question of writerly intent and readerly attribution is more than usually tricky with regard to Rilke. Even so, if it is true, as Sean O'Brien expressed it in *Poetry Review* 95:3, that 'A New Age Rilke would not be Rilke at all, of course', his conspicuous lack of interest in, or withdrawal from, almost everyone's everyday life – the world of work, for obvious example, but also family life and other social and political realities – is perhaps his most serious limitation. At the same time, it is much less of a problem, one sometimes feels, in the world which his poetry creates, to view the artist and especially the poet as a kind of hero or inspired seer than it is in the world which most of us have to cope with day by day. Presumably because his mind was for the most part so intent on higher things, Rilke could also be surprisingly heartless ... Of course, every reader will decide for him – or herself about the actual value of Rilke's values but, for all his emotional and spiritual acumen, he remained relatively indifferent to questions of ethics. And yet in the absence of a shared ethic, whose emotional or even spiritual life can flourish for long? On the other hand, this may be precisely what appeals to us in Rilke's writing when we feel indifferent ourselves to the needs of others or to our familial or social or political responsibilities in general. To guard against this sort of reading, it is sometimes necessary to sift the poems – including some very fine ones – with considerable care:

Abishag

> Now David was old and stricken in years; and they covered him
> with clothes, but he begat no heat.
> Wherefore his servants said unto him, Let there be sought for my
> lord the king a young virgin: and let her stand before the king,
> and let him cherish her, and let her lie in thy bosom, that my
> lord the king may get heat.
> So they sought for a fair damsel, throughout all the coasts of
> Israel, and found Abishag a Shunnamite, and brought her to the
> king.
>
> *I Kings 1.1–3*

i

She lay there. And her child-like arms were made
Secure by servants round the withering man –
On whom she sweetly lay as time dragged on.
He was so old she almost felt afraid.

And now and then she'd turn and push her face
Into his beard, whenever an owl hooted;
And all that Night was came, crowding the space
Which terror and desire had now transmuted.

The stars were trembling just as she was trembling.
Across the chamber wafted a curious scent.
The curtain moved by itself, like something resembling
Something in search of which her quiet look went.

But she held on tight as he grew darker, older;
And, out of reach of quintessential night,
She lay, feeling his kingly limbs grow colder,
A virgin and as light as a soul is light.

ii

He sat enthroned and thought the whole dull day
Of things he'd done, of pleasure and frustration,
Indulging his favourite bitch's wish to play. –
But, in the evening now, Abishag swayed
And arched above him. His crazy life lay
Like a coast abandoned to its reputation
Beneath her silent breasts' curved constellation.

And sometimes, as the lover of many women,
He'd recognize through brows which needed trimming
Her unexcited, kissless mouth. He found
Her callow feelings' green divining rod
Was not to be tugged down to his deep ground.
He shuddered coldly; hearkened like a hound,
And sought himself in his last blood.

Well, yes, no doubt David *was* a great king and a great poet and here
achieves, in Heidegger's famous phrase, 'an impassioned FREEDOM
TOWARDS DEATH'. But what happened to the girl? And is her unexcited
kisslessness under these circumstances really likely to have been a question
of her *callowness?* Like other artists of the period, Rilke not infrequently
underrated or discounted or, alternatively, idealized women in relationship
to male energy or creativity (his poetry rather obviously suffers from his
not having lived *with* a woman for any length of time)... And what, for
that matter, about the rest of King David's dying? One has only to read
on in *I Kings* 1–2 to encounter the gory details, the familial in-fighting
and political power-play, surrounding the accession of Solomon, and the
removal by assassination of his and his father's enemies. At times, one
prefers the tough-minded worldliness of Heine, for example, as even the
most devoted admirer of Wordsworth – equally high-minded and
magnanimous, and another Romantic who transcended Romanticism –
may sometimes prefer Byron:

King David

Now the days of David drew nigh that he should die; and he
charged Solomon his son, saying, I go the way of all the earth:
be thou strong, therefore, and shew thyself a man;
And keep the charge of the Lord thy God, to walk in his ways,
to keep his statutes, and his commandments...:
That the Lord may continue his word which he spake concerning
me, saying, If thy children take heed to their way, to walk before
me in truth with all their heart and with all their soul, there shall
not fail thee (said he) a man on the throne of Israel.

I Kings 2.1–4

Smiling despots, passing on,
Know their power is never gone:
Though they die, it changes hands.
Human bondage never ends.

Poor plebeian nags and steers –
Hauling carts for years and years!
And the stubborn neck gets broken
Which won't keep its proper yoke on.

Solomon watched as David lay
On his death-bed: 'By the way,
You had better keep an eye on
General Joab, o my scion.

'That old ruthless die-hard gets
Generally on my tits.
But he's weathered wars and purges,
And I daren't indulge my urges.

'You, my son, are wise and strong,
Godly and, above all, young –
And you shouldn't have much trouble
Bursting Joab's hoary bubble.'

A frequent and unashamed fibber in his life, Heine was incapable in his poetry of fudging a moral issue. What we would all love, I imagine, would be a poetry for our time as capable of ethical as of emotional and spiritual acumen. In the meantime, we had better be grateful for the poets we have. And if one were asked to choose? Well, if the ethical can – wittingly or unwittingly – help to conserve or even lead us to the waters of the spirit but can't make us drink them, the spiritual can baptize or subsume the ethical. And so it's clear which is – if not in fact, at least potentially – the more comprehensive:

'O sage, Dichter, was du tust?'

Say, poet what it is you do? – I praise.
But Death and nightmare mar our days:
How can you stand, how stomach them? –I praise.
But all that lacks a name, the Anonymous,
How, poet, can you summon it? – I praise.
Masked and disguised in ever-changing ways,
What right have you to claim the truth? – I praise.
And why should star and storm both recognize
In you their peace and strife? – Because I praise.

A related piece: sonnets of Gaspara Stampa: Jessica Harkins

Jessica Harkins teaches at the College of St Benedict/St John's University and earned an MFA in Poetry at Washington University, where she is currently completing a dissertation in Medieval Literature. She lived for several years in Italy, where she first began the project of translating and recovering Gaspara Stampa's complete poems. Her work has appeared, or is appearing, in *Stand* in the UK and in several journals in the US. A native of rural Oregon, she lives in Minnesota with her husband and dog.

> Have you imagined the love of Gaspara Stampa?
> Recalled it so intensely that any girl – deserted
> By her lover – might emulate her fine example
> And might say to herself: Let me be like her!
>
> – Rilke's First *Duino Elegy*, translated by Martyn Crucefix

46

High hill, sacred river, you have sheltered
the virtues, the Graces, and the cherubs
from the day you gave him to the world,
he who makes me and himself bright and praised.

You soothe your slopes, you raise your horns,
you with new flowers, and you with new waters,
now that your lord and mine returns to you,
also filled with new honors.

And after he has stayed with you, please
see that he quickly returns to me,
since without him I can barely live.

In this way winter may always be far from you;
in this way Flora and Pomona, as companions,
may make you always April and always August.

47

I am so tired of waiting by now,
so overcome by pain and by desire
for the little faith and great forgetfulness
of the one whose return, miserably, I want,

that I call to her for my cool reprieve,
she who turns the world pale and whitens
with her scythe, and gives the last punishment:
so does the pain in my chest strengthen.

And she makes herself deaf to my cries,
scorning my misled and foolish thoughts,
just as he too is deaf to returning.

So with the grief that softens my eyes
I make these waves and this sea compassionate,
and he lives at ease among his hills.

54

If the fire of my heart were not tempered
by the tears that pour so often from my eyes,
I would have already seen my soul, outside
of myself, ready to obey death's messenger;

because hope by now cedes to fearfulness,
and every part of me is subjugated to it,
since one can see expressed by a thousand signs
that he who can hurt me desires my pain.

So if I live, it is by the grace of my tears;
if I die, it is the fault of the fierce desires
of my lord, so sweet in appearance.

He bound me so that others might not loosen me;
he wants to be able to boast of my death.
O scarcely shining or honored spoils.

When the sun brings dawn at a later hour,
and when, in time, it brings us a later nightfall,
when it shows its golden crest, when the night
reveals the silvered horn of the moon,

my heart, miserably, returns to its sighs,
to the voices, to the fitful tears;
so has his absence gathered them all
under one sign, he who now adorns France.

And such heated desire to see him again
presses and stings among all the other torments
so that I no longer know how to withstand it.

And it pains me most that he is so far from me
that the ability to call him back, or move him
to pity, is beyond the reach of cries.

101.

With what worthy greetings or words
will I receive my pleasing lover,
who returns to me with so many glories,
perhaps more than the sun ever saw in one man?

Which colour, now of roses, now of violets,
might be mine? Which heart now firm, now trembling,
may be led before his divine image,
he who gives me fear and desire as he pleases?

Will I dare with these faithful arms
to clasp the precious neck and draw
my trembling to his lively face?

Wretched, that even as suffering brings such glory,
I am afraid this joy may destroy my heart;
whoever has felt this knows it so.

153

If you could, lord, with the eyes of your soul,
perceive the secrets of my heart
as you see these external shadows
openly, with your body's eyes,

you would see the pains of hell:
an abyss of infinite pain,
and as much jealousy, as much fear
as Love has given, or could give in eternity.

And you would see yourself seated as ruler
in the middle of my soul, where torments
could never remove you, nor ever will;

and you would see all my desires are spent,
or oppressed by heavy and noble sleep,
save those for you, lying awake and burning.

203

Since it was my destiny for you to turn aside
your feet and your desire, so that I lost the hope
of ever seeing again those serene lights
that I have already praised in many pages,

I turned myself to the great Sun, and with the art
and the light, which come only from Him,
I have drawn out of the shallows and of the sands
my wooden boat, with oars and ropes.

Reason was the rope and the oars were
the desire, which then made a dyke and a wall
against the rage and the pride of Love.

And so without fear of drifting onto the rocks
I live in a port now quiet and secure;
I praise only one, and I suffer for no one.

It was near the port that Love, who so unfairly
delights in my pains and injuries,
took me back to the middle of the sea
where I had sailed three years in doubtful winds.

And to double the wings of my desire
he brought such a bright horizon to my eyes
that I am comforted watching him,
and the absence of pain makes me breathless.

I feel a fire equal to the first fire,
and in so little time so strong
that I fear it may be greater than the other.

But what can I do, if I am fated to burn,
if I consent to go voluntarily
from one fire to the next, from one to another harm?

Gaspara Stampa (1523–1554) of Padua wrote a number of sonnets to the Count Collatino di Collalto, and was one of the first recognized female poets in Italy. As well as the reference to her in the First of the *Duino Elegies*, in a letter from Rilke to Annette Kolb written on 23 January, 1912, she is mentioned as an example of a 'lover' much more pure, more explicit and 'less adulterated' than Saint Theresa. She represents, for Rilke, an example of an unrequited lover whose love is objectless and infinite and therefore a good example to follow. Her book, published posthumously, was radically reordered by an editor in 1913 both to fit Petrarchan conventions and to accuse her of being a prostitute. Contemporary Italian scholarship refutes these changes, and in newly translating Stampa, Jessica Harkins follows the original order of the 1554 text. Unlike the 1913 editorial narrative of prostitution and religious repentance, this newly-restored order reveals Stampa's concern with her emotional equilibrium and a tentative apprehension of a new secular subject and model of love.

Clive Wilmer

Clive Wilmer is a poet and lecturer, who lives and teaches in Cambridge. His most recent collection is *The Mystery of Things* (Carcanet, 2006), which is reviewed in this issue.

Remembering Leishman's Rilke

When the first English translation of Rilke's *Duino Elegies* appeared, it was reviewed in the United States by W.H. Auden. The date was September 1939. Auden commented on 'the growing influence of Rilke upon English poetry'. 'Rilke,' he wrote, 'is probably more read and more highly esteemed by English and Americans than by Germans.' In German-speaking countries the wider consequences of that September have made for a steep decline in Rilke's status, in spite of the fact that he was not a nationalist. Rilke, the post-Nietzschean and celebrant of quasi-mystical inwardness, represents exactly those aspects of German culture of which modern liberal Germans feel most suspicious. But this has not been a problem for English-speakers. Indeed, as if to prove Auden's point, his influence on English poetry seems at the moment to be increasing. As I write, a new translation of the *Sonnets to Orpheus* by Don Paterson has recently appeared, and many a new collection includes the odd version from his work, Seamus Heaney's *District and Circle* being just one example. There is not much sympathy for Germanic culture in England, and yet a number of key German writers have exercised disproportionate influence on modern English literature. As far as poetry is concerned, Rilke is overwhelmingly the most important figure, and his main rival of a later generation, Paul Celan, was himself something of a Rilkean. (It is, incidentally, interesting that neither Celan nor Rilke was a German national. Rilke was born in Austro-Hungarian Prague, while Celan was a German-speaking Romanian Jew.) Auden does not have the space to enlarge upon the reasons for Rilke's influence, but he does draw attention to one of Rilke's major discoveries: his solution to the problem of how to express the abstract in concrete terms:

> While Shakespeare, for example, thought of the non-human in terms of the human, Rilke thinks of the human in terms of the non-human, of what he calls Things (*Dinge*), a way of thought which, as he himself pointed out, is more characteristic of the child than of the adult.

Auden goes on to show how one of the poet's 'most characteristic devices is the expression of human life in terms of landscape': a striking feature of Auden's own poems.

What all this suggests is that there is something in Rilke to which English poets respond – something previously absent from our poetry but in keeping with it. But Rilke could not have made the impact he did without effective translations. Auden commented in these terms on the version he was reviewing:

> What a scholar's opinion of these translations may be I do not know and do not very much care. There is no such thing as a perfect translation; it is a job that has to be redone for every generation. But I am confident that this translation by Mr Leishman and Mr Spender will remain definitive for our own.

Auden was to prove exactly right about this. No one today deciding to read the *Iliad* will turn first of all to Alexander Pope. But Pope's Homer is great poetry and still ought to be read. The translator Auden was praising, J.B. Leishman, was not a poet of that quality, but for a term his versions of Rilke did their job effectively. During the last twenty years or so, they have been steadily superseded, but they should not be forgotten. Forty or fifty years ago, if you wanted to read Rilke and lacked good German, you turned to the set of fourteen volumes published by the Hogarth Press. Seven of these volumes were translated by Leishman, just one of them – the *Duino Elegies* – in collaboration with Stephen Spender. In five of them the German text was valuably included. The *Duino Elegies* is probably the most distinguished volume; its particular success may be attributable to Spender's contribution, though it is just as likely to be due to the absence of rhyme in the original and the closeness of Rilke's loosened dactylic hexameter to the kind of English free verse that favours a longer line. In other words, the exigencies of form are less constricting in the *Elegies* than they tend to be in Rilke's other poems. Today, most translators assume that their job is, regardless of structure, to get at the core of the poem's meaning. Leishman clearly thought the form was of at least equal importance, the result at his weaker moments being unnatural expressions and a syntax that distorts the original emphases. There *were* distinctive virtues none the less. Leishman often succeeds in capturing the movement of the German without contortion, as a glance at the *Elegies* and even some of the rhymed lyrics will easily show. (The marvellous 'Going Blind' from *New Poems* is a good random example.) In any event, back in the 1960s, with this battery of easily readable texts, it was possible for a reader like myself, with minimal German, to be as familiar with

Rilke as I was with Yeats or Eliot. For a time, Leishman was indispensable. There *were* other translations in existence, but no one else had done the job so comprehensively or established so convincing and consistent a manner and tone.

*   *   *

I owe Leishman a debt of gratitude. Forty years ago, when I was seriously learning to write poetry, there was a handful of books I depended on. At that time, two slim paperbacks were seldom out of my pocket: Michael Alexander's *The Earliest English Poems* and Leishman's selected Rilke – among the first of a classic series, the Penguin Modern European Poets. Before long I began collecting the Hogarth volumes and getting to know the German as well as the English. I soon discovered that Leishman taught English at Oxford and had written books on such poets as Donne and Milton. He was not in his own right much of a poet, but the depth of his intimacy with English poetry enabled him to give his Rilke an English style of his own, and he did this without domesticating him, maintaining a sense of his foreignness.

Old English is Low German, and German like English is a stress-time language. You can imitate Rilke's rhythms syllable for syllable, as you cannot with, let us say, Paul Valéry. Traditionally, English readers looking for inspiration from outside their native language turn to French or Italian, but we are much nearer to home with a German poet like Rilke. That is why, for me, Leishman's versions went so well with Alexander's book. Young poets, it seems to me, need a poetry to inspire them that is neither the stuff they were taught at school nor whatever it is that is currently fashionable. They need something that will encourage them to look more deeply into their language: something that will lead them to explore its essential character. Rilke in English sounded like the sort of poet – Hopkins, for instance – who, rather than rely on any sort of mainstream, looks to the ancient and the marginal. An enthusiasm for Anglo-Saxon alone, on the other hand, might have led me to literary nostalgia or worse things. Rilke did not encourage that. Intrinsically German though his poetry is, he was not satisfied with being merely Teutonic. He was a cosmopolitan who was steeped in, for instance, French and Russian poetry. He made me feel there was no reason why loving 'The Ruin' or 'The Seafarer' should prevent me from reading Baudelaire.

*   *   *

In 1967, fresh from first reading the *Duino Elegies*, I wrote a poem called

'Three Movements'. It was heavily influenced by Rilke – particularly by his sense of the potential for transcendence inherent in the actual, physical world. Here is the first 'movement', with an epigraph from the *Elegies*:

For Beauty's nothing
but beginning of Terror we're still just able to bear
– Rilke, Duino Elegies I

> I am fearful of peaks:
> they own such fallings. Why
> then do they draw
> me mad to them?
>
> As with music, I'm saved
> yet drawn by the constant
> negation of sheer ascent.
> But still it is upward.
>
> Up there,
> gazing from almost
> nothing, down on the all of be-
> lowness, might I not mountingly melt
> in the rarefied air?
>
> Cry with me here
> like the girl on the dance-floor,
> more to herself than her lover:
> 'Please, please, don't let it ever
> stop!'

There is something a little absurd about this poem. It is perhaps the absurdity of insecure identity, which afflicts most of us in adolescence. Nevertheless, in recognising that, I am also recognising something authentic. Whenever I read it, it brings back the feeling of that period of my life. It was Rilke who made that possible for me – or more accurately, the Rilke of Leishman's translations. The language of the poem has been learnt from the language of those translations: 'such fallings', 'the all of belowness', 'mountingly' – these slight deformations of English are Leishman's way of rendering German qualities, of capturing a distinctively German way of saying things. One of the things a good translation does is extend the range of what one's own language can do or say. It thereby extends the range of our experience: if we become able to say things we

79

couldn't say before, those things enter our consciousness. Rilke says things that English doesn't seem to notice, though there seems to be no reason why it shouldn't. Again, I am a little reminded of Hopkins, who is constantly stretching the language, subjecting it to strain. Leishman's Rilke has the same energy and spiritual intensity: that improbable combination of restlessness and contemplative discipline.

The obvious source for my poem is late Rilke: the *Elegies* and the uncollected poems in free verse – what Michael Hamburger calls *The Unofficial Rilke*. But the qualities I am interested in can more easily be isolated in the earlier, more traditionally formal poems. Take this lovely sonnet from *New Poems*, composed in Paris in 1908.

Spätherbst in Venedig

Nun treibt die Stadt schon nicht mehr wie ein Köder,
der alle aufgetauchten Tage fängt.
Die gläsernen Paläste klingen spröder
an deinen Blick. Und aus den Gärten hängt

der Sommer wie ein Haufen Marionetten
kopfüber, müde, umgebracht.
Aber vom Grund aud alten Waldskeletten
steigt Willen auf; als sollte über Nacht

der General des Meeres die Galeeren
verdoppeln in dem wachen Arsenal,
um schon die nächste Morgenluft zu teeren

mit einer Flotte, welche ruderschlagend
sich drängt and jäh, mit allen Flaggen tagend,
den grossen Wind hat, strahlend and fatal.

Here is Leishman's 'Late Autumn in Venice':

The city drifts no longer like a bait now,
upcatching all the days as they emerge.
Brittlier the glassy palaces vibrate now
Beneath your gaze. And from each garden verge

the summer like a bunch of puppets dangles,
headforemost, weary, made away.

Out of the ground, though, from dead forest tangles
volition mounts: as though before next day

the sea-commander must have rigged and ready
the galleys in the sleepless Arsenal,
and earliest morning air be tarred already

by an armada, oaringly outpressing,
and suddenly, with flare of flags, possessing
the great wind, radiant and invincible.

Leishman's limitations here are clear and characteristic. One cringes a
little at such artificial locutions as 'upcatching' and 'oaringly outpressing',
yet for me at 19 or 20 – as I think my poem indicates – it was precisely
such expressions that caught the genius of Rilke. They are not, it should
be emphasised, affectations. They are actually more or less literal renderings.
Grotesque as they are, their meaning and purpose are both clear and
clumsily expressive. Clumsiness, I would argue, has it virtues. Indeed,
Leishman is at his weakest when he gives in to English fluency. The
Latinate 'volition' in line 8, for instance, has none of the force of Rilke's
'Willen', and it is surely important that Rilke's sea-commander toils
overnight ('über Nacht'), not 'before next day'.

To dwell on these flaws, however, would be to demand perfection: the
one thing which, as Auden reminds us, translators can't deliver. A translator
today would probably offer something less than Leishman's detailed
replication of Rilke's structure. It is possible to suggest the rhyme-scheme
and rhythmic pattern without achieving a syllable-for-syllable equivalent.
In noting Leishman's deficiencies, moreover, we should not miss the
beauty of the poem over all, its energy, grace and sheer readability. The
sestet, in particular, has beauties which brilliantly survive one feeble rhyme
('ready/already') and the single ludicrous phrase already noticed.
Translators, particularly those who are not themselves famous poets, get
little glory. Some of them – Leishman outstandingly – deserve a great
deal more.

Charlie Louth

Charlie Louth is a Lecturer in German Language and Literature at Queen's College, Oxford, where he is a Fellow. His research interests include poetry from the eighteenth century onwards, especially Hölderlin, Rilke and Celan, translation and comparative literature. He has had numerous publications including in *The Modern Language Review* (2003), in *Modern Poetry in Translation* (2004) and in Oxford *German Studies* (2004).

What is particular about Rilke?

Part of the job of criticism must be to try to determine what is particular about a given writer or work, what distinguishes them from other writers or works. Of Rilke it is often said that his virtues, his strong points, what is especially typical of him and thus what we read him for, correspond to the strengths and peculiar characteristics of the German language. Michael Hofmann, echoing Robert Musil, even suggests that he 'may well be the apotheosis of the German language: the poet in whom its persuasions, abstracts and music are most triumphantly effective' (in *Behind the Lines*, p. 60), which would mean that Rilke not only grows out of the texture and complexion of German but teaches us what they are, brings them into a new clarity and power. To some extent it is true of any great poet that they exploit and actually unfold the possibilities of the language they are writing in, but it might be worth dwelling for a moment on some of the aspects of German that come most sharply into focus in Rilke's writing.

One is German's capacity of compressed and compact utterance, the ability to make one word contain a complex of thought and feeling. I'm not thinking so much here of German's habit of building words together out of shorter words, more of the way a word can be altered by changing a vowel or adding a prefix or suffix. Rilke's fondness for the conditional tense, and the effectiveness of his use of it, derive much from the fact that it can be identifiably expressed in one word, as an inflection of a more straightforward tense to which it points, so that it holds within itself both what it departs from and what it could one day be resolved into. The opening of the first of the *Duino Elegies* depends on that kind of complexity of tone:

> Wer, wenn ich schriee, hörte mich denn aus der Engel
> Ordnungen? und gesetzt selbst, es nähme

einer mich plötzlich ans Herz: ich verginge von seinem
stärkeren Dasein.

[Who if I cried out would hear me among the angels'
orders? and even if it happened that one of them
took me suddenly to his heart: his existence, stronger than mine,
would end it.]

The underlining of the subjunctive mood announces the significance of
it for the cycle as a whole and alerts us to its presence even in the weak
forms that cannot be inflected (such as 'hörte'). The importance of its
being one word rather than two, and a modified sound rather than just
one to which an addition has been made, is that it is better able to reflect
or express a mode or state of being as something in flux or in suspension.
The altered vowel-sound comes to correspond to a mood, particularly in
the *Elegies*, of questioning and longing that is more pervasive, and more
complete, because of its economy of expression. At the risk of being
unclear, I would say that the German one-word conditional, especially as
used by Rilke, is more concrete and fundamental, and at the same time
more resistant to being pinned down, than the compound form (which is
also possible in German). It also has a greater scope of meaning, as at
the end of the second Elegy, where it is used with an optative force:

Fänden auch wir ein reines, verhaltenes, schmales
Menschliches, einen unseren Streifen Fruchtlands
zwischen Strom und Gestein.

[If only we too could find – pure, contained, narrow –
something human, a strip of our own fertile soil
between river and stone.]

The *Elegies* run through the whole scale of implications and possibilities
contained within the conditional, but it is already a common feature of
the *New Poems* where, particularly in the 'as if' mode, it often forms the
hinge between the thing or situation and the viewer's mind working upon
them. The famous final injunction of 'Archaic Torso of Apollo' – 'You
must change your life' – gets a lot of its power from the way it emerges
from a background of conditionals.

The lines from the end of the second elegy contain another instance
of German compression, the adjectival noun 'Menschliches'. This possibility
of turning an adjective into a noun, which often involves the making
concrete of an abstract quality, or the flitting or wavering between the

two, is something Rilke often exploits and which corresponds to a general tendency of his poetry, which is a fixing of the fluid, the transient, into a form in which a provisional quality, a process, is still palpable. The abstract, the uncontained, is held just enough to become what Hölderlin calls 'feelable and felt', but without its losing its movement, its unfixability. It's not unlike the one-word conditional: in the adjectival noun the adjective is still present, we don't quite have the self-sufficiency of a noun, a quality is half-turned into a substance just as a substance is seeping off into a quality. And similarly in the infinitive-made-noun, another form favoured by Rilke, the verb has not been completely taken up into the noun but continues to make its presence felt, to unsettle the natural fixity of a noun. Both forms hesitate between different states, belonging to both, and this, again, particularly in the *Elegies*, but really throughout, is Rilke's mode. The particular status of such words can be seen quite clearly in the lines from the second Elegy: 'Menschliches' seems to grow out of the three adjectives that precede it, a little more affirmative than them but only distinguished from them by a capital letter, a capital letter that, even though Rilke doesn't capitalize the first words of his lines, is almost disguised by standing at the beginning of the line. It is arrived at through a kind of litany of adjectives, and provides the transition to the definite nouns of 'einen unseren Streifen Fruchtlands'. Grammatically it points both backwards and forwards, and carries in its make-up the fragility and tentativeness of being between fluidity and fixity, 'zwischen Strom und Gestein'. Again, the concentration of this into one word is important for the way it focuses complexity and refuses to let the elements of that complexity separate. German's ability to do this is clearly useful to lyric poetry, which is partly about economy and concentration, and Rilke's attention to that possibility has a lot to do with the difficulty of translating him into English. These couple of lines are a compaction of difficulties since 'Fruchtland' is a neologism, perhaps a shy at the French *verger*, whose absence from German Rilke regretted (a possible reason for Leishman and Spender's going for 'orchard' in their version). So the noun that then does come to stand for the mid-position is itself provisional, unsettled, aptly inventing itself for a place not yet found. Leishman/Spender translate the lines:

> If only we could discover some pure, contained,
> narrow, human, own little strip of orchard
> in between river and rock!

This pulls 'Menschliches' wholly to its adjectival pole so that it becomes indistinguishable from the preceding adjectives, and orchard is too oddly specific for something that is precisely yet-to-be-defined. Mitchell in his generally closer version (though he omits 'narrow', perhaps because it seems more negative than German 'schmal'), settles for 'human place', moving more towards the substantival pole, and 'fruit-bearing soil', a kind of spelling out of the original density:

> If only we too could discover a pure, contained,
> human place, our own strip of fruit-bearing soil
> between river and rock.

Another feature of German that everyone recognizes is its tendency to form long intricate sentences. This is mainly due to the strictness and clarity of conjugation and declension, which allows the relations between words and clauses to remain traceable even when they are spun out over several lines. Rilke is a master of the short sentence, usually summing up a previous movement and marking a pause, such as 'Sonst war nichts Rotes' [Nothing else was red] or 'Sie war schon Wurzel' [She was already root] in 'Orpheus. Eurydice. Hermes', or 'Denn Bleiben ist nirgends', 'Hiersein ist herrlich' in the *Elegies*, but he also makes great use of the long, meandering sentence. Many of his poems, particularly sonnets, are formed from one sentence, conducted over the line-endings and through the stanzas to make a contrast, again, between the fluidity of a continuous stream of unfolding meaning and the firmness of the structure it both creates and overrides. This tension, again not unlike the tensions held in a single word, is essential to what Rilke is doing in his poetry, to his exploration of states of mind and body that resist definition, that can only be indicated tentatively or momentarily, within the changing course of sentences that partly describe, partly mimic and at their best enact the processes they attend to. One fairly straightforward example of the long sentence combining with strict form is the sonnet 'Roman Fountain' from *New Poems*, in which the single sentence, each element connecting to the next, equates to the continuous cycle of water in the fountain, animating it, while the sonnet structure represents the marble form itself, with its different tiers holding up and passing on the flow. The poem's last word is 'Übergängen', 'transitions' (neatly converted into 'flow' in Stephen Cohn's translation). In a fountain water connects everything, and in this poem syntax does, so that it becomes its verbal equivalent. Much of what the poem conveys to us about the fountain comes not from what the words mean or say, but from what they do, and they do what they do through being interconnected into a whole sentence that is both tenuous, like the drops in lines 11–12 ('nur manchmal träumerisch und tropfenweis // sich niederlassend an den Moosbehängen' [only letting itself down the mossy hangings // occasionally, dreaming drop by drop]), and, vitally, coherent, one.

Rilke uses the reach of German syntax not just to obtain length and so to achieve the kind of effect discernible in 'Roman Fountain' and other poems where there is sense in containing a fluid motion within a tight structure, but more generally to reproduce in the movement of his verse the patterns of thought, or at least patterns that can convince us they are akin to those of thought. So the opening of 'To Hölderlin', a poem that talks of 'learning from the provisional' ('am Vorläufigen … lernen'), gives the impression as we read it of enacting its own thoughts, reproducing a rhythm of thinking as much as giving a particular content. The lines refer to Hölderlin's poetry: borrowing elements from a famous poem, they try to retrace the effect of reading him:

> Verweilung, auch am Vertrautesten nicht,
> ist uns gegeben; aus den erfüllten
> Bildern stürzt der Geist zu plötzlich zu füllenden; Seen
> sind erst im Ewigen.

> [Dwelling, on even the most familiar things,
> is not granted us; out of images fulfilled
> the spirit plunges to images suddenly to be filled; lakes,
> only in eternity.]

Movement, the impossibility of stasis, is realized in the syntax, in the fluctuations and contradictions: 'nicht', at the end of the first line, belongs with 'ist' (negates it) but is separated from it by a comma, so that the possibility of dwelling, of lingering pause, is both presented and withheld. 'Am Vertrautesten' condenses something abstract, intimacy, so that it seems to become concrete, a place or a hold, but offers no purchase and slips away nonetheless; the only images that can hold the course of the spirit are those that are becoming, those that are not yet full images, as is implied by the fact that they are understood rather than reiterated before the semi-colon in the third line (lost in my translation); and so 'lakes' catches at the water imagery but immediately defers itself into a never-attainable future. Coming at the end of the long line, 'Seen' again seems to offer a pause, collecting the previous lines, but then resists being read as such. The effect is similar to 'Denn Bleiben ist nirgends' [Nowhere we can remain]: a pause, a resting-place, is provided and removed in one moment.

These lines are a good example of something we can value in Rilke, the way we become more conscious of the knotty and actual texture of his language, of its moves and pauses, when it is combined with pure idea. It then gives us a very real and immediate sense of how the mental and the physical, or the abstract and the concrete, interact and are not in fact separate. It is this kind of knowledge, in hundreds of varied instances, that he allows us, at least for the duration of the reading of a poem, to put on. One instance of such a reminding that mental, emotional and physical states are intermingled is 'Leda' from the second part of the *New Poems*. 'Leda and the Swan' is also the subject of a poem by Yeats, and a comparison of the two poems will serve as a final way of attending to what is particular about Rilke. Both poems are sonnets: treating the same theme independently in the same form they offer good ground for comparison.

Leda

Als ihn der Gott in seiner Not betrat,
erschrak er fast, den Schwan so schön zu finden;
er ließ sich ganz verwirrt in ihm verschwinden.
Schon aber trug ihn sein Betrug zur Tat,

bevor er noch des unerprobten Seins
Gefühle prüfte. Und die Aufgetane
erkannte schon den Kommenden im Schwane
und wußte schon: er bat um Eins,

das sie, verwirrt in ihrem Widerstand,
nicht mehr verbergen konnte. Er kam nieder
und halsend durch die immer schwächre Hand

ließ sich der Gott in die Geliebte los.
Dann erst empfand er glücklich sein Gefieder
und wurde wirklich Schwan in ihrem Schoß.

[Leda

When the urgent god slipped into it
the swan's beauty filled him with dismay;
he vanished in it, senses all awry.
But his deception rushed him to the deed

before the feelings of his new existence
could be tried. And she, shot through, undone,
saw and knew him as he came a swan
and knew at once, confused in her resistance,

what he wanted, that she could not hide
it from him now. He came down onto her
and necking through her loosening hands the god

released himself into the girl he loved.
Then he felt the glory of his feathers
and truly became a swan between her thighs.]

Leda and the Swan

A sudden blow: the great wings beating still
Above the staggering girl, her thighs caressed
By the dark webs, her nape caught in his bill,
He holds her helpless breast upon his breast.

How can those terrified vague fingers push
The feathered glory from her loosening thighs?
And how can body, laid in that white rush,
But feel the strange heart beating where it lies?

A shudder in the loins engenders there
The broken wall, the burning roof and tower
And Agamemnon dead.
                Being so caught up,
So mastered by the brute blood of the air,
Did she put on his knowledge with his power
Before the indifferent beak could let her drop?

Looking at the two poems side by side, it's immediately obvious that
while they are both Petrarchan sonnets they make very different use of
the form. In Yeats's poem the tercets are run together (and oddly broken)
but otherwise the syntax complies with the sonnet's inner divisions, with,
particularly, a pause between octave and sestet. Rilke's poem on the other
hand overrides all the natural pauses between stanzas, so that there is
constant tension between articulation and confusion of the form, a tension
that relates both to the poem's central encounter and, especially, to the

struggle of manifestation the poem mostly concentrates on: just as Zeus is trying to find his way fully into the form of the swan, so the poem seems to be working its way into the form of the sonnet – only at the end, with the last line and rhyme, 'und wurde wirklich Schwan in ihrem Schoß', are the two processes complete, the god swan and the poem sonnet. By then, the poem has not just shown it is a sonnet, but shown the necessity of the form to its theme.

The running-on of line into line and verse into verse is also expressive of the impetuosity of Zeus's desire, which Rilke has made turning into a swan a metaphor of. Very characteristically, his interest in the myth is almost confined to wondering what it would be like to become a swan. He imagines his way into this by comparing it to desire, so that in the end it is impossible to say whether in this poem the metamorphosis is a metaphor for the growth of desire or whether desire is a metaphor for becoming a swan. In the myth they are one manifestation, and the poem folds both ways and won't unravel into figurative and literal strands. Once the process has begun it cannot be stopped. Leda has a kind of knowledge, but Zeus has suspended all understanding, he has become swan for one purpose and is consumed by it. The surrendering to the senses is experienced as confusion that needs clarification. At first, not quite a swan, he is divided, made other by his desire and by his new state, he is *on his way* towards something. Only at the end, in the fulfilment of his desire, does he become fully other and so himself. In the German, the entering into the swan and the penetration of Leda are connected by the words 'ließ sich' (lines 3 & 12) so that the one is clearly the continuation of the other. And *betreten*, as well as meaning to enter, to step into, is also, like the English tread, the proper word for a cock-bird's mating with a hen-bird. Rilke's poem is an exploration of the changes, the fusing of mental, emotional and physical aspects, in sexual desire, which taking on the form of a swan helps us to understand at the same time as they give us some imaginative sense of what it might be to shift shape. The repetition of the word 'verwirrt', used first of Zeus then of Leda, indicates the nature of the poem, in which there are no clear distinctions. And the poem is of course called after Leda, and she is at its literal centre. She is introduced with the odd phrase 'die Aufgetane' (another aspect of Rilke's particularity – just how peculiar a lot of his language appears beside more conventional German). 'The opened one': being defined entirely by her openness makes it unlikely that the word refers only to Leda's physical attitude, she seems to be exposed in and by her insight and receptiveness and experiences a kind of epiphany. She is laid open by what she knows because what she knows is that she cannot resist a god.

Yeats's version of the theme is quite different. 'Laid in that white rush' might, to someone coming from Rilke's poem, appear ambiguous at first, expressive of a confusion between god and mortal, but within the economy of Yeats's poem there can be no reading of the words as referring to the cygnean god. The sonnet is used as a structure in which opposition and distinction can, through violence, be resolved. As against Rilke, there is a terrifying clarity. Yeats presents the encounter incontrovertibly as rape, and dwells on its physicality. And although he tends to keep closer to Leda's perspective than to Zeus's, especially in the questions of the second quartet, his perspective is essentially an outside one. Whereas Rilke doesn't look beyond the act and barely assumes knowledge of the myth, for Yeats it is precisely a mythical event, in which personal violence opens onto a whole vista of future history. (According to most versions of the myth, Leda goes on to produce an egg from which Helen hatches out, and in some versions Clytemnestra is also produced, so the fall of Troy and the death of Agamemnon at the hands of his wife on his return home are made a direct consequence of the 'sudden blow' the poem relates.) Violence engenders violence and destruction, but also a new age: with Troy and Agamemnon we have the hesitant beginnings of a historical time. Yeats's poem is all about the mastering and bounding of force, and has a dramatic grandness about it that is quite alien to the Rilke poem. Its final question, which seems to ask whether there is any possible equation between knowledge and power, and whether Leda partakes for a moment of the god's omniscience and omnipotence, is purely speculative, and the poem lets it drop as the swan does Leda. We are left external to the event, whereas Rilke has taken us inside.

But to return to the sonnet form: what is surprising about the Yeats poem is its break. The poem seems to spend itself in the words 'And Agamemnon dead', with the following lines, staggered, as a sort of coda. We are made to look back at the mastery of the poem from a distance like that which separates us from the mythical event, and it is precisely that distance which makes the event of words appear with such clarity while resisting the analysis of the question. To emphasise the stepping back the poem even ends on an imperfect rhyme. Instead of wondering that it is possible for 'masterful images, because complete' ('The Circus Animals' Desertion') to be set off or revoked by the mastery of imperfection, we can compare the ending of Rilke's sonnet, which rather than breaking with the conclusiveness of the form exploits it, Zeus finding embodiment in the lines which complete the poem. It is this correspondence that lends the final image its predominantly positive force, so that the poem seems to end in fulfilment. But in keeping with the rest of the poem's attention to process, and with what we might see as Rilke's ideal of poetic language, there are different ways of reading the closing lines. First, 'dann erst' ('only then') might mean 'only at that moment' or 'only *after* that', so that satisfaction might come in or after desire, or both. And then there is the wording of the last line: 'wurde wirklich Schwan'. Each word is elusive. 'Wurde' oscillates between 'was becoming' and 'became'; 'wirklich' between each of its adjacent words, suggesting both 'actual becoming' and 'real swanhood'; and 'Schwan', without article, seems more quality than thing, only the capital S prevents 'wirklich' from qualifying it as an adjective. (Another possible translation of the last line might be: 'becoming really swan between her thighs'.) The iridescence of the language works against finality, so that the lines hold in balance the question of whether the god's process of becoming ends in his animal confinement, or whether it continues fully fledged.

Patrick Bridgwater

Patrick Bridgwater is Emeritus Professor of German in the University of Durham. He has published widely on modern German poetry (*Penguin Book of Twentieth-Century German Verse*; *The German Poets of the First World War*; *The Poets of the Café des Westens*; *The Life and Work of Georg Heym*; *August Stramm, Twenty Two Poems*; *Rainer Maria Rilke, Duino Elegies*). His most recent book was on De Quincey.

English Poets and Rilke

Rilke was introduced to Keats by Rudolf Kassner's genial collection of essays on English poets of the nineteenth century, *Die Mystik, die Künstler und das Leben* (1900), which he read in 1901. Rilke knew and admired Kassner, to whom he dedicated his Eighth Elegy, and who, in a sixtieth-birthday tribute to the Austrian poet, written in 1935,[1] was to describe Rilke as a poet in the Keats tradition. Kassner saw Rilke as bringing to a close the series of European visually oriented poets which began with 'the poet who can never be sufficiently praised, John Keats'.[2] The two poets are linked by a fundamental affinity that goes beyond the visual to include both Rilke's 'perfecting of that marvellous narcissistic lyricism which begins in England with Keats' and, what is more important, the 'negative capability' that Rilke himself embodied to such a striking degree.

Keats took Locke's view of the human mind as a passive sponge soaking up impressions, which he found discussed in Hazlitt's *Essay on the Principles of Human Action* under the suggestive heading of 'identity', and developed it into his own idea of the poet's 'negative capability', by which he meant the impressionability and in that sense lack of personal identity which he believed to mark all great poets. It was necessary, Keats believed, for the poet to be forever open to impressions, sensations or whatever, which means that the 'camelion' (chameleon) poet is forever changing his/her ideas, a fact insufficiently pondered by many of those who have expounded the *Duino Elegies* as though they contain a philosophical system, whereas they embody a poetic argument, which has more to do with mood than with self-consistency. If he knew it – and he could have known it from Kassner – the ever vacillating Rilke would surely have drawn comfort from Keats's view that poets ought never to make up their minds about anything, but should remain open-minded. Keats's 'let us open our leaves [petals] like a flower and be passive and receptive'[3] is Rilke's approach too. Indeed, in 1920 Rilke wrote that 'Art can proceed only from a purely anonymous centre',[4] which is strikingly close to Keats's remarks on the poet's lack of 'character', and therefore on his ability at any time to assume the identity of 'any one particular beauteous star'. Rilke, who, like his Austrian fellow-poet Hugo von Hofmannsthal,[5] was a notable example of the chameleon-poet, possessed that ability to an uncanny, exemplary degree:

> Keats defined the poet as the most unpoetical thing in existence because he had no identity but was always open to invasion from the multiplicity of experience. This dilemma became the burden of Rilke's unceasing complaint during the critical years [...] 1907–14: 'Au lieu de me pénétrer les choses me percent' [Instead of soaking in, things cut me to the quick] [...] The crux of the matter is that the psychic structure of the two poets was equally grounded in an unusual degree of emphatic reaction to experience which in turn determined the kind of poetry they wrote.[6]

Kassner's tribute to Rilke was written in 1935. Two years later Maurice Betz, a friend of the poet, wrote:

> Rilke told me one day that he had learnt English in a few months in order to be able to read Keats and Browning, but that on being disappointed by these poets he had [...] felt himself so alienated from England and the English language that he almost as quickly forgot everything he had just learnt. He had realized that England lay without the magic circle of his nature and its experiences and possibilities.[7]

This brings us back to 17 January 1914, when Rilke saw, in André Gide's house in Paris, a reproduction of Joseph Severn's famous sepia drawing of Keats on his deathbed. Apparently greatly moved by it, Rilke the next day wrote his poem on Keats, 'Zu der Zeichnung, John Keats im Tode darstellend' ('On a Drawing depicting John Keats in Death'):

> Nun reicht ans Antlitz dem gestillten Rühmer
> die Ferne aus den offenen Horizonten:
> So fällt der Schmerz, den wir nicht fassen konnten,
> zurück an seinen dunklen Eigentümer.
>
> Und dies verharrt, so wie es leidbetrachtend,
> sich bildete zum freiesten Gebilde,
> noch einen Augenblick, – in neuer Milde
> das Werden selbst und den Verfall verachtend.

93

Gesicht; o wessen? Nicht mehr dieser eben
noch einverstandenen Zusammenhänge.
O Aug, das nicht das schönste mehr erzwänge
der Dinge aus dem abgelehnten Leben.
O Schwelle der Gesänge,
O Jugendmund, für immer aufgegeben.

Und nur die Stirne baut sich etwas dauernd
hinüber aus verflüchtigten Bezügen,
als strafte sie die müden Augen Lügen,
die sich an ihr ergeben, zärtlich trauernd.

(A look, faraway as open horizons, reaches the silent poet-praiser's face. Thus does the pain we could not take in flow back to its own dark source.

And for a moment the face retains the sovereign look it assumed when contemplating pain, regarding life and death with a new-found forbearance.

A face, then, but whose? No longer the face that so recently made those [poetic] connexions. O eye that can no longer conjure such beauty out of the life it has left behind. O source of song, O young man's mouth, now abandoned forever.

Only the brow constructs out of bygone insights something to take across into death, as though sadly giving the lie to those tired, submissive eyes.)

That Rilke misinterpreted Severn's drawing as showing Keats after death is less important than the nature of the poem and its place in Rilke's work, for this tailed sonnet is a variation on the poem 'Der Tod des Dichters' ('Death of the Poet') (1906), which was inspired by Rodin's group of the same name, and was written at a time when Rilke was, even for him, in a particularly self-reflective state. The two poems are very much of a piece. 'Zu der Zeichnung, John Keats im Tode darstellend' is not really about Keats at all. It is about a legend. It is about a great poet who dies young. It is about the death of a poet. In other words, it is about Rilke's attitude towards his own death, a subject which greatly preoccupied him. The poem not only exhibits his habitual way of translating other artists' experience into his own terms; it goes further, appropriating the dead Keats into his private mythology of himself as one whose task is praising. Rilke has identified with Keats in a way that shows more concern for himself than for his dead brother-in-art.

Kassner, no doubt disappointed by Rilke's response to the great English poet, must also have realized that there were linguistic, cultural and personal reasons why Rilke, in the event, did not respond more positively to Keats and his work. Rilke was, notwithstanding his veneration for Baudelaire and Hölderlin, and his tumultuous enthusiasm for Elizabeth Barrett Browning's *Sonnets from the Portuguese*, potentially jealous of other poets. Notwithstanding his versions of *Sonnets from the Portuguese* (which, based on preliminary translations by Alice Faehndrich, themselves triggered by Marie Gothein's translations of 1903, betrayed no great knowledge of the English language), English was not a language with which he was comfortable, and Keats's work was culturally inaccessible to the poet whose heart was closer to Baudelaire and Manet than to Lemprière. Besides, when Keats was drawn to his attention in 1914, Rilke was so much wrapped up in his own affairs, that he saw in Keats merely a pale reflection of himself. Of course Keats 'ought to' have appealed to Rilke, one of whose watchwords was 'sensualité de l'âme', and might have done so if all the circumstances had been right, although I doubt it, for Keats was too far from Rilke's poetic stamping-ground. He remained interested in the Keats legend, as he was interested in the Shelley legend and the Wilde legend, but his concern was, at bottom, the Rilke legend and how it would turn out to be. That was always his subtext.

As the most original and powerful of modern German poets, Rilke has had a profound impact outside German-speaking Europe and a not inconsiderable one in the English-speaking world. In the 1940s in particular he was a considerable presence in English poetry. W. H. Auden noted in 1939 that Rilke's influence on contemporary diction and imagery was growing (which certainly applies to his own work of the time, e.g. the sequence 'In Time of War'), and in 1946 Stephen Spender stated, in a talk on the BBC Far Eastern service, that Rilke's work had been considered by most English poets as deeply as 'that of Eliot himself'. The implied analogy between Rilke and Eliot remains valid: readers of the *Duino Elegies* will not infrequently find both *The Waste Land* and *Four Quartets* called to mind. The 'intolerable wrestle / With words and meanings' of the *Four Quartets* is clearly heard in these elegies in which the self-absorbed poet-aesthete struggles, alone, on the very edge of language, often finding words for the 'unsayable', though, inevitably, words occasionally fail him. Although he has always been all things to all men and women, Rilke is very much a poet's poet. Most strongly influenced by him were Sidney Keyes, who revelled in his poetic ideas, and W. H. Auden, who borrowed extensively from him before rejecting his whole poetic persona; other poets of the 1930s–1950s (among them Alun Lewis, Edith Sitwell [whose bower-bird poetry includes many a jewel from Rilke], Stephen Spender, C. Day Lewis, Hugh MacDiarmid and Randall Jarrell) were affected by his example to a lesser extent. It is on Keyes and Auden that I focus.

In his tragically short career Sidney Keyes more than once acknowledged his indebtedness to Rilke, whose poetry he appears to have come across at Tonbridge (School) in the late 1930s. Leishman's translation of Rilke's *Later Poems* (1938) was evidently among the books recommended to him by Tom Staveley: This is suggested by the fact that one of Keyes' earliest poems, 'Prospero' (1938), is reminiscent of Rilke's 'Der Geist Ariel': not only is the poetic technique similar, but the attitude to death – an abiding preoccupation of both poets – is very similar. For the schoolboy poet-in-the-making who discovers him, Rilke cannot but be a potent, heady influence: the emotional rhetoric, the introspectiveness and preoccupation with loneliness and death, and the artistic self-awarenesss are likely to sweep the teenage poet off his feet. This was clearly the case with the young Sidney Keyes, who lived in a dream-world inhabited by his poetic heroes. His friend and editor Michael Meyer wrote that

> Blake, Schiller, Wordsworth, and, above all, Yeats and Rilke, were more intimate to him than the contemporary world. He was in the closest and most constant contact with their minds through their writings, and he preferred their company to that of the living.[8]

In a letter to fellow-poet David Wright dated 30 December 1941 Keyes wrote: 'My *ideas* come from Yeats and Rilke, as you probably realize!' It is echoes of Rilke's and Yeats's ideas that we see in his early poems. The fragment 'Shall the Dead Return?' relies on Rilke's requiem 'Für eine Freundin' for its general conception of death, and contains lines such as 'They stray wearily, grey faces wistful / Seeking and yearning for eternity' that echo Rilke's First Elegy ('And being-dead is difficult / and needs to be worked at, before one begins to feel / a little eternity.'). By the same token the lines 'But remember / Never a man of you fought as I those years / Beside the incarnation of mortal pride / The yearning of immortals for the flesh' in the poem 'Gilles de Retz' are strongly reminiscent of Rilke's lines in the Seventh Elegy, 'The sunken are ever / seeking the earth again.' We have Michael Meyer's word for it that 'The yearning of immortals for the flesh', which Keyes found in Rilke, seemed to him a theme of the greatest importance. In 'Gilles de Retz', however, the most significant borrowing from Rilke is the idea of the 'community of love without giving or taking'. In a letter to Milein Cosmann written in July 1942 Keyes said that in his 'crushing boredom and hopelessness' he had turned again to Rilke, 'who says in *Malte Laurids Brigge* [that] 'to be loved is to be consumed [...] to love is to endure.' But it is so hard to love, in the right sense of accepting the world without the desire for possession.'[9] The ideal of love without possession is inspired by *Malte Laurids Brigge* and the *Duino Elegies*:

> Is it not time that we, loving,
> freed ourselves from the beloved and, trembling, endured it:
> as the arrow endures the string to become, tensed in the sudden release,
> something *more* than itself. For staying is nowhere.' (First Elegy)

'Gilles de Retz' was to have been included in a series of elegies modelled on Rilke's *Duino Elegies*, with pain as one of the central themes. Keyes' love-poem 'The Gardener' ends with an echo of the key-line of the First and Second Duino Elegies, 'Every angel is terrible': 'O it is terrible to dream of angels'. When he wrote 'The Gardener', Rilke was very much in his mind: 'I have just read *Weise von Liebe u. Tod des Cornets Cristoph Rilke*, and partially translated it,' he wrote. 'Perhaps it is a little Romantic and ninetyish, but obviously the work of a great poet [. . .] Not a major work, but like nothing else I have read.' At the same time he had the *Duino Elegies* echoing in his mind, and was also reading *Malte*. Even singly these are potentially overwhelming reading for an emotional young poet with increasingly insistent presentiments of his own early death.

In tandem with a series of elegies modelled on the *Duino Elegies* Keyes planned a sonnet sequence modelled on the *Sonnets to Orpheus* that was to have included sonnets dedicated to figures from the past who had influenced him, including Rilke, as well as Rilkean sonnets about things seen and events experienced and inwardly appropriated (cf. Rilke's *Dinggedichte*). He abandoned the plan because he found the sonnet form cramping, concluding that it would have been 'as if I had shut myself up in a number of little boxes', which should be considered together with the point later made by John Heath Stubbs, that Keyes made the mistake of taking Rilke's free treatment of the sonnet form as his model, without first understanding the dynamics of the sonnet, with the result that while Rilke's sonnets observe the basic sonnet structure, Keyes' imitations have little in common with the sonnet save the requisite number of lines. Keyes' poetic immaturity is shown by the fact that while he realized he was cramping his style by trying to force himself into the the strait-jacket of the sonnet form, it seems not to have occurred to him that he was also doing so by modelling himself on Rilke.

Keyes only translated one poem by Rilke, 'Der Dichter' (The Poet). Here is his version:

> The hour slips from me: the wingbeats of the hour
> Wound me and take my peace away.

I am alone. Yet what strange power
Inhabits all my life, my night, my day?

Unhoused and loverless I live
In no sure place, lacking all centre:
I give myself and as I give
Possess the world by that surrender.

The first six lines are a straightforward and successful translation: Keyes has changed nothing of the original while unobtrusively updating and improving the diction. With the last two lines it is a different matter. Rilke's lines ('Alle Dinge, an die ich mich gebe, / werden reich und geben mich aus' [All the things to which I give myself / Are enriched and pass me on in turn]) have been altered because they express a kind of passive acceptance of life for which Keyes, like Alun Lewis, but unlike W. H. Auden, had no time. Keyes made his own position clear in 'Time will not Grant' (1941):

Rilke tenderly
Accepted autumn like a rooted tree.
But I am frightened after every good day
That my life must change and fall away.

The last line here alludes to the last line of Rilke's 'Archäischer Torso Apollos'.

When Keyes came to write his first really ambitious poem, 'The Foreign Gate', his model was again Rilke. The poem takes its motto, quoted in German, from Rilke's Sixth Elegy:

The Hero is strangely akin to those who die young. Duration
does not concern him. His rise is existence; he's constantly
setting out and entering the changed constellation
of his perpetual peril. There few would find him. But
that which is grimly silent about us, sudden god-given fate,
hymns him into the storm of its upsurging world.

Rilke's Hero is a private cult-figure, the poet's super-ego, but also an ideal figure pointing to the ideal of perfect self-realization, the man who is forever ready for his destiny, the genetically programmed death that lurks inside him from conception. This is the point, for 'The Foreign Gate' urges the need for courageous submission to death (Rilke's 'acceptance'), which now for the first time appears as a real presence in

Keyes, who has clearly fallen under the spell of Rilke's great landscape of death in the Tenth Elegy, to say nothing of its precursor and successor tributary images. Meyer was right to speak of the poem being dominated by Rilke: there are many echoes of Rilke's thought, diction, and imagery here, and then in the fifth section there is a direct reference to Rilke:

Once a man cried and the great Orders heard him:
Pacing upon a windy wall at night
A pale unlearned poet out of Europe's
Erratic heart cried and was filled with speech.
Were I to cry, who in that proud hierarchy
Of the illustrious would pity me?
What should I cry, how should I learn their language?

Keyes is referring to the conception of the First Elegy when Rilke, standing alone on the ramparts of the Castle of Duino in a storm, seemed to hear through the pounding of the Adriatic far below a voice which gave him the now famous opening of the *Duino Elegies*: 'Who, if I cried, would hear me among the Orders of Angels?' The *Duino Elegies*, to which we are continually referred in Keyes' poetry, are concerned with Keyes' own preoccupations: Love, Time, and Death.

The many references to Rilke in Keyes' letters and notebooks explain his attitude to the Austrian poet. In June 1942, for instance, he compares his three great literary models:

Wordsworth and Rilke were not troubled by [Yeats's] violent need for possession: one was himself expressed in mountains, the other in a more urban imagery which embraced a whole culture. They are, for this reason, more powerful poets, though they lack Yeats's magnificent violence. Yet the more subtle revelations of Wordsworth and Rilke are less actual to us than Yeats' direct oracular statements: for Rilke's culture of carved tables and personal relationships like works of art is temporarily eclipsed, and we have come to see nature as disordered and menacing.

While the sculptural quality of Keyes' own poetry owes much to Rilke's 'culture of carved tables' in the form of the objective *New Poems* written under the influence of Rodin, it is hardly surprising that in 1942 some at least of Rilke's work should strike Keyes as too arty, not sufficiently direct, a point made more forcefully by Auden It must be stressed, however, that the whole point of the *Duino Elegies*, the work by which Keyes was most powerfully influenced, is that nature is there seen as 'disordered and menacing' precisely. A few weeks before his death Keyes wrote of himself in words that might have been written by Rilke:

> I should have been born in the last century [...] because then I might have been a good pastoral poet, instead of an uncomfortable metaphysical without roots. The trouble is, that a thing of beauty isn't a joy for ever for me; nor am I content to imagine beauty is truth, etc. All I know is that everything in a vague sort of way means something else, and I want desperately to find out *what*.

He is here defining himself in terms of an implicit identification with Rilke, the archetypal 'uncomfortable metaphysical without roots'.

Although he claimed not to follow the early 1940s trend towards 'a new and overwrought Romanticism', Keyes was in his way very much a Romantic, compare his letter to Richard Church of January 1943:

> As to the question of my symbolism: the best clue I can give you is to say that I believe the greatest and most influential poets in the last hundred years or so to be Yeats and Rilke. These two brought back reports from a kind of Ultima Thule of Romanticism, which suggest that there is even more – much more – to be discovered there, and the starting point of my quest is therefore an attempt to synthesize this information.[10]

Implicitly Keyes links the 'Ultima Thule of Romanticism' with the inspiriting mountains of the Ninth Elegy. What marks Keyes as a Romantic is his awareness that 'everything in a vague sort of way means something else', and above all his obsession with the Ultima Thule of Death:

> The Romantics raised a spectre they could not lay; it was, broadly speaking, death as a part of life, conceived in terms of sensual imagery. To the Midddle Ages and the Elizabethans, death was merely the Leveller; to the 17th century, a metaphysical problem; to the 18th century, the end of life. The Romantics tried to think of it as a state of existence. By the 1840s, this had become an obsession, and had degenerated into curiosity. By the later 19th century, and up to our own time, it had resulted in a clearly apparent *Death Wish*, as the only solution to the problem – since the solution must come in sensual terms [...] It was left to necrophilous Germany, to Rilke, in fact, to provide the best solution short of actually dying. That is why there had to be a 'Poet of Death' in the 20th century; and why Rilke is the most important poet since Goethe and Wordsworth.[11]

The background to this diary-entry is, of course, Rilke's Tenth Elegy.

Keyes' view of Rilke as *the* modern 'Poet of Death' is a limited one, but it does summarize what Rilke was for Keyes (and for Alun Lewis too, who was confirmed by Rilke in his central preoccupation with the 'single poetic theme of Life and Death'). Keyes' ideas came from Rilke, it being Rilke's ideas on love, time and death which he found most stimulating, but he was naturally also influenced by the form in which these ideas were expressed, for they only become remarkable when Rilke clothes them in words of poetic grandeur; when the chips are down, it's the words that count, not pre-poetic ideas or feelings. Keyes' plans to write a series of elegies and a sonnet-cycle modelled on the *Duino Elegies* and the *Sonnets to Orpheus* respectively, the 'sculptural quality', 'resonance' and 'grandeur' which a contemporary reviewer noted in his poetry, his contributions to the traditions of the landscape poem and of blank verse, and some of his symbolism, are all indebted to Rilke. Meyer's statement (in the prefatory 'Memoir' to Keyes' *Collected Poems* of 1945) that Keyes was the first truly English poet effectively to marry continental symbolism to the English Romantic tradition is certainly arguable. Keyes is the first English-language poet to penetrate the enigmatic arcana of the *Duino Elegies* and *Sonnets to Orpheus* and make them his own. He discovered Rilke early and was helped by him in his own poetic development. His tragically early death, the presentiment of which does so much to explain the attraction of Rilke, meant, however, that he never had time to outgrow his early Rilkean poetic persona. Given more time his attitude towards his early master would have changed, perhaps bringing it closer to that of W.H. Auden, who was both more influenced than Keyes on the poetic level and far more critical of Rilke on the public one, but then Auden, unlike Keyes, lived to move away from Rilke.

Auden probably always had private reservations about Rilke and his ultra-aesthetic works, but he became vocally opposed to Rilke's whole poetic persona, stance and view of poetry only after learning not a little from him. For a start, Rilke was an influential model for the early Auden's treatment of the sonnet form: in *Poems* (1928), we find something that was to dominate Auden's work of the 1930s, the Rilkean sonnet that Monroe K. Spears was to describe memorably well as

> a sonnet or the recognizable equivalent (often highly irregular in form) in the manner of Rilke's *Sonnets to Orpheus* [...] the characteristic device he takes over from Rilke is that of putting unidentified persons, indicated only by pronouns [...] in usually symbolic landscapes, with the sonnet beginning in the middle of an unexplained dramatic situation.[12]

101

The *Sonnets to Orpheus* are characterized, as Rilke himself said, by 'the greatest freedom and [...] the most extreme variations that can be comprehended under that otherwise so sedate and stable form'; strictly speaking they are not so much sonnets as free variations on the sonnet form. Auden's sonnets exhibit the same formal irregularity.

The 'Rilkean sonnet' as seen in 'Control of the Passes' was, he said, the key (in *Poems*, 1928) and 'Sir, no man's enemy, forgiving all' (in *Poems*, 1930) becomes one of the dominant forms employed by Auden throughout the thirties; it is extensively used in the sequences 'In Time of War' and 'The Quest', where the phrasing and the imagery alike betray the hold Rilke had on him at the time. Both Auden's architectural imagery (buildings, fountains, aqueducts, etc.) and the images of the doll, child, animal, bird, rose, mirror, mountain, etc. recall Rilke and often have Rilkean symbolical values. In the Foreword to his *Collected Shorter Poems 1927–1957* (1966) Auden admitted that in the 1930s his 'addiction to German [meaning Rilkean] usages became a disease'. 'In Time of War' (in *Journey to a War*, 1939) consists of 28 sonnets in the Rilkean 'portrait' mode, and, as Spears has said, 'The Rilkean abrupt beginning, unfixed pronouns and imagery from mythology and legend serve to counteract what would otherwise be almost too explicit a presentation of ideas'.[13]

The use of unfixed pronouns in a symbolical or allegorical setting, which provides Auden with a new way of linking abstract and concrete, general and particular, while carrying with it the danger of obscurity, brings us to what is, after the Rilkean sonnet as such, the most significant single technique that Auden appropriated from Rilke, *paysage moralisé*. In a review of the American edition of Leishman and Spender's translation of the *Duino Elegies*, Auden wrote:

> one of the constant problems of the poet is how to express abstract ideas in concrete terms [...] Rilke is almost the first poet since the seventeenth century to find a fresh solution [...] While Shakespeare, for example, thought of the non-human world in terms of the human, Rilke thinks of the human in terms of the non-human, of what he calls Things (*Dinge*) [...] Thus one of Rilke's more characteristic devices is the expression of human life in terms of landscape. It is this type of imagery which is beginning to appear in English poetry.[14]

Although this type of imagery was beginning to appear in Auden's own poetry well before 1939, he was confirmed by Rilke in his own tendency to use physical objects as projections of human qualities. It was from Rilke that he learned the use of psychic geography or landscape to express emotional states, this being seen at its clearest in the poem 'Paysage Moralisé'. In brief, Rilke helped Auden to discipline his moralist's tendency toward abstraction.

There are, in the sonnet sequence 'In Time of War' (1939), a number of direct allusions to Rilke. Sonnet XXIII in particular shows that Rilke was much in Auden's mind at this time:

> To-night in China let me think of one,
>
> Who through ten years of silence worked and waited,
> Until in Muzot all his powers spoke,
> And everything was given once for all;
>
> And with the gratitude of the Completed
> He went out in the winter night to stroke
> That little tower like a great animal.

By the time of the sonnet-sequence 'The Quest' (in *New Year Letter*, 1941; see Sonnets X and XVI) such allusions have been forced by the pressure of outward event into the ironical mode. Newly ironical allusions to Rilke's Angel, Hero, and Acrobat characterize Auden's whole approach to the Austrian poet once the initial purely poetic magic has worn off. Veering from ambivalence to hostility, most of them are found in the 'Letter' in *New Year Letter* (1941). The first such reference is notably ambivalent:

> *Rilke*, whom die Dinge bless,
> The Santa Claus of loneliness.

Rilke is here dolled up to resemble the modiste Madame Lamort of the Fifth Elegy because Auden's decade-long admiration for Rilke's poetic technique is, in a typical 'thirties reaction to the poetry of the previous generation, rapidly giving way to the idea that poetry à la Rilke is 'not enough'.

The passage in *The Dyer's Hand* (1962) in which Auden makes clear his view that 'Poetry is not magic. In so far as poetry, or any other of the arts, can be said to have an ulterior purpose, it is, by telling the truth, to disenchant and disintoxicate,' goes back to his changed attitude to Rilke twenty years earlier. In the same passage he goes on to attack 'the poet who comes [implicitly: like Rilke] to think of himself as the god who creates his subjective universe out of nothing'. Having come, by 1941, to consider there to be something diabolical about aestheticism, he wrote in *New Year Letter*, of the Devil, that

103

He puts a Rilke in my hands.
'You know the Elegies, I'm sure,
– *O Seligkeit der Kreatur*
Sie immer bleibt im Schosse – womb
In English is a rhyme to tomb.'
He moves on tiptoe round the room,
Turns on the radio to mark
Isolde's Sehnsucht for the dark.

It is because, in his view, 'All vague idealistic art / That coddles the uneasy heart, / Is up his alley' that the Devil quotes Rilke in these uncomplimentary terms; yet, given that the Devil is the prototypical liar, Auden's view is, I think, less clear-cut than it seems: shades, here, of the poem 'Spain' (1937), which was less committed than many of his friends would have expected.

There is no need to invoke the other acknowledged and unacknowledged references to the Eighth Elegy in Auden's 'Letter', for we have already seen that he ultimately rejected Rilke not because he saw him as a 'Poet of Death' in Keyes' sense of a poet whose major theme was death, but because he had been forced to the conclusion that Rilke was not a 'life' poet, that his very art, by its purity, placed him on the side of death rather than life. It is a point of view with which Thomas Mann would have agreed. The early Auden and the late Rilke are, of course, complete opposites, but the fact is that Auden turned his back on Rilke only after spending the thirties in his company. That the English-language poet who had least in common with Rilke, was, for a decade or so, the most influenced by him, is one of the ironies to which reception history is prone.

Notes

[1] Reprinted in a revised form in Kassner's *Buch der Erinnerung* (Leipzig: Insel-Verlag, 1938, new edition 1954).

[2] On the reception of Keats in Germany, see my *Anglo-German Interactions in the Literature of the 1890s* (Oxford: Legenda, 1999), 123–44.

[3] Letter to Reynolds of 19 February 1818, see *Letters of John Keats*, ed. Frederick Page (London: OUP, 1968), 80.

[4] R.M. Rilke, *Briefe aus den Jahren 1914 bis 1921* (Leipzig: Insel-Verlag, 1937), 335.

[5] In the important essay 'Der Dichter und diese Zeit' (in Hugo von Hofmannsthal, *Blicke. Essays* [Leipzig: Reclam, 1987], 156) Hofmannsthal followed Keats in arguing that the poet, the silent brother of all things, takes his colour from the things on which his eye comes to rest.

[6] Frank E. Wood, 'Rilkes Keats-Bild', *Germanic Review*, 25 (1950), 211. For Rilke's complaint, see his *Briefe 1907–14* (Leipzig: Insel-Verlag, 1933), 265.

[7] Maurice Betz, *Rilke vivant* (Paris: Editions Emile-Paul Frères, 1937), quoted from E.C. Mason, *Rilke, Europe and the English-Speaking World* (Cambridge: CUP, 1961), 41f.

[8] *The Collected Poems of Sidney Keyes*, ed. Michael Meyer (London: Routledge,1945), 12.

[9] See Rilke, *The Notebook of Malte Laurids Brigge*, tr. Johm Linton (London: The Hogarth Press, 1978), 234.

[10] *Collected Poems*, xviif.

[11] *Collected Poems*, xviii.

[12] Monroe K. Spears, *The Poetry of W.H. Auden*, 1963, 254

[13] Spears, 149

[14] *The New Republic*, 6 Sept, 1939.

Manfred Engel

Manfred Engel has the Taylor Chair of the German Language and Literature, University of Oxford. His selected publications are: *Rilkes 'Duineser Elegien' und die moderne deutsche Lyrik (1986); Der Roman der Goethezeit*, vol 1: *Anfänge in Klassik und Frühromantik (1993);* co-ed. *Rilke, Werke. Kommentierte Ausgabe*, vol. 1 & 2 (1996), 5 (2003); co-ed. *The Enlightenment and the Dream* (2002); co-ed. *KulturPoetik.Zeitschrift für kulturgeschichtliche Literaturwissenschaft Poetics* (2001 ff.); essays on Blake, Goethe, Hölderlin, Novalis, C.F. Meyer, Rilke, Eliot, Kafka, Arp, et al., and on the cultural and literary history of the dream.

T.S. Eliot and Rilke

Polyphony and Dialogism in *The Waste Land* and the *Duineser Elegien*

T.S. Eliot's *The Waste Land* appeared in 1922, Rilke's *Duino Elegies* in 1923. So both belong to the great decade of 'classical' Modernism in which many authors tried to account for, or even to compensate for the breakdown of the European cultural tradition, which the Great War had completed rather than caused. In this cultural crisis, doubt in the vitality of the occidental tradition and a sceptical attitude towards the newly risen forces of modernisation led to a wide-spread interest in myth and in ancient and foreign cultural traditions.

This, in short, is the historical background of my essay. I will try to show that *The Waste Land* and the *Duino Elegies* use dialogical poetics (which can both be described in the terminology of the Russian critic Mikhail Bakhtin[1]) in very different ways, and that the difference between these versions of dialogism can help to elucidate basis differences between Eliot's and Rilke's versions of poetic Modernism.

I

Obviously, there are various levels of polyphony in Eliot's *The Waste Land*:[2] (1) *Polyphony and heteroglossia of voices, ideologies, sociolects*

---

[1] Of course, Bakthin believes poetry to be a monological genre (Bakhtin 1981, 286); in my opinion, however, this is certainly not true, at least as far as modern poetry is concerned

[2] All quotations from *The Waste Land* are given by verse-number from: Eliot 1974. For a brief survey of interpretations cf. the editors' introduction in Cuddy and Hirsch.

and dialects: Instead of the traditional poetic self or narrator, we encounter a multitude of different persons and voices, belonging to different social groups, different nations and cultures and to different times. (2) *Polyglossia of national languages*: There are, for instance, passages in French, German, Italian and even Sanskrit. (3) *Polyphony of texts and genres*: Some of the poem's voices are obviously quotations[3] or allude to other texts and genres.

This evident polyphony and heteroglossia has been puzzling interpreters for years. Even today, most critics are looking for psychologically plausible characters[4] and for the protagonist or main speaker who could function as the unifying centre of the poem.[5] This clearly neglects Eliot's most important poetic innovation: *The Waste Land* is not organized around one or several coherent characters; it is a dialogical interplay of voices representing different ideologies, value systems, and world-views.[6]

The basic opposition, which forms, so to speak, the deep-structure of *The Waste Land*'s dialogism, is the opposition between *voices of the present* and *voices of the past*. These two groups represent two different forms of societies or cultures, two different types of world-views and social values. The *present* is the 'Waste Land' of modern European culture; its inhabitants are isolated subjects, incapable of communication, love, empathy, compassion, weary of life, deprived of any metaphysical values, searching for material gain only, functioning mechanically like human machines.[8] The cultural worlds of the *past* – reaching back from aristocratic childhood experiences in pre-war Europe (v. 8–18) to the mythical time of the *Upanishads* (v. 395 ff.) – were organic wholes, integrated into the

---

[3] For a brief survey of all quotations – equalling well over 10 percent of the poem – cf. Frank and Bödeker 57; for Eliot's sources in general cf. Smith.

[4] Cf. e.g. the recent study by Brooker and Bentley.

[5] Of course, Eliot himself started this hunt for a traditional poetic self by calling Tiresias 'the most important personage in the Poem, uniting all the rest' (note to v. 218). Astonishingly enough, even a recent study by Bedient – which seems to be the first to use Bakhtin for an interpretation of *The Waste Land* – is looking for something like a single ventriloquist behind the different voices. In an orthodox Bakhtinian view, only the author could be this organising centre.

[6] 'The speaking person in the novel is always, to one degree or another, an ideologue, and his words are always ideologemes. A particular language in a novel is always a particular way of viewing the world' (Bakhtin 1981, 333).

[7] This second group presents itself mainly by direct or indirect quotations; it consists, so to speak, of the 'speech of another' (Bakhtin), i.e. authentic voices from the past. Eliot quotes various English authors, mainly of the 16th and 17th century, such as Shakespeare, Marvell and Webster, but also Dante, Augustinus and texts of Buddhism and Old Indian mythology.

[8] The only scene in which the present appears as positive is v. 257–265.

cycles of nature. It was a time when metaphysics worked and formed a bond between human beings and between man and nature, when people participated in meaningful myths and rituals, and were still capable of love and romance.

In Eliot's poem, these two worlds are confronted on three levels. Firstly (and rarely), in explicit discussion, in lamentations about the loss of the past or in hopes of its future revival; this is what we may call the *rhetoric level* of *The Waste Land*. A second form of confrontation occurs on a *metaphoric level*, founded largely on the tropology of the fertility rites described by Jessie L. Weston and George Frazer; most important here, of course, is the opposition between barrenness and fertility, death and rejuvenation. The third level of confrontation – the only one I am going to deal with here – can be described in Bakhtinian terminology as the *dialogic level* of the poem where the two groups of voices are brought into different versions of dialogical interaction.

This dialogism extends to all three logically possible relations between the two groups. I give one example only for each: a) *past – present* (the most important variant): At the end of a pub conversation in vernacular English we encounter a quotation from *Hamlet* in quite different a tone: 'Good night, ladies, good night, sweet ladies, good night,/ good night' (v. 172–73); b) *present – present*: The present relationship between man and women is first described in a middle, then in a lower class surroundings (v. 111 ff. and 139 ff.); c) *past – past*: especially in the confrontation of different religious and mythological system, e.g. v. 307–311 which alternates between quotations from St Augustine's *Confessions* and Buddha's *Fire-sermon*. A special group is formed by indirect quotations of old myths via modern artistic adaptations, e.g. the reference to the myth of Perceval via Verlaine (v. 202), to the myth of Tristan and Isolde via Wagner (v. 31–34 passim) or to Shakespeare via the 'Shakespearean Rag' (v. 128–130). These show that the past is still present in our cultural memory.

Here we can find many of the forms of dialogism described by Bakhtin: There are, for instance, examples for *stylization* ('an artistic representation of another's linguistic style' Bakhtin 1981, 362) – e.g. when a voice belonging to the present suddenly assumes the authority of biblical prophecy (v. 19–30), indicated by a fragmentary quotation from the Bible ('son of man' v. 20).[9] There are different versions of what Bakhtin calls *variation* (which 'joins the stylized world with the world of contemporary consciousness' 1981, 363) – for instance when the love between Tristan

---

[9] Other examples are the description of the female boudoir in the language of high love poetry (v. 77 ff.) or the Spenserian tone in the description of the wintry Thames (v. 173 ff.).

and Isolt (v. 31–34) is infected[10] (v. 42) by the present failure of love (v. 35–41). Especially important is the so-called *hybrid*, defined by Bakhtin as:

> an utterance that belongs, by its grammatical (syntactic) and compositional markers, to a single speaker, but that actually contains mixed within it two utterances, two speech manners, two styles, two 'languages', two semantic and axiological belief systems (Bakhtin 1981, 304; cf. also: 358–362).

The function of this constant dialogical interplay of voices is fourfold: (1) The voices of the past and present respectively 'carve out a living image' (Bakhtin 1981, 361) of the other language and its ideology. (2) The dialogism between the voices of the past creates ambivalence: no single voice is in itself the (monologic) centre of authority and truth. (3) The dialogism between past and present voices throws a polemic light on the depravation of present society. (4) The most important function of Eliot's hybridization, however, is to present *all* voices as part of our collective cultural memory.[11] So, in a way, the past is still present – and can therefore still exert an influence.

This brings me to the intercultural hermeneutics of Eliot's dialogism. The culture most distant from us in time and space in *The Waste Land* is the Old Indian world of the *Upanishads*.[12] It is presented in the second part of the last section entitled 'What the Thunder said'. After numerous Christian allusions in the first part – to the crucifixion of Christ, the journey to Emmaus or the Chapel Perilous of the Grail legends – the second part leads us to the world of Buddhism: An Indian landscape is sketched out in an alien language – Eliot uses the old Sanskrit names like 'Ganga' (for Ganges) and 'Himavant' (for Himalaya) – and we hear the Sanskrit onomatopoeia for the sound of the thunder ('da') and three interpretations of this sound from one of the *Brihadaranyaka Upanishads*: datta, dayadhvam, damyata. Only the notes supply a translation: give, sympathize, control; the poem itself confronts us directly with the alien 'voice of another' (Bakhtin).

Eliot does not even try to present a portrait of Old-Indian culture. We may infer that it must have believed in 'natural' laws – laws decreed by

---

[10] The term 'infection' ('Ansteckung') was first used by Leo Spitzer in his analysis of reported speech.

[11] The old mythological traditions, for instance, survive in various forms of superstition – like the Tarot cards of Madame Sosostris (v. 43 ff.).

[12] For Eliot's profound knowledge of Old Indian culture cf. Sri.

nature, by the authoritative voice of the thunder god – and that it may thus have been able to curb individualism and egotism. Yet we receive no direct explanation, or picture, or symbol of Old India but are merely confronted with the dialogical interplay of voices, with a special type of double-voiced speech which is, by the way, missing in Bakhtin's system: namely *interpretation* as an attempt to find the approximate equivalent for one voice in another by paraphrase. In fact, we even encounter two types of interpretation: Whereas the Old-Indian interpretation of the thunder's voice is given in an obviously consonant voice – here the human speech is almost echoing the voice of nature[13] – the modern interpretation of the Buddhist imperatives in the paraphrase which Eliot provides, is clearly dissonant: modern language, modern thinking and feeling are directly confronted with the alien Sanskrit words. Eliot's interpretation is thus of a very special, dialogic kind: it does not try to understand what the Indian words meant in their Buddhist context – this, according to Eliot, we will never know;[14] instead, it asks what they *could* mean *to us* and tries to find a modern analogy for them in our idiom and our realm of cultural experience. The Sanskrit voice and its modern interpretation combine – to use Bakhtin's terminology – to form a 'double-voiced word', a cultural hybrid, merging two 'voices' – two different cultures – with only one 'accent', one value-system.[15] So Eliot uses dialogism as a hermeneutic tool which combines the attempt to understand with an awareness of unbridgeable strangeness and difference.[16] Unlike Weston or Frazer Eliot is not looking for a trans-cultural authentic and authoritative arch-myth; instead, he uses the accumulated alien voices of the past to convey an 'accent', a world-view for which the present voice still has to be found.

[13] Allusions to a natural, onomatopoetic language are frequent in *The Waste Land*; cf. the Philomel-myth (v. 103, 203–206), the Thames-daughters' 'weialla' (v. 277–78 and 290–91), the 'water-dripping song' of the hermit-thrush (v. 357), the Portuguese version of a cock's cry (v. 392).

[14] Eliot categorically rules out any possibility of adequately understanding past cultures; cf. his early (unpublished) seminar paper on 'The interpretation of primitive ritual and his introduction to Savanorola', qtd. in Brooker and Bentley 50, 117, 154–158.

[15] For details cf. Bakhtin 1984, 199 passim. Bakhtin does not, to my knowledge, give an explicit definition of 'accent'. Whereas 'voice' means the complex of utterance (a specific use of language) and ideology; accent – or, as Bakhtin sometimes says, an 'accent system' (1981, 328) – stands for ideology only. So there can be combinations like 'two voices, two accents' (e.g. 'hybrid'), 'one voice, two accents' (e.g. 'stylization'), or 'two voices, one accent' (the last combination seems to be missing in Bakhtin's system). Cf. the explanation of 'accent' given in Voloshinov 103–106.

[16] This method is illustrated in the final lines of *The Waste Land*, a sort of coda which in its forced heteroglossia is a *mise en abîme* of the whole poem.

II

The relevance of Bakhtin's dialogism to *The Waste Land* is, I think, fairly obvious. The case of the *Duino Elegies*,[17] however, is a much more dubious one: The language of the poem is fairly homogenous; certainly, there are not even traces of Eliot's polyphonic fragmentarism, there are no quotations and comparatively few cultural references. And there is, so it seems, one coherent and constant poetic self, reasonably close to the author, at the centre of the cycle, whose voice is omnipresent, unbroken and uncontradicted. So the *Elegies* seem to be an arch-example for the monological diction of traditional poetry.

But although there is hardly any heteroglossia in the *Elegies*, there are, indeed, dialogic structures. A closer scrutiny will show that the seemingly monological poetic self of the cycle oscillates, chameleon-like, between three different personae: (1) An *auctorial self*: speaking – and sometimes narrating – with the voice of authority, evaluating, counselling or even commanding the reader, and often changing to a collective 'we'. (2) A *personal self*, close to the author: expressing his feelings and presenting personal reminiscences. This second persona differs from the first not so much in 'voice', but in 'intonation' – as Bakhtin calls the 'emotional-volitional tone' which attaches an utterance 'to a unified and singular being-event'.[18] Whereas the auctorial self is representative and generalized, the personal self is marked off as an individual; therefore the details of his experience must remain opaque and 'alien' to the reader. (3) A *dialogical self*: this third self enters into a multitude of dialogues with the mythic and para-mythic *dramatis personae* of the *Elegies*: the Angel, the lovers, the hero, the child, the mother, etc.[19] As these figures represent

---

[17] Quoted by Roman number of elegy and Arabic verse number from Rilke 1975. For important self-comments, a selection of interpretations and documents of reception cf. Fülleborn and Engel; for an interpretation of the cycle see Engel and Rilke 1996–2003, 591–702.

[18] From: 'K filosofii postupka' (Toward a philosophy of the act); untranslated Russian essay, qtd. in Morson and Emerson 133 f.; cf. also Bakhtin 1990, 311 f.: 'Under the intonative aspect of the word, we understand its capacity to express all the diversity of the speaker's axiological attitudes toward the content of an utterance (on the psychological plane – the diversity of the speaker's emotional-volitional reactions)'. Cf. also Voloshinov 103, where intonation is defined as the 'expressive' subcategory of 'evaluative accent'.

[19] In Bakhtinian terms this amounts to a special version of the 'active double-voiced word' (1984, 199 passim). Most of these dialogic relationships – a partial exception is *Duino Elegies* IV, 37–52 – lack the polemic and aggressive elements, which dominate in Bakhtin's concept of active double-voiced words. In this aspect, the dialogism of the *Elegies* is much closer to Martin Buber, cf. his: *Ich und Du* (Leipzig, 1923); there are, however, analogous conceptions in the Russian philosophy of religion (Vjaceslav Ivanov and Pavel Florenskij), which may have been known to Bakhtin and may have influenced him, cf. Clark and Holquist 120–145.

aspects of the poetic self, or rather of the human condition, so the 'dialogues' of the *Elegies* may be interpreted as a sort of self-dramatization of the central self. They represent an empathic understanding, a hermeneutics in which the speaker projects himself into the world-view of his partner. Here, again, there is not so much a difference of voices, but of intonations and, moreover, of 'accents', of world-views and evaluations. These accents may be ordered into two main groups: (1) the accent of *lamentation* ('Klage') – bewailing the present human condition, the sufferings of loss and death, the impossibility of love, the inconstancy of feeling, the estrangement from nature; (2) the accent of *praise* ('Rühmung') – a past and, hopefully, future world-view which affirms and integrates all aspects of human existence.[20]

This basic opposition between the accents of praise and lamentation brings us to the second important element of dialogism in the *Elegies*. Like Eliot, Rilke ascribes to past cultures an ability to create mythical equivalents for human experiences, equivalents which shaped life into a meaningful whole. This ability is lost forever; what we can and must do, however, is create a sort of new, *inner* mythology. Rilke calls this the task of 'transformation' ('Verwandlung'). Again, much as Eliot, Rilke considers 'transformation' as a work in progress; the new mythology is still absent and has to be suggested by quoting and transforming the voices of many past mythologies.

Once more, I have to restrict myself to a single example for these intercultural hermeneutics: the treatment of Egyptian culture in the *Tenth Duino Elegy*.[21] Its first part – after an introductory exposition of the desired transition from 'lamentation' to 'praise' – presents the 'City of Pain' ('Leidstadt' X, 16), which closely resembles the 'unreal city' of Eliot's *Waste Land*. The second part leads us 'behind the last hoarding' into the region of the 'real' (v. 38) and further into 'the spacious landscape of Lamentation',[22] which seems to form an intermediary realm between the moment of death and some unspeakable 'soundless' ('tonlos' v. 105) beyond. This landscape clearly resembles the world of Old Egypt and its cult of the dead,[23] yet, as Rilke

[20] In their emotional-volitional aspect ' lamentation' and 'praise' are, of course, basically intonational. In the *Elegies*, however, they acquire the quality of two world-views, two 'systems of accents'.

[21] Egyptian culture is alluded to also in: II, 74–79, VII, 73 and IX, 58. For Rilke's knowledge of Egypt – which he visited in 1911 – cf. Hermann, Nalewski, and Grimm.

[22] 'Die weite Landschaft der Klagen' (v. 61).

[23] The 'elder lament' (v. 96 f.) resembles the Egyptian goddesses Isis and Nephytis, the 'landscape of Lamentation' (v. 61–71) combines elements of the ruins of Memphis and the Thebean desert. Most important, of course, is the sphinx (v. 72–87) – 'Twin-brother to that on the Nile' ('Brüderlich jenem am Nil' v. 74) – of which, at the time of Rilke's visit to Egypt, only the gigantic head was visible above the sands (cf. his letters to Clara Rilke, January 20, 1907, and to January 20, 1907, and to Magda von Hattingberg, February 1, 1914, quoted Fülleborn, Engel I, 94–98).

himself cautions, it 'is not to be identified with Egypt, but only to be regarded as a kind of reflex ion of the Nile country into the desert-clarity of the dead's consciousness'.[24] So again – like in Eliot's *Waste Land* – there is no attempt to give a direct picture or interpretation of an alien culture. Instead, we are again confronted with a cultural hybrid: The 'landscape of Lamentation' combines the mythic integration of life and death in the Egyptian culture – which is only alluded to as one example for other past cultures – with the modern repression of death, just as it combines – in poetical terms – the voices of myth and of allegory. Unlike Eliot, however, Rilke does not quote the authentic voice of Egypt:[25] Egyptian culture speaks to us not through its texts but through its monuments. Yet again these monuments have to undergo a very special type of interpretation: The 'indescribable outline' of the gigantic face of the sphinx – symbolizing the lost integration of mankind into cosmic relations (v. 78–79) – is communicated to the spectator by the sound of an owl's flight, 'brushing [. . .] along [the sphinx's] cheek'.[26] The meaning of the sphinx – which is and is not the sphinx of Old Egypt – is interpreted by a non-verbal voice transforming the sublime view into an orphic sound. The voice of culture, we might say, is translated by the voice of nature.

This is certainly the most important difference between our two authors. For T.S. Eliot the voices of nature and the – closely affiliated – voices of the mythic past cannot be assimilated to our modern consciousness (cf. note 14), whereas for Rilke, reared in the great tradition of German hermeneutics, nature and cultures of the past are still accessible – at least to persons who are capable of a certain degree of empathy. That is why Eliot confronts us with heteroglossia as the strongest version of polyphony, whereas Rilke can restrict himself to the 'weak' version of different accents only. Yet even for him the gap between past and present cannot be closed completely. This is marked by the existence of different poetic codes within the *Duino Elegies*: Rilke uses different kinds of symbolic speech – much as Eliot uses different voices – combining them dialogically as picture and interpretation, or as myth and allegory, or as a never-ending chain of signifiers, which mutually interpret each other, none of them a

---

[24] Rilke 143; German: '*nicht* Ägypten *gleichzusetzen* ist, sondern nur, gewissermaßen, eine Spiegelung des Nillandes in die Wüstenklarheit des Toten-Bewußtseins' (to Witold Hulewicz, Nov. 13th 1925; Fülleborn, Engel I: 322).

[25] There is only one exception: the untranslated and unexplained word 'pschent' (v. 82), that is: the double-crown of Upper and Lower Egypt, worn by the sphinx.

[26] 'Und sie [die Eule],/ streifend im langsamen Abstrich die Wange entlang,/ jene der reifesten Rundung,/ zeichnet weich in das neue/ Totengehör, über ein doppelt/ aufgeschlagenes Blatt, den unbeschreiblichen Umriß' (v. 82–87). Cf. also: 'manchmal schreckt ein Vogel und zieht [. . .] weithin das schriftliche Bild seines vereinsamten Schreis' (v. 67–69).

full-fledged representation of meaning, but merely what Rilke calls a 'Gleichnis' (v. 107), a likeness, a simile. Thus he creates a new version of dialogism, which Bakhtin had considered impossible:

> No matter how one understands the interrelationship of meanings in a poetic symbol (a trope); it is impossible under any conditions or at any time to imagine a trope (say, a metaphor) being unfolded into the two exchanges of a dialogue, that is, two meanings parcelled out between two separate voices. For this reason the dual meaning (or multiple meaning) of the symbol never brings in its wake dual accents (1981, 327f.).

Rilke's *Tenth Duino Elegy* – like many other modern poems – proves, I think, that Bakhtin is wrong. It starts with an allegory of the modern world (v. 16–40), recreates in its main part a heavily allegorised version of the mythical past (v. 54–105), and ends by using a symbol from the realm of nature as a mere hypothetical simile:

> And yet, were they waking a symbol [rather: a simile] within us,
> the endlessly dead,
> look, they'd be pointing, perhaps, to the catskins, hanging
> from empty hazels, or else/ to the rain downfalling on dark soil-bed in early Spring. –
>
> And we, who think of *ascending*
> happiness, then would feel
> the emotion that almost startles
> when happiness *falls*. (v. 106–113).[27]

This blending of myth and allegory, symbol and simile – and, of course, of the related 'accents' or world-views – is an impressive example of a special kind of dialogism: the dialogism of tropes as a 'hybrid' of different kinds of poetic codes.

---

[27] 'Aber erweckten sie uns, die unendlich Toten, ein Gleichnis,/ siehe, sie zeigten vielleicht auf die Kätzchen der leeren/ Hasel, die hängenden, oder/ meinten den Regen, der fällt auf dunkles Erdreich im Frühjahr. –// Und wir, die an *steigendes* Glück/ denken, empfänden die Rührung,/ die uns beinah bestürzt,/ wenn ein Glückliches *fällt*.' Leishman and Spender wrongly translate 'Gleichnis' as 'symbol'; 'likeness' or 'simile' would be much more adequate.

References

Bakhtin, Mikhail. 1981. *The Dialogic Imagination: Four Essays*, ed. Michael Holquist, tr. Caryl Emerson and Michael Holquist. Austin.

———. 1984. *Problems of Dostoevsky's Poetics*, ed. and tr. Caryl Emerson (Minneapolis, 1984).

———. 1990. *Art and Answerability: Early Philosophical Essays*, ed. Michael Holquist and Vadim Liapunov, tr. Vadim Liapunov and Kenneth Brostrom. Austin.

Bedient, Calvin. 1984. *He Do the Police in Different Voices: The 'Waste Land' and Its Protagonist*. Chicago.

Brooker, Jewel Spears, and Joseph Bentley. 1990. *Reading 'The Waste Land': Modernism and the Limits of Interpretation*. Amherst.

Clark, Katerina, and Michael Holquist. 1984. *Mikhail Bakhtin*. Cambridge/Mass.

Cuddy, Lois A., and David H. Hirsch, eds. 1991. Critical Essays on T.S. Eliot's *'The Waste Land'*, Boston.

Eliot, T.S. 1974. *Collected Poems 1909–1962*. London.

Engel, Manfred. 1986. *Rainer Maria Rilkes 'Duineser Elegien' und die moderne deutsche Lyrik*. Stuttgart.

———. 2004. 'Rilke als Autor der literarischen Moderne'. *Rilke-Handbuch*, ed. by M.E. and Dorothea Lauterbach. Stuttgart and Weimar. 507–528.

Frank, Arnim Paul and Birgit Bödeker. 1991. 'Trans-culturality and inter-culturality in French and German translations of T.S. Eliot's *The Waste Land*', *Interculturality and the Historical Study of Literary Translations*, ed. Harald Kittel and Arnim Paul Frank. Berlin. 41–63.

Fülleborn, Ulrich, and Manfred Engel, eds. 1982/83. *Rilkes 'Duineser Elegien'*, 3 vols. Frankfurt/Main.

Grimm, Alfred. 1996. *Rilke und Ägypten*. München.

Hermann, Alfred. 1966. *Rilkes ägyptische Gesichte*. Darmstadt.

Lehmann, Jürgen. 1977. 'Ambivalenz und Dialogizität. Zur Theorie der Rede bei Michail Bachtin', *Urszenen*, ed. Friedrich A. Kittler and Horst Turk. Frankfurt/Main. 355–380.

Morson, Gary Saul, and Caryl Emerson. 1990. *Mikhail Bakhtin: Creation of a Prosaics*. Stanford.

Nalewski, Horst. 1976. '"… diese unerbittlich großen Dinge Ägyptens". Rilkes Anschauen der ägyptischen Welt', *Rilke-Studien*. Berlin/East. 216–230.

Rilke, Rainer Maria. 1975. *The Duino Elegies*. The German text, with an English translation, introduction and commentary by J.B. Leishman and Stephen Spender. London.

———. 1996–2003. *Werke: Kommentierte Ausgabe in 4 Bänden und einem Supplementband*, ed. Manfred Engel et. al., Frankfurt/Main and Leipzig.

Smith, Grover. 1983. *The Waste Land*. London.

Spitzer, Leo. 1928. 'Zur Entstehung der sogenannten "Erlebten Rede"', *Germanisch-Romanische Monatsschrift*, 16: 327–332.

Sri, P.S. 1985. *T.S. Eliot, Vedanta and Buddhism*. Vancouver.

Voloshinov, Valentin N. 1973. *Marxism and the Philosophy of Language*. Transl. Ladislav Matejka and I.R. Titunik. New York.

Martyn Crucefix

See his biography in the Translations/Versions section where he has some new translations.

Still-Recognisable Form: the dialogue between Romantic and Modern in Rilke's *Duino Elegies*

I

In January 1912, Rilke wrote what was to become the opening of his tenth *Duino Elegy*. Even then, with astonishing foresight, he knew these lines would form part of the finale of the great work he projected. The mechanistic, industrial-scale horrors of the First World War were still barely imaginable and (in an English literary context) Hardy was composing for his dead Emma, the first of the *Georgian Poetry* anthologies had just appeared. Yet it is hard not to believe Rilke sensed something of the apocalyptic changes imminent for himself and for Europe: 'One day, at the close of this fierce inspection – / that I might sing out in celebration and glory / to affirming angels'. But if Modernism is characterised by its iconoclastic breaking with past habits and values, with past artistic forms, if the Modern is recognisable by its fragmentation, difficulty and allusiveness, do we hear it in lines such as these?

> How we squander our pains.
> How we gaze beyond them into the miserable
> distance to see if there is not, perhaps, an end.
> Yet they are winter leaves, our dark evergreen,
> *one* season of our secret year – not only a season,
> but a site, settlement, camp, soil and resting place.

The fact that Rilke waited ten years before he could finish the *Elegies,* is far more significant than being merely one of the most famous writer's blocks in literary history. Not until the year of Eliot's *The Waste Land* and Joyce's *Ulysses,* could Rilke complete what he called the great white sail of the *Elegies* (the accompanying *Sonnets to Orpheus* were in comparison a little rust coloured sail). The composition of the *Elegies* straddles the years that ushered in what we recognise as the Modern era and the fingerprints of two very different worlds lie all over these great poems.

116

It is usual to consider the opening lines of the *Elegies* as articulating one of the great cries of the Modern alienated individual. Standing as it does at the opening of what Rilke knew was a great, sustained artistic project, these lines are best regarded as corresponding to the invocation to the gods traditionally sung by earlier, happier poets. It was originally intended as a humble request for divine assistance and its formulaic nature betrayed their confidence in receiving a response. Riding a wave of anticipation, Homer's *Odyssey* opens, 'Sing to me of the man, Muse, the man of twists and turns' (Penguin, 1996, tr. Robert Fagles). Rilke, on the battlements of Duino Castle, hears only his own contrasting interrogative: 'Who, if I cried out, would hear me among the ranks / of the angels?' The lines that follow detail the way in which (even 'if' a response was to be forthcoming) the spark gap between human and divine at the opening of the twentieth century is so wide that 'Every angel is terrifying'. The artist – the Modern individual – must 'hold back ... swallow back the bird-call / of black grief that would burst from [him/her]' and the sequence of poems that has been initiated is no longer inspired by the higher realms but is rather a meditation on what the response must be to its resounding silence: 'Ah, who is it we can turn to for help?'

And yet this careful creation of an angel-shaped hole in the poem harks back to older certainties. For comparison, Marinetti had three years earlier produced his bullish, even violent *Manifesto of Futurism* (1909) with its passionate loathing of the past. Rilke is engaged in something very different. His advice to an aspiring writer in 1903 deploys imagery more in keeping with the Romantic ethos of organic creation: 'To carry, come to term, give birth, is *everything*. To allow each thing its own evolution' (*Letters to a Young Poet,* Carcanet, tr. Cohn). At the opening of Elegy 2, Rilke draws on the apocryphal Book of Tobit, in which Tobias is unwittingly accompanied on a journey by the angel Raphael and although T. S. Eliot's use of myth as ironic contrast to the Modern is familiar enough, Rilke's tone is very different:

> Where are the days of Tobias, when one of these
> most radiant creatures stood at the simple doorway
> ready to travel, in part disguised and so not
> as frightening?

Such lines are bathed in a retrospective envy of an earlier, more secure world and this is made all the more poignant by the frank and dramatic admission that follows:

> If the archangel bent down now, dangerously

bent from behind the spread of stars, took one step
towards us, we would be beaten to death
by our own high-beating heart.

II

The influence of Marx and Freud is definitive in the development of
Modernism and there is no doubt that Rilke writes under the influence
of Freud whose *The Interpretation of Dreams* was published at the turn
of the new century. The *Elegies* take up the sex issue explicitly and
bravely:

> Lovers – do you not grow
> ever more present in each other's passion until,
> overwhelmed, you beg – 'No *more!*' –
> you, who at the touch of the other's hands swell,
> fill out to such abundance like grapes
> in a great vintage – you, who sometimes vanish,
> though only in moments the other is so fully present.

Jo Shapcott has illustrated with her subversive responses to Rilke's later
love poems, *Tender Taxes* (Faber, 2001), how far this viewpoint is narrowly
male: men are driven by 'the hidden, guilty river-god / of the blood', by
unfathomably deep desires towards sexual union. The imagery Rilke uses
here is that of a nightmarish descent into the human psyche towards the
Freudian Unconscious, a world that lies 'tangled in the spreading tendrils
of inner events / already entwined into patterns of choking / undergrowth,
threaded by hunting bestial shapes.' Rilke's typical male is irresistibly
drawn deeper: 'He waded deeper, deeper, still loving it, / to ancient blood,
toward ravines where terrors / lay in wait, gorged still with his own
fathers / and every horror knew him, winked in complicity. / Oh yes, the
horrors smiled...'
　　Nevertheless, there are strikingly few signs here of Freud's notion that
a more open acknowledgement of the role and power of sexual feeling
must resolve the tension and destructiveness that Rilke communicates so
vividly through his imagery. Rilke offers only limited and curiously
nineteenth century notions of how to deal with the passionate, Dionysiac
nature of man. Though the *Elegies* adopts a particularly scathing tone
towards the sentimental idea of the 'saving' woman, a closer reading
suggests there are few other alternatives. In Elegy 2, Rilke can be found
admiring Classical statuary and what he envies in the 'Attic stelae' is

their possession of 'such self-control'. In the final lines of Elegy 3, addressing a woman, he declares:

> What do you know?
> That you stirred prehistory in your lover?
> What passion was it welled from the long-dead
> in him? What women were there who hated you?
> What men of darkness did you rouse in young veins?
> What dead children reached their arms to you?
> O gently, gently, then! Let him watch you
> at some steady, everyday task – lovingly, lead him
> close up to the garden, give him whatever might
> outweigh the nights ...
> Hold him back ...

Rilke's treatment of romantic and sexual love draws these quietist and conservative conclusions. His pessimism is elsewhere translated into the strange enthusiasm for unrequited, intransitive relationships since these allow more scope for self-development, more freedom to become. Requited love – even when it avoids the 'horrors' of sexuality – seems to run too great a risk of a kind of closed-circuit introversion, perhaps falling into stifling 'conventional' behaviours associated with marriage. It is in such ways that love is 'difficult' as he confided to Franz Xaver Kappus in 1904.

III

One element of Rilke's thought that Auden was later to absorb ultimately derives from Friedrich Schiller's seminal essay *On Naïve and Sentimental Poetry* (1795). It is Elegy 8 where Rilke presents a sustained meditation on this subject that again nostalgically harks back to earlier (mythical) Edens. Schiller argues that creatures *'are what we were*; they are *what we should once again become.* We were nature just as they, and our culture, by means of reason and freedom, should lead us back to nature'. Similarly, in perceptual terms, Rilke postulates the 'Open' ('das Offene'). This is what lies 'so deep in the face / of an animal. Free from death ... The freed creature's doom / stands behind it and ahead lies God / and when it begins to move, its movement / is through an eternity like a well-spring'. The absence of the consciousness of death is essential to this state of ignorant bliss. However, over 100 years after Schiller, Rilke finds he cannot sustain the optimism inherent in his predecessor's outlook. The

Elegies lament the way we 'face always World / and never Nowhere without the No: / that unsurveyed purity we might breathe / and *know* without limit and not desire.' Though such a condition contributes to the alienated state of humankind (here traced to its real source in self-consciousness and an awareness of death) it is again the grief-stricken tone of Rilke's writing that suggests the backward glance: 'Even for a single day, *we* do not have / that pure space before us into which flowers / endlessly bloom'.

The second half of Elegy 8, goes on to present a taxonomy of the Open and it emerges that Rilke's earlier statements were exaggerated for effect, since not all creatures live in such unrelieved bliss. The warm-blooded mammals share something of our 'melancholy' and, as he details this, the nostalgic nature of his thinking is clear. The mammal also:

> feels
> the presence of what often overpowers us –
> a recollection, as if what we push for
> endlessly, once was closer and more true,
> our links to it infinitely more tender.
> Here, all is distance; there, it was breath.
> After that first home, this second
> seems to be windswept and uncertain.

It is really a reminiscence of the womb since the bird (born from a shell but sheltered by the mother bird) experiences 'half-certainties' while the gnat (born into the open air) possesses an enviable bliss as it '*remains in the womb that bore it*'. The poem returns to something akin to the human condition with the justly famous description of the bat ('womb-born and yet has to fly'). Our own jittery, troubled existence is brilliantly reflected in the bat's flight:

> As if frightened of itself, it must hurtle
> through the air the way a crack goes
> through a tea-cup – so a bat's track
> streaks through the porcelain of evening.

Likewise, we remain mere 'spectators' of our own lives; 'It spills from us. We arrange it. / It falls to pieces. We arrange again. / We ourselves fall to pieces.'

Modernism partly defines itself in the confrontation with this fragmented world. Pound urged the breaking of the pentameter in Canto LXXXI and it is worth remembering that free verse – loose and organic as we often now perceive it to be – was intended to reflect this difficult encounter with a broken world. Eliot insisted on the need to 'dislocate if necessary' ('The Metaphysical Poets') and wrote poetry full of hesitation, false starts and fractured repetition. As artists, the Modernists broke the aesthetic mould in order to say new things but suffered a failure of nerve when it came to the social and political implications. Modernism's attraction to the Right is well-documented and the least that can be said for Rilke is that with his nostalgic orientation, his idealisation of the truly strong man comes as no surprise. It is in Elegy 6 that the qualities of the Rilkean hero are enumerated. In contrast to us, he is decisive in the 'urge to action'. There is an impetuosity derived from a carelessness about his Fate. Yet, ironically, it is Fate that 'sings him forwards into the storm / of his on-rushing world'. In one of those images that leave Rilke open to mockery (and accusations of blinkered gender bias), the hero betrays his superiority even in the womb where his 'imperious choosing' wins the race to fertilise the egg. What is striking here is Rilke's complete lack of interest in how this kind of behaviour might play out in real (social and political) life. The tone of the poem suggests unreserved hero-worship ('I hear of none like *him*') and the gulf between the heroic and the masses is decisive and insuperable. In personal terms, like some macho modern-day celebrity, the hero draws 'grief-stricken girls' to sacrifice themselves, but in general he remains aloof, he is something 'quite other' ('anders').

IV

So politically, Rilke is conservative and anti-democratic. His distaste for the modern world of the early twentieth century is palpable and based on the belief that new forms of living divide us ever further from the authenticity of experience that he so values.

> The spirit of the age has engineered for itself
> vast reservoirs of power, though they are shapeless
> as the charged force it draws from all things.
> Temples are no longer known...

His dislike of America – as a technologically advanced and democratic society – is obvious. In a letter he declared, 'from America, empty indifferent things are pouring across, sham things, *dummy life*'. Modern living lacks solitude and silence. Rilke harks back to traditional forms of thought – the great cathedrals, the music, the books. In English poetry, Shelley's *A Defence of Poetry* presents an interesting comparison to the heroic artist's role of forging new forms of perception that then ossify and require further artists to make it new. Shelley perceived the need for a kind of continuing revolution in human consciousness led by the 'unacknowledged legislators' – the poets and artists – and with greater consistency this leads him to corresponding political conclusions. Rilke is more intent on preserving the good artistic work of the past and so, rather than revolution, he upholds an aristocracy of artists handing on their work, each generation building on what went before it. Elegy 7 argues that we 'should not become / confused by this, rather strengthened in preserving / the still-recognisable form'. This fits well with his individualistic perception of the role of heroes in which there is more than a touch of the Nietzschean *ubermensch*. These remote but always admired figures overcome the tyranny of the conventional and act as figureheads for a return to lost values.

This brand of conservative revolution is to be found in Rilke's treatment of that other great nineteenth century theme, mankind's relationship with the natural world. If we attend to the structure of the *Elegies*, it is the renovation of this particular aspect of human life that constitutes one of the great imperatives of the sequence. This is what the opening denial of Elegy 7 is concerned with: 'No more wooing, enough of this courting'. In suitably aggressive and iconoclastic tone, the poem turns its back on the angel-shaped hole of its opening sections. Ironically it does this in order to savour the natural world and, in contrast to the grief-stricken alienation of the opening of Elegy 1, Rilke's second great cry is one of joyful experience: 'Just being here is glorious!' ('Hiersein ist herrlich!'). This is not the world observed from afar, but transformed in its interaction with human consciousness: 'within'. Watching a falling star from a bridge in Toledo, Rilke reported the sensation of it falling through his 'inner space: the body's dividing outline was no longer there'. This is vividly reminiscent of hundreds of Romantically-tinged epiphanies back to Rousseau's *Reveries of the Solitary Walker*. The resultant evangelical energy and joy in Elegies 7 and 9 offer the reader some of greatest pleasures of Rilke's work:

> Not only all the summer's dawns – not only
> the transformation into day, radiant with beginning.
> Not only such days, so tender around flowers
> and above, in tree-shapes, huge and powerful.
> Not only the reverence of these unfolding forces,
> not only pathways, meadowland in the evening,
> not only, after late thunderstorms, the breath
> of cleared air, not only the on-coming of sleep
> and a premonition in the evening...

but the nights too. Those tall nights of summer
and the stars, stars around the earth.

Of course, this joy is intentionally interrupted by the reservations of Elegy
8 with its astringent awareness that we are 'forever bidding goodbye'.
Death itself is the second great subject of Rilke's most ambitious work.
For English readers, it is the frail figure of Keats who surfaces, declaring
that this world is a Vale of Soul-making, that it takes a 'World of Pains
and troubles ... to school an Intelligence and make it a soul'. Similarly,
Rilke anticipates that 'nights / of grieving' will become more dear to
him, that he will learn how not to 'squander' pain, but make of it 'a site,
settlement, camp, soil and resting place'.

V

Though Keatsian parallels reveal the Romantic nature of the theme of
death, Elegy 10, where it is further developed, deploys a far more
fragmented and non-linear style than any other. After the rather formal
opening (with which this essay began), the poem spins away into a wholly
new mode of topographical symbolism, a satirical tone and passages of
extended personification. We are swept to 'Grief-City' ('Leid-Stadt') with
its shallow and obfuscating attitudes towards personal death, the Christian
church magnificently and haughtily dismissed as 'clean, closed,
disappointing as a Post Office on Sunday'. For Rilke, this is the contemporary
Western world of commerce, consumerist advertising, sharks and swindlers,
partly fuelled by alcohol such as 'Neversaydie bitter that tastes sweet to
drinkers / as long as they chew fresh distractions with it...' Such blackly
comic details show the rotten heart of this state is its avoidance of the
reality of death. Yet for Rilke there are those who preserve the old ways.
The personification he introduces is identified by the word 'Klage'. It
signifies an individual, her tribe and their land and is often translated as
'Lament' which has always struck me as conveying a rather affected,
almost poetic kind of emotional posturing – precisely what Rilke is urging
us to avoid in our confrontation with these difficult aspects of life. For
my translation, I chose the word 'Keening' to better convey the raw
edginess of authentic feeling preserved by these people living 'far off ...
way out there'. The Keening tribe's elders give a guided tour of their
realm where (in Keatsian fashion) even the darkest human emotions
('polished lumps / of original grief ... a petrified clinker of rage') can
be given full rein. In fact it is ultimately Rousseau's image of the noble
savage Rilke draws on here to suggest an atavistic wisdom, abandoned

by the contemporary world, offering the possibility of a condition in which the realms of life and death are one. Writing to his Polish translator, Rilke argued that *'Affirmation of life AND death appears as one in the 'Elegies'* ... we must try to achieve the fullest consciousness of our existence, which is at home in the *two unseparated realms'*. The *Elegies* in the end postulate such a unified state of being.

And yet, there is something willed about these final moments. Rilke wrote in 1922 though there are many elements that would not have been out of place 100 years earlier. Is it an awareness of this that leads Rilke to disrupt its concluding moments, switching from the grand drama of the Keening personifications to the fragmentary coda, returning to a more tentative lyrical mode?

> ... we, who conceive of happiness
> as something that must be *rising*,
> find in us feelings almost of dismay
> when a happy thing *falls*.

These are obscure lines, but the stanza that precedes them is clearer in its import. What we perceive as wasteful and proleptic of an ending may be more truly perceived as the beginnings of transformation. The whole sequence argues this and it is for this reason Rilke can be (too) easily taken up by those seeking a kind of self-help spiritualism. In fact, Rilke faces brutal truths as befits his living through the opening years of the twentieth century. But in doing so he is able to identify the possibilities of a joyful renovation in the individual human life which re-synthesises beliefs from an earlier, more confident age.

Stephen Cohn

See his biography in the Translations/Versions section where he has some new translations.

Rilke Where Art Thou?

Robert Lowell, in introducing his book *Imitations*, ends with this statement of his own faith: '... for the excellence of a poet depends on the unique opportunities of his native language. I have been almost as free as the authors themselves in finding ways to make them ring right for me.'
Richard Davenport Hines (writing of Proust in *A Night at the Majestic*), on the other hand, tells us with some eloquence and no less clarity that he has been been affronted '... by the high-handed re-writing or slipshod approximations to which several other translators have resorted ... others seem confident that they have a surer mastery of words ... and produce sentences that for all their flourishes are faithless, complacent and false.'

Could anyone find common ground anywhere between such very opposed positions? Where exactly does 'free' inflate into 'high-handed'? Who has the authority to make such a judgement? Has 'free', furthermore, become a cant-concept, by now gone rotten in the mouths of politicians? Can poetry be 'free'? When poetry has liberated itself to the edge of its possibilities, beyond rhyme and beyond any kind of rhythm, does it inevitably grade into prose-poetry, and from then on into post-poetry, into meta-poetry, into prose?

Why, too, does Lowell call his verses *Imitations* rather than *Translations* or *Versions*? – (the last a dangerously slippery classification, sometimes greedy to assign itself privileges to which it is not in the least entitled).

When I was a young sculpture student and was working in the life-room, a tutor advised me kindly and credibly: 'The exercise isn't to copy the model – eyebrows, fingers, ankles, belly-button. It is *equivalents* that we're looking for. Remember, you're working in clay – clay has different valency from flesh and blood and bone!'

Jacob Epstein, on quite the other hand, when a student in Paris was energetically directed by Bourdelle, his teacher: 'Il faut toujours copier le modèle – bêtement!' There is some contradiction here.

Reflecting about how I've gone about things in trying to translate Rilke and Brecht, and about what I might have believed I was doing, I can decide fairly swiftly that of these positions, each of which has its own integrity, I like Lowell's the best and feel most sympathy towards it. It may be true that 'learning' has to be mimesis, in its early stages at least, but to attempt 'translation' as, on the whole, an exercise in transcription, has not been what I've set out to do. To attempt to achieve a sensitive and responsible trot is something difficult enough, and well worthwhile, but this hasn't been my own intention.

Rilke's 'Orpheus. Eurydike. Hermes' begins:

> Das war der Seelen wunderliches Bergwerk.
> Wie stille Silbererze gingen sie
> als Adern durch sein Dunkel. Zwischen Wurzeln
> entsprang das Blut, das fortgeht zu den Menschen,
> und schwer wie Porphyr sah es aus im Dunkel. Sonst war nichts
> Rotes.

Lowell's 'imitation' starts with:

> That's the strange regalia of souls.
> Vibrant
> as platinum filaments they went,
> like arteries through their darkness. From the holes
> of powder beetles, from the otter's bed,
> from the oak king judging by the royal oak –
> blood like our own life-blood, sprang.
> Otherwise nothing was red.

> The dark was heavier than Caesar's foot...

Rilke's first line ('That was the amazing mine of souls', in an accurately literal transcription) requires unexpectedness in its language to come alive in English: Lowell provides it. But Lowell isn't 'translating', what he is doing is something much more like painting from another painting, something akin to Picasso when he was working from *Las Meninas* or from *Le Déjeuner sur l'herbe*.

It is clear enough that Picasso isn't 'copying' the Manet or the Velasquez. The Lowell is wildly other than the Rilke but it possesses a similar energy and it speaks a similar incantatory magic. And the 'foot', like the 'dark', is as heavy as Rilke himself might have meant it to weigh.

Lowell's Orpheus poem ends:

> He stood and stared at the one level, inevitable road,
> as the reproachful god of messengers

looking round, pushed off again.
His caduceus was like a shotgun on his shoulder.

Here we have anachronism as well as anatopism. There were very few shotguns in the Underworld of Ancient Greece, but the serpent-staff of Hermes *can* be like a shotgun and we can see him toting it, wonderfully clearly. There was no Caesar in the Greek Underworld, either, and yet – who does not feel the weight of that foot?

A puzzle remains, and this may be its explanation: the Greeks believed that the spirits of the dead were accompanied and protected on their journey to the Underworld by the *psychopompos*, the conductor of souls, and psychopompos is one of the prime vocations of Hermes. So it may be that, in Lowell's chain of association, Hermes, Eurydice's guide and protector, is 'riding shotgun'. New Englanders, too, watch cowboy-movies.

Imitations? One translator will work diligently to achieve a literal exactness, an exact lateral movement (insofar as that may be possible) from the O- to the T-language, a transpositioning. Very often that leads to a language on its own – the sometimes absurd language of translatorese. Otherwise, one might set out to try to remake the original so that it will read as if the T-language were its *own* language. This is closer to what Lowell means to do, but he proceeds a great deal further into territory of his own. The poems in *Imitations*, whether Rilke, Valéry, Rimbaud or Pasternak have been more thoroughly appropriated by Lowell himself than the word 'translation' can respectably signify. Had they in the first instance been his own poems, this is how Lowell might have written them. 'My first two Sappho poems', he writes in his Introduction, 'are really new poems based on hers'. It is just as as true of many, many others in the collection – perhaps even of most of them.

Imitations was published in 1962. In it there is Lowell's imitation of Valéry's 'Hélène' ('once more I see the galleys bleed with dawn / and shark with muffled rowlocks into Troy'), itself one of Lowell's great poems. How can that be? a translation? *Everything* is translation, said Pasternak, and he was surely right.

In the view of one formidable lettré, there are really only these alternatives: either you can give your own literal prose translation or you must write your own poem. There is truth in that dictum, too, but in my own much-less-formidable and also less-lettré view, there are a very great number of possibilities before, between, and after those alternatives; a rich spectrum of choices that might be made.

'Blesse thee Bottome, blesse thee; thou art translated!' exclaims Peter Quince when he first catches sight of his fellow-mechanical wearing the ass-head. The creature can sometimes be as crude and asinine as Bottom himself and, like Bottom, nevertheless still find love.

Rilke himself, at a crossroads in his life and work, translated a number of poems by Paul Valéry: '... one day I read Valéry and I knew that my waiting was over'. *Charmes ou Poèmes par Paul Valéry* was published as a collection in June 1922, but most of its poems date from between 1917 and 1921. Rilke's *Sonnets to Orpheus* were written between 2 and 23 February 1922, during Rilke's annus mirabilis, the year in which he also completed the long-stalled *Duino Elegies*. (Eliot's *The Waste Land*, Joyce's *Ulysses*, Edith Sitwell's *Façade* and Lawrence's *Birds, Beasts and Flowers* belong to the same vintage.)

Valéry's 'Le Cimetière Marin' is among the most often-attempted translations of the twentieth century and with good reason for it is a most wonderful poem. Rilke's own translation of it is as masterful as one would expect. But it has some unexpected weaknesses. Valéry's second stanza has:

> ... Ouvrages purs d'une éternelle cause,
> Le temps scintille et le songe est savoir.

Rilke translates this:

> als reines Werk der ewigen Bedingung
> wird Zeit zum Glanz und Traum zur Wissenschaft.

In Valéry's as in Rilke's own vocabulary, 'knowing' lies a very long way from 'knowledge' and further still from 'science', which is what 'Wissenschaft' has, for a very long time, come to mean. But the second example is, if anything, even more unexpected, and it comes in Valéry's teenage-sex stanza (which holds, in miniature, a great deal of what this great poem is setting out to say). I cannot resist giving the whole stanza:

> Les cris aigues des filles chatouillées,
> Les yeux, les dents, les paupières mouillées,
> Le sein charmant qui joue avec le feu,
> Le sang qui brille aux lèvres qui se rendent,
> Les derniers dons, les doigts qui les défendent,
> Tout va sous terre et rentre dans le jeu!

For the third line, Rilke has:

> die süße Brust die glüht und sich erfrischt...

It is as if Rilke had not in the least understood what is meant by 'playing with fire'.

There are many echoes of the Valéry poem in Rilke's *Sonnets to Orpheus* and in every case they seem to me to cross-resonate, making both poems even more profound and expansive. The last stanza of the Valéry begins:

> Le vent se lève! ... Il faut tenter de vivre!
> L'air immense ouvre et referme mon livre...

It has a kinship with the ending of Rilke's own very much earlier poem 'Archaischer Torso Apollos', the first poem of *Der Neuen Gedichte Zweiter Teil* which dates from 1908. The translation below is my own:

> We never knew his legendary head,
> nor saw the eyes set there like apples ripening.
> And yet his torso, as a lamp turned low
> still shines, still sees. For how else could the hard
>
> contour of his breast so blind you? How could
> a smile start in the turning thighs and settle
> on the parts which made his progeny?
> This marble otherwise would stand defaced
>
> beneath the shoulders and their lucid fall;
> and would not take the light
> like panther-skin; and would not radiate
>
> and would not break from all its surfaces
> as does a star. There is no part of him
> that does not see you. You must change your life.

Rilke's clarion-call, his imperative to live (and there is little real distance between 'life' and 'change') comes almost ten years before Valéry's poem. The Apollo poem has lines (the last two, especially) that cannot be translated in any other way. The alternatives simply are not there. The first stanza of the Rilke poem has:

> ... Aber
> sein Torso glüht noch wie ein Kandelaber,
> in dem sein Schauen, nur zurückgeschraubt,
> sich hält und glänzt.

My lines have lost 'Kandelaber'. It is a decorative word and I was most unwilling to let it go; but no-one can regulate a candelabra's light by 'screwing it back', as one can an oil-lamp or gas-lamp. Furthermore, 'Kandelaber' was the word used for street gas-lamps; not yet, in 1908, replaced by electricity. I owe that piece of information, and much else, to J.B. Leishman to whom more respect is owed than has recently been paid.

What is lost in translation is occasionally less harrowing than what has been found but had better been left unfound. When 'the same word' seems to impose itself, it may be better to turn it down and to go on seeking. In the *Neue Gedichte Zweiter Teil* there is a sonnet, *Die Flamingos*, which is one of the group of poems which resulted from Rilke's visits to the Jardin des Plantes in Paris. 'In Spiegelbildern wie von Fragonard...' it begins, and then describes the leggy, shrimp-pink birds in terms of a bed-warm sexiness, erotic and alluring. Then there is trouble in the aviary, a bird-fight (cat-fight wouldn't do here) among rivals, and the birds teeter away on their stick-slender legs:

> Auf einmal kreischt ein Neid durch die Volière;
> sie aber haben sich erstaunt gestreckt
> und schreiten einzeln ins Imaginäre.

> A jealous screech shrills through the aviary:
> they spread their wings and stretch out necks, surprised.
> And each alone stalks silently away
> on slender legs, out into fantasy.

'Das Imaginäre' is an offer that a number of translators haven't been wary enough to refuse. Three of them give 'the imaginary' and another 'the imagination'. But what sounds alike very often does *not* mean alike, and here Rilke means to walk us on our own readers'-legs into another, a fantastic world. The flamingos here are stepping into other-world, into fantasy, into Fantasia! What's required is something far more strange, unreal, bizarre, than imagination alone.

Harry Mathews, in his novel *My Life in CIA*, offers the following formulation: If you're translating Proust into English you don't want to get caught in the trap of the too-close equivalent and the faux ami that you can't get out of your head once you've thought it. So the trick is to take in the original and then say it as if it were your own thought expressed in your own voice to a friend in a coffee-shop.

Proust: Longtemps, je me suis couché de bonne heure.

Scott Moncrieff: For a long time I used to go to bed early
Howard: Time and again, I have gone to bed early.
Harry Mathews: When I was a kid it took me years to get my parents
to let me even stay up till *nine*.

The four samples above aren't really about faux amis; but it isn't too
hard to imagine (or even to fantasize) the effect that the last of them
would have on Richard Davenport Hines. As for Mathews himself, is
he joking or is he in earnest? Both, would be my guess. I believe that
there is something important within the humour, something serious to be
learned.

Local language, too, alters the effect of poetic diction. American speech
is flatter by far than is English English: we are much more staccato,
especially when we are trying to impress. Auden's rhythms had changed
perceptibly after quite a short time living in the States. Furthermore,
Rilke's own German was never the *Hochdeutsch* that modern readers
might take for granted; it was rather a kind of *Pragerdeutsch*, a
Sudetendeutsch which is by now more or less extinct. When Rilke wrote,
in the *Second Elegy*:

'O Aufschaun: / neue, warme, entgehende Welle des Herzens...'

I believe that the word *Aufschaun* stood for being careful, taking notice,
being circumspect, and that it was not meant to stand for its present
dictionary meaning. In the attempt to turn Rilke's German into credible
English or American, into paraphrastic language, one may easily wander
too far in the paths of righteousness: one translation of the *Elegies* takes
Rilke's 'die Leidstadt' and turns that into 'Pain City'. I would guess there
may well be a Pain City, Arizona, or perhaps one in Wyoming. Does it
matter? Yes it does. It distracts from and it subverts the poem's mood
and direction.

Edward and Vita Sackville-West worked together on an early English
translation of the *Duino Elegies* and this was published in a luxurious
edition for Count Harry Kessler, by the Hogarth Press. It was bound in
white vellum, the initial letters were engraved by Gill, and the book was
printed on paper made by the Maillol brothers, Aristide and Gaspard. But
'the Rilke' by which the poet became best known in these islands was
the *Duino Elegies* translation made by J.B. Leishman and Stephen Spender,
and published by the Hogarth Press in 1939. Spender wrote, in a letter
to myself, that the collaboration hadn't been easy and that, in the end

and in his own mind at least, he had withdrawn from the co-authorship and now thought of the book as Leishman's. It is not hard to understand how and why the two collaborators had found themselves pulling against one another, one concerned with poetry, the other with accuracy of diction. Nevertheless, the *Duino Elegies*, in that same English translation, attracted enormous attention and respect and became an important cultural marker among the British. The Germans on the other hand, seemed for a long time to show very much more enthusiasm for Rilke's *Neue Gedichte* of 1907 and 1908, and especially so for the Jardin des Plantes poems such as 'The Panther', 'The Gazelle', 'Parrot House' and others. These were among the poems which schoolchildren were regularly set to learn-by-heart. But to say this needs to include the reservation that it can really be said only in relation to the pre- and post-Hitler years: the Nazis disapproved of Rilke. He was in their eyes 'not ideologically correct', a fact for which we ourselves should be thankful. (There have always been and will always be thought-police and art-police, and they flourish rampantly in our own time. Perhaps we should think of them as wardens; as an ugly element in the logistics of population control.)

Rilke, then, has moved in and out of western cultural fashion. Here, it was first of all the *Duino Elegies* which people came to know: the *Neue Gedichte*, the *New Poems Part One* and *Part Two*, are still a prized treasure of the German-speaking world but remain much less known among the Anglophones.

The *New Poems* are the poems people have particularly in mind when they speak of Rilke's *'Ding-gedichte'* – his 'thing-poems'. In those, it is as if the poet had been forever seeking to enter deeply into objects, creatures, buildings, landscapes, people: into their essences and presences: a supremely narcissistic poet entering, at last, into the life and valency that lies *outside* the self. But Rilke's extraordinary focusing on things, and on the real, has absolutely nothing to do with what might be thought of as 'materialism'. He is pointing us in almost exactly the opposite direction. In showing us what he shows us, Rilke, far from innocently, leads us into the most profound questioning about all that is not shown.

In the *Sonnets to Orpheus*, something subtly different may be going on underneath the surface of the poems. The *Sonnets* grew primarily from the tap-root of the 'Orpheus. Eurydike. Hermes' of the *Neue Gedichte*. It would not, I think, be monstrous to suggest that a degree of narcissism had returned in these poems, for Rilke has plainly written himself into the person of Orpheus; and his sonnet-cycle (*Sagenkreis?*) celebrates the Singing God quite as much as it mourns the lost Eurydice – who in her turn doubles for the young Vera, destroyed by leukaemia just as Rilke was fated to be destroyed himself.

I believe that Rilke is ever-enchanted by the entire possibility and by all the possibilities of legend, of story, of tradition. He is literally spell-bound by the Old and New Testaments, by Shakespeare's *Tempest*, Ovid's *Metamorphoses* – the last of these being the source for the *Sonnets*. Furthermore, it is not merely that the profession of story-teller is one that pleases him and is felt by him as his vocation: it is rather that Rilke may believe in legend itself (together with recall) as the mould for very much of what makes us human.

'Ce n'est point avec des idées qu'on fait des sonnets, Degas, c'est avec des mots'. That was what Mallarmé had to say, and Rilke might or might not have agreed with him. The marital tussles and epiphanies which lie between form and content, between what-may-have-been-sought and what (instead!) was found, between overt message and evident self-contradiction – such things may be described and, even, up to a point be understood. Beyond that point every genuine work of art is likely to resist or utterly confound explanation. Works of art, whether literature, painting or sculpture, music or architecture, how they tempt the taxonomist and, especially, the theorist, and oh how they refuse in the end to give answers to – What is it, what is it for, what does it mean? and why? and why?

We may just as well ask those questions about a fellow human being, a person, which is what we do all the time socially, and what biographers do in their trade. It is for exactly those reasons that those exercises, too, are so frequently so death-handed. What requires a midwife finds, all too often, an undertaker.

'Most phenomena are unsayable,' wrote Rilke, 'and works of art are the most unsayable of all ... mysterious presences whose lives endure alongside our own perishable lives...' But what does 'poetry' do? It tries to say. Amazingly, it often succeeds. Easy to be persuaded that 'mystery' has to be learned, demands an apprenticeship. Does it? If we are to accept Rilke's own account of the *Sonnets*, something that is surely mystery may simply arrive, as a gift, as a given, as 'dictation'. Can it really be as simple as that? It can't. It isn't. In the case of Rilke's *Sonnets* and *Elegies*, there had already been a lifetime of preparation followed, at the near-end, by something like the bursting of a dam.

Always behind Rilke's *Sonnets* lies the *Doppelbereich*, the double kingdom of life and death, this world and other-world, worldliness and other-worldliness, the here against the not-here. Mystery is what makes mysteries mysterious: whether spiritual, carnal, religious, secular, rationalist or metaphysical.

In letter number VII to Officer Cadet Kappus, Rilke admonishes him at length to welcome difficulty: '... that something is hard must be just one more reason why we should do it'. But eighteen years later he

declares, at the end of the wonderful *Third Sonnet* of *Part I*: '... True
singing / is whispering; a breath within the God; a wind.'
Alive in the very argument, the contradiction, deep-rooted.
A text? A mystery?

Wissen wirs, Freunde, wissen wirs nicht?
Beides bildet die zögernde Stunde
in dem menschlichen Angesicht.

Texts cited in this essay are listed below:

Rainer Maria Rilke:
Elegies from the Castle of Duino, tr E and V Sackville-West, printed by Kessler
    at the Cranach Press for the Hogarth Press, 1931
Duino Elegies, tr JB Leishman, Hogarth Press, 1939
Neue Gedichte, tr JB Leishman, Hogarth Press, 1964
Duino Elegies, tr Stephen Cohn, Carcanet, 1989
Neue Gedichte, New Poems, tr Stephen Cohn, Carcanet, 1992
Sonnets to Orpheus, with *Letters to a Young Poet*, tr Stephen Cohn, Carcanet 2000

Du Côté de Chez Swann, Marcel Proust, Paris, 1913
Charmes ou Poèmes par Paul Valéry, NRF, 1922
Mallarmé, the Poems, tr Keith Bosley, Penguin, 1977
My Life in CIA, Harry Mathews, Dalkey Archive Press, 2005
A Night at the Majestic, Richard Davenport Hines, Faber, 2006

Rüdiger Görner

Rüdiger Görner is Professor of German at Queen Mary University of London, and founding Director of the Centre for Anglo-German Cultural Relations. Between 1999 and 2004 he was Director of the Institute of Germanic Studies and founded the Ingeborg Bachmann Centre for Austrian Literature. His main research areas comprise representations of science and music in the German language literatures, from the late eighteenth century to the present day, poetic theory at the turn of the centuries, the literary aesthetics of repetition and the conception of pluralectics in German (late) Romanticism. He has published studies on Hölderlin's poetics, the Goethezeit, Austrian Literature from Stifter to Thomas Bernhard, on Rilke, and on Thomas Mann and his notion of finality in culture. He has initiated many post-graduate research programmes at major universities in Germany. His publications are too numerous to list.

Dancing the Orange

Notes on Rilke's praise of sensuality

When in February 1922 Rilke had accomplished the exhilarating but exhausting task of completing his *Duineser Elegien* he felt the need to step out of his ancient tower of Muzot castle (nr Sierre) that had protected him and his work during those months of exceptional creativity. He stroked, even caressed, the grey walls of this poetic fortification like an old animal as he put it in a letter to his confidante, Lou Andreas-Salomé. With this truly touching gesture, he paid his thanks to the very place that had granted him the right space for the inspiration which he needed to finish what had been on his mind since he had written his first elegy in Duino Castle in January 1912.

What does this small but significant episode tell us about Rilke? That sense and sensitivity, sensibility and sensuality constituted but one experience in his life and work; and that he, the poet, was still able to relate to the Orphic myth and its suggestion that inspiration can make even stones respond. As it happened, Jean Cocteau was to finish his surrealist play *Orphée* in the year of Rilke's death (1926).

Rilke's gesture towards the stone echoes his early preoccupation with matter that turns to art in the hands of an artist. This is particularly evident in his impressions of Medieval art and the world of the Renaissance that he gave expression to in his *Florenzer Tagebuch* (Florence Diary) of 1898, especially in respect of Michelangelo's sculptures. Incidentally, this very impression led to his prose 'Von Einem, der die Steine belauscht' (Of One who listens to stones). The idea that the sculptor freed the shape contained within the stone that he works on, after he has touched it and listened to its morphic resonances, to borrow Rupert Sheldrake's phrase, was to dominate Rilke's reflections on Rodin, arguably the most sensual of artists that he met.

Rilke's fascination with the visual arts informed the motifs of his poetry and the nature of his discourses on the arts in letters and essays, stretching from the Worpswede artists (Heinrich Vogeler, Otto Modersohn including his future wife and Rodin disciple, Clara Westhoff) to Cézanne, and from Picasso to Klee. In his reflections on art Rilke introduced a renewed sense of the visual to German literature and provided a refined conception of synaesthetic expression in poetry that tuned down the (post-)Wagnerian and Neo-Romantic notion of a total work of art to something symbolically more tangible.

It is interesting though to find in his early Florenzer Tagebuch a number of references to synaesthetics whose message remained valid for him and unchanged throughout his poetic career. They represent a telling modification of the 'total work of art' ideology and read as follows:

> In every piece of one of the arts all effects of art must be accomplished. A painting does not need a text and a statue will not require painting-like colour, and a poem is not in need of music; it is rather that in each of them everything else should be contained.

In this passage Rilke sides with Gotthold Ephraim Lessing in this respect who, in his defining treatise on *Laokoon and the limitation of painting*, argued that the mixing of the arts was dangerous for them because in this process they would lose their identity. The more rewarding artistic endeavour, Rilke claims with explicit reference to Lessing, is to devote oneself to exploring the transitions between the respective forms of art.

But now, in 1922, when the world was still trying to come to terms with revolutionary changes in political, social and cultural terms, as well as utter fragmentation of consciousness connected with (post-) war traumata, alongside with severe doubts about the validity of language as a means of authentic communication, Rilke insisted, through completing the *Duineser Elegien* and *Sonette an Orpheus*, on the very unity of experience, entrusting his metaphors with representing just that. But this is not to suggest that Rilke had ignored those radical changes that had occurred during his lifetime; nor did he fail to give expression to them in his poetry and letters. But he demanded from himself that this expression should still take the shape of a perfectly crafted and deeply inspired work of (poetic) art. No talk therefore of the 'death of the author' in his œuvre; nor was there any trace of the distinctly modern idea that the reader of a text should be regarded as its true author, a conception however that can already be found in the writings of the early Romantic poet Novalis. In a letter to a young poet, the type of correspondent that suited at times Rilke's pedagogic calling, the author of the *Duineser Elegien* stated quite categorically and quite in line with what he had written in his *Florenzer Tagebuch* some twenty-five years **before**: 'The poem does not intend to excite the potential poet in the reader ... as the completed picture tells him: look, you do not have to paint me; I already exist!'

In the years 1922, or so it seems, modernism took a new turn with Rilke's contribution of the *Duineser Elegien* and the *Sonette an Orpheus*, with Joyce's *Ulysses* and Eliot's *The Waste Land*, not to speak of the completion of Proust's *Recherche*. Even though a sense of fragmentation is present in Rilke's *Duineser Elegien*, too, Eliot (with crucial help from Ezra Pound) was the poet who articulated that feeling in more dramatic poetic terms. But the essence of this 'new turn' within Modernism was the fusion of sensuality and abstraction, most prevalently so in the Vorticist movement but also in Surrealism as a more sophisticated continuation of the Dadaists.

Rilke, Proust and Joyce contributed crucially in their distinctly different ways to a new poetic and narrative quality of sensuality in texts. These texts contained the entirety of modes of artistic expression, from the sublime to the crude, from sophisticated speech to the vernacular and from engaging in mythological image (re-) making to the exploration of the ordinary, which of course owed a great deal to Naturalism and Symbolism. The three writers in question attempted to merge the naturalist and symbolist approach to representing the inner *and* outer worlds as well as memory and love for things present.

Rilke's work on the *Duineser Elegien* and the *Sonette an Orpheus* were accompanied, and perhaps partly inspired, by his ongoing passion for Michelangelo's sonnets, which he continued to translate until 1923 when he began to grace Paul Valéry's texts with his considerable, if not ingenious, translating skills. One question that informs Michelangelo's sonnets is the relationship between the senses and true love. 'Voglia sfrenata el senso è, non amore,/Che l'alma uccide'. Rilke translates this core phrase of Michelangelo's poems thus: 'Was seelentödlich aus den Sinnen bricht,/ist keine Liebe.' Rilke, interestingly, creates a new adjective from what Michaelangelo describes as the effect of something that bursts out of the senses. That very 'something' kills the soul and cannot be regarded as love. A literal translation of this adjective would read 'soul-deadly'. And even though Michelangelo's sonnet establishes a clear dichotomy between genuine love and mere sensuality, Rilke's rendering of this line and, in fact, most of the sonnets, achieves a distinctly sensual effect.

The senses are the antennae of being; they function as receivers but Rilke ascribed to them their very own ontological status. Similarly, Rilke instrumentalizes the sonnet as a finely-tuned instrument of perception attributing the five senses and, at his most divinatory, the sixth sense, too, to individual sonnets. Don Paterson in the afterword to his ingenious 'version' of Rilke's *Die Sonette an Orpheus* (*Orpheus*, 2006) argues that this corpus of Rilke poems constituted 'a kind of meta-essay on the possibilities of the sonnet form.' Paterson is right in identifying the 'singing' within these sonnets as Rilke's key statement on a distinctly human activity that connects Man with myth and that can be called Man's most sensual and, at once, spiritual form of expression.

One cannot praise Paterson's 'version' of Rilke's sonnets enough, which includes his afterword and 'Fourteen Notes on the Version'. Both amount to an eminently appealing poetology of a poet whose renderings of the German texts are not only eminently musical but capture intelligibly the essence of Rilke's composition. What Rilke's translations did for Barrett-Browning's *Sonnets from the Portuguese* and for Michelangelo's sonnets in German, Paterson has done for Rilke in English; for he *has* turned them into agents of an eminently inspired language that invite the reader to measure his own spiritual sensuality and sensual spirituality against this array of Orphic images. Paterson's decision to give each sonnet a title was a particularly fortunate one; for it signals to the reader what the names of these very essences of Orphic poetry are; and the senses feature prominently with sonnets on 'Tone', 'Taste', 'The Look', and 'Breath' that are flanked by sonnets on 'Orange', 'Mirror' or 'Cut Flowers' that challenge our senses. If the *Duineser Elegien* provide us, according to George Steiner, with the 'master-text of modern ontological solitude', Paterson's 'version' of *Die Sonette an Orpheus* present them as a compendium of sensual poetry that underwrites the permanency of change.

Like other poets and critics Paterson remarked on the ferocious speed with which Rilke wrote his Orphic sonnets ('Rilke was flying his kite in a thunderstorm'). But the point is that speed is not one of the sonnets' subject matters. In fact, most of them radiate a sense of calm and concentration but also a gratifying relaxation. Rilke claimed to have written these sonnets as if under a 'verbal dictation'. If this was true the reader is unaware of it. One of Rilke's sonnets wonders 'Giebt es wirklich die Zeit, die zerstörende?' (in Paterson's rendering: 'Is there really such a thing as time-the-destroyer?') as if it wants to question that the ruptures of time could ever be a threat to us. The point of Rilke's Orphic sonnets is instead that we need to know how the essences of life 'tick'; we need to be within them and outside of them at the same time *in order* for us to be in charge of them. Rilke's famous phrase 'Sei allem Abschied voran, als wäre er hinter/dir, wie der Winter, der eben geht' (in Paterson's version 'Be ahead of all departure; learn to act/as if, like the last winter, it was all over') epitomizes this feeling of mastering circumstances, which is one 'paraphrasable sense' of this unique poetic cycle. The other is undoubtedly the significance of change and transformation for the development of life, thought and emotion.

Paterson suggests that we need to engage with poetry and appreciate the relation of the words with each other. The implication is that, ideally, when reading poems we ought to write versions of them. In so doing we would extend the possibilities of the words interacting with others on the basis of what the original poem had prescribed in terms of structure, verbal mode and mood. 'Mädchen [...] tanzt den Geschmack der erfahrenen Frucht', Rilke writes in his fifteenth *Sonett an Orpheus*, which Paterson, in an attempt to enhance the sensual impact of this line even further, interprets thus: '[...] dance what you know on your tongue'. In his 'Fourteen Notes' Paterson refers to Robert Schumann's response to a query about a piece's meaning which was to play the piece again. In more than one way this also seems to be Paterson's preferred hermeneutic tool. In order to comprehend the meaning of a Rilke sonnet to Orpheus he reads, writes and 'sings' it once more. However, his versions, like Rilke's translations, do not overwrite the originals but write into them as it were. They establish a sensual and intellectual relationship with them, thus creating the impression of an authentic approach to the object of transposition.

'Tanzt die Orange', Rilke writes in the same sonnet. The idea of dancing the taste of the orange, even the orange itself, meaning not only its taste, but shape, form, inner structure and juiciness, may be called the pinnacle of Rilke's poetically attempted performance of his ontology of the senses. Scent after scent, shape after shape, the poet celebrates the intoxicating effect of the presence of the senses. What Rilke calls for is a choreography of sensual abstraction and abstract sensuality with his poetry being the 'music' for that dance. Rilke's *Sonette an Orpheus* thus invite us to dance to the poetic music of the senses and reflection. In that scenario we are not to ask with Yeats 'who can tell the dancer from the dance' but who can tell the taste from the moving sense.

Rilke was the passionate 'perceptionist' among the poets. His poetry is imbued with perceptions and desires to be perceived by the reader in the way in which a viewer sees a still life and sets it into motion through the intensity of his perception. The Orphic sonnets in particular challenge the sense of movement and of hearing. The very beginning of this extraordinary cycle requires particular attention: 'Da stieg ein Baum. O reine Übersteigung!/O Orpheus singt! O hoher Baum im Ohr!' Almost any translation, transposition or free rendering of this sequence cannot but fall flat. Even Paterson's 'version' cannot really give the rich impression of the original: 'A tree rose from earth. O pure transcendence -/Orpheus sings: O tall oak in the ear!' To begin with, this rendering loses all exclamation marks but one. But the exclamatory nature of this sequence is crucial for its meaning. The exclamations simultaneously interrupt and interconnect the parts of this sequence. The rising of the tree turns into a 'pure over-rising' suggesting the utmost intensification of rising. Through Orpheus' singing the tree (and not only the 'oak tree'!) enters the ear, perhaps even as a late or faint echo of the Genesis' tree of recognition.

Rilke's poetry in praise of the senses can be regarded as his contribution to a project that many of his contemporaries were engaged in – from Richard Dehmel to Franz Werfel, not to speak of the expressionists in poetry, painting and even philosophy. They all subscribed to what Nietzsche's Zarathustra had proclaimed under the heading the 'innocence of the senses', namely the emancipation of sensuality, which was to be connected by Henri Bergson with his conception of the *élan vital*. The sheer dynamics of 'life' were allowed to be unleashed in art and thought. In the minds and eyes of many an artist this affirmation of life and the glorification of its forces were, in principle, not even shattered by the horrors of the First World War. Some writers, Ernst Jünger for one, regarded even destruction as a manifestation of life's forces that would have to be seen, in a pre-Socratic sense, as the origins of the new.

This pronounced emancipation of the senses in the arts and philosophy countered the neo-Kantian renaissance of thought that assumed a world beyond the senses and with it a form of purely intellectual perception. It is quite evident from Rilke's approach to writing poetry that he seemed to have attempted some reconciliation between those two alternative forms of perception. His early concern for objects, which he never lost, reveal his interest in establishing a poetic equivalent to phenomenology to which he came close during his brief study period in Berlin under the tutelage of Georg Simmel, who would not only discuss the sociology of space and art but also the meaning of picture frames, mugs and their handles.

Rilke appeared to have responded almost instinctively to this approach, appropriating Simmel's idiosyncratically phenomenological method and 'translating' at least some of it into his 'poetry of objects', most notably in his *Neue Gedichte* of 1907/08, but equally so in the *Duineser Elegien*. The emerging impression of Rilke's treatment of objects and the act of perception is that of a deliberately subtle sensuality. Take, for example, this passage from *The Fifth Duino Elegy*:

Ach und um diese
Mitte, die Rose des Zuschauns:
blüht und entblättert. Um diesen
Stampfer, den Stempel, den von dem eignen
blühenden Staub getroffen, zur Scheinfrucht
wieder der Unlust befruchteten, ihrer
niemals bewußten, – glänzend mit dünnster
Oberfläche leicht scheinlächelnden Unlust.

Ah, and around this
centre, the rose of watching
flowers and un-flowers. Round this
stamp, this pistil, caught in the pollen
of its own flowering, fertilised
again to a shadow-fruit of disinterest,
their never-conscious, seeming-to-smile, disinterest,
gleaming lightly, on surface thinness.

(A.S. Kline, 2001)

What this elegiac segment illustrates is an almost excessive subtleness of observation that literally unpicks layer by layer this object of quasi-analytical perception in a manner that is entirely unique in (German) poetry. But at the same time the poetic analysis itself retains its sensual appeal. It does not come across as coldly analytical but as entirely appropriate for the object in question, a flower with its innermost revelations.

There is a short flower sequence, too, in the *Sonnets to Orpheus*, devoted to the 'Anemone', the 'Rose' and to 'Cut Flowers' to use the titles of Paterson's 'versions' or transliterations. But what the reader gets in those poems is both sensual imagery, poetic analysis of a flower and an interpretation of what the identified segments stand for, thus contributing to the impression that the Sonnets attempt to be self-contained and, poetically and hermeneutically, self-sufficient.

Rose, du thronende, denen im Alterume
warst due in Kelch mit einfachem Rand.
Uns aber bist du die volle zahllose Blume,
der unerschöpfliche Gegenstand.

141

In deinem Reichtum scheint du wie die Kleidung um Kleidung
um einen Leib aus nichts als Glanz;
aber dein einzelnes Blatt ist zugleich die Vermeidung
und die Verleugnung jedes Gewands.

These two quartets read in Paterson's version as follows:

Enthroned one: in the ancient understanding,
you were no more than a cup with a plain rim.
But for us, you are the full-blown, infinite bloom,
the wholly indefatigable thing:

impossible richness, silk dress on silk dress
laid upon a body of pure light –
and yet one naked petal will negate
all attire, all show of outwardness.

The rose is presented as the inexhaustible object that defies interpretation.
But two possible yet juxtaposed 'interpretations' introduce this particular
sonnet – an 'ancient' or conventional one ('Kelch mit einfachem Rand')
and a modern version that sees in the rose an emblem of the flower per
se. The real point is, however, that each of the rose's petals appears like
a piece of cloth only to deny itself. Instead, it advocates bareness and
the exposure of beauty and abundance, thus indicating vulnerability. This
is the main difference between Rilke's poetic advocacy of the senses and
his poetics of sensuality on the one hand and, on the other, the notion
of senses liberated on behalf of the élan vital by many of his contemporaries:
Rilke shows the fragility of sensuality and points to the fact that the
senses, albeit still intact, are an endangered species that require careful
protection for they cannot be taken for granted any longer, especially not
after the silencing shock of the world war devastation. Rilke's *Duineser
Elegien* and his *Sonette an Orpheus* testify to his attempt to regain his
language after this barbaric onslaught on humanity and culture without
actually mentioning the war explicitly. More sobering still was the
recognition that such barbarity was contained in that very culture with
all its sinister drives and half-conscious desires and the ultimately self-
destructive will to unlimited power. In his *Third Duino Elegy* Rilke coined
the phrase of the 'schuldige Fluß-Gott des Bluts' (the guilty river God
of blood) to describe these precarious drives. In a sense the *Sonnets to
Orpheus* and many of the later poems tried to engage again in identifying
modes of linguistic sophistication, be it in the context of the re-vitalised
sonnet-form and the Orphic myths, or in the shape of challenging abstractions

that dominate so much of his more experimental late poetry. Yet, he insisted on retaining a measured degree of sensuality even in his abstract poetry, on making new sense of the power of the senses, and on re-cultivating sensitivity through poetry as his very particular response to the coarser aspects of civilization.

Alison Croggon

See her biography in the Translations/Versions section in which two of her translations of the *Duino Elegies* appear.

Dear Rilke

Dear Rilke. If he were not a great poet, he might be one of the most purely annoying figures in the literary pantheon. Few poets have been responsible for as much bilge as Rilke has: he seems to be a magnet for a certain kind of literary narcissism. His invocations to self-insight and solitude can be easily softened into exhortations to mere self-regard or soft-centred spirituality, in the same way that Hollywood celebrities assure themselves that God loves them personally through determinedly vague readings of the Zorah. And Rilke's moments of self-pity or mere fatuousness can seem to confirm your worst suspicions about the self-indulgence and preciousness of poets.

Not all of this is Rilke's fault (although some of it is). Moreover, who of us could survive intact the reverent mythologising that has haunted Rilke's legacy? And how many could survive his naivety? For one of his greatest strengths is his refusal to eschew what William Carlos Williams called 'the essential naivety of the poet'. No one, not even a great poet, can survive this naivety without appearing at some point to be a fool. And perhaps only the very best and the very worst poets have the strength of mind to continue with that naivety once the world begins to mock it: the best because they see quite clearly that they have no choice but to seem foolish if they place their faith in poetry, and the worst because the world's base mockery confirms them in their vain purity.

But I am already flinging around some big words – 'faith', 'great'. It seems impossible to think about Rilke without them; but they apply in very contradictory ways. Contradiction, after all, lives in the heart of Rilke's poetics. As William Gass points out, for a poet who hated organised Christianity, Rilke populated his poetry with enough Virgin Marys and angels to rival the Catholic Church. And I have no doubt that Rilke is a great poet: but what do I mean by that? I think I mean two things: his lack of embarrassment in the face of the numinous, by which I mean a certain courage (the other face of poetic naivety); and his sheerly beautiful language, which enacts the inarticulate vortices of passionate being. Nowhere are these qualities more evident than in the ten poems that comprise the *Duino Elegies*.

The turbulent currents that make the *Elegies* so enthralling are generated by the dynamic contradictions of a mind acutely conscious of its own movements. There is nothing static in the *Duino Elegies*: direction, velocity, is all. This is why it is such a mistake to read them as if Rilke were dispensing philosophy, as if a meaning can be accurately paraphrased away from the texture of the language itself. Rilke is not a philosopher, still less a sage: he is a poet. The poems are not 'about' life: rather, they are a startling mimesis of its instability and transience.

In my struggle to translate these poems, which seems to have taken longer than it did for Rilke to write them, one thing has come very much to the foreground. The intractability of some lines or images, their often stubborn refusal to resolve into a clarity that I knew existed within the most difficult or obscure of them, depended to an crucial extent on my comprehension of the spatial relations within them. The relationship between the poems' elements is fluid and in constant motion: everything is above, below, before, behind, within, without. Things and people leave and arrive, approach and depart, climb over or vanish behind each other, restrain or release each other. Every surface is permeable, every physical or psychic state in a process of flux. Even matter itself exists in state of dynamic transformation: Rilke makes you constantly aware of its weight or lightness, its viscosity or airiness or solidity. This stanza, from 'The Second Elegy', is not untypical:

For we, when we feel, evaporate; ah, we
breathe ourselves out and away; from ember to ember
giving a fainter smell. Here perhaps someone might say
yes, you enter my blood, this room, the spring
feels itself with you ... it's no use, he can't hold us,
we dwindle in and around him. And those who are beautiful,
o who holds them back? Appearance continuously
enters and leaves their gaze. As dew on the early grass
what is ours rises from us, as the heat of a
steaming dish. O smile, where do you go? O upturned glance:
new, warm, vanishing wave of hearts –;
alas, that's what we *are*. Does the universe
in which we dissolve, taste of us? Do angels capture
only their realness, streaming towards them,
or sometimes, in error, a little
of our being? Are we only diffused
in their features, like a vagueness in the gaze
of pregnant women? Unremarked in the vortex
of their recoil to themselves. (How should they remark it.)

145

The complexity of the transitions here is not merely a question of the supple turning of the metaphor of feeling as an evaporation of the self. Rilke is constantly interrupting himself, as if – to borrow an image from Mandelstam – a thought in flight evolves in mid-air to something else, in a constant process of improvisation. In this stanza Rilke moves restlessly from an abstract thought to a specific place ('this room'), from first person to third and back again, from an image of dew rising to the domesticity of a hot dish of food; and then, without warning, he flings us into the immense ocean of the cosmos, where the faint traces of our felt life are absorbed into the dynamic vortex of angelic being.

The complexities Rilke articulates are very particular, and to my mind are at the core of his modernity. Rilke's modernity is not of the kind that embraced the machine age, and perhaps for that reason has been difficult to recognise. As an aside, it has occurred to me that the *Duino Elegies*, rather than being thought of in terms of a late Romanticism in uncomfortable collision with modernity, might be more fruitfully imagined as the poetry of a man who thoughtfully observed the kinds of phenomena that are mapped in the complex sciences: cloud formations, the flocking of birds (human beings are not, he says, as 'intelligent' as flocking birds), turbulences of air or water: the energies that are traced in fluid dynamics or chaos theory. He is not mapping Platonic abstractions so much as finding ways to express complex, often organic, patterns of flow – eddies, currents, seasons, growth, consciousness.

The urgency this sense of motion generates is reinforced by the *Elegies'* mode of insistent address. Again and again Rilke demands: Look! See! Hear! But, again, the 'you' in the poems is under constant, explosive pressure: it may shift mid-line or remain ambiguous: it may conjure the lover, the angel, the father, the child, the seasons, the stars, death, the poet himself. And as the addressee is in constant flux, so is the poet: and as the poet transforms, so he demands a concomitant responsiveness in the reader. The elusiveness of these poems doesn't come from obscurity so much as a quality of *speed*. And here I admire Rilke's poise: for this dizzying motion is in dynamic relationship with a great stillness that exists in the very centre of his poems.

One of the things that prevents the *Duino Elegies* from disintegrating under their own centrifugal force is their rhythmic power. From the very first lines of 'The First Elegy', Rilke grabs the whole of your attention:

Wer, wenn ich schriee, hörte mich denn aus der Engel
Ordnungen? und gesetzt selbst, es nähme,
einer mich plötzlich ans Herz...

The first translations I read (and still, to my mind, the best I have encountered) were the Spender/Leishman collaborations. They are very beautiful; but when I read the German out loud, I felt a jaggedness, a bitterly disciplined economy, a tough directness, that was obscured in the English. To my ear, the English was *too* beautiful; sometimes this conception of beauty glossed the precision of Rilke's movement through the poems, taming the exact unruliness of their dance. On the other hand, translations which render the *Elegies* into a kind of sudsy prose, leaning on angelic imagery and a faux philosophical weight to carry the poetry's meanings, do Rilke a much greater disservice: they seem to dispense with poetic beauty altogether. They express an unspoken baggage of apology for the poem's excesses; perhaps it's a rather Anglo-Saxon embarrassment towards its intensities of feeling, which are most carnally felt in its rhythms. There's no doubt that the sonic texture of Rilke's language is the most difficult quality to render in English, the aspect which most reminds you that translation is an expression of impossible desire, an inevitable appointment with failure. But the beauty and exhilaration of Rilke's rhythmic variations were probably the major reason I embarked on the folly of translating the *Duino Elegies*; perhaps it was even more significant than my ardent desire to understand them better.

Given their complexity and precision, the meaning of these poems is irreducible. They mean, as every poem does, exactly what they say: or, perhaps more accurately, exactly what they *are*. With this caveat firmly in mind, I'll briefly attempt to draw some trajectories of meaning out of the turbulence.

Rilke is the consummate poet of faith: no one else describes its compelling and unreasoning force with such clarity as he does in the *Duino Elegies*. For Rilke, faith is a kind of forgetting, like the flight of a bird lifted by the 'heightening seasons', 'almost forgetting / that he is a pitiable animal and not just a single heart / they fling into brightness, into the ardent sky.' Lovers, with 'their long-since groundless ladders, leaning / on only each other, tremulously', gloriously ignore their own irrationality. Faith is its own groundless reason, lifting itself into its own reality:

Hear, my heart, how otherwise only
the holy hear: so when the immense cry
lifted them up from the ground, they kept kneeling,
impossibly, more deeply attentive:
such was their listening.

And yet, this faith, far from being transcendent, is grounded in – even

147

depends on (or from) – the finitudes, the ordinary stench, of physical existence. I couldn't disagree more with Robert Hass's comment that the *Duino Elegies* are 'an argument against our lived, ordinary lives', that he is 'always calling us away' from 'the middle of life'. No: rather, the *Duino Elegies* generate an urgent gravity towards that very middle, towards that very ordinariness: for there is nowhere else to be alive. If anything, Rilke argues himself *away* from the dizzying universe of the abstract and transcendent, the self-consciousness that hides from us the deeper knowledge of belonging that glows behind human alienation.

This is Rilke's naïve assertion: that we are human, and belong in this world. The *Duino Elegies* argue against the mediations that bar us from that humble threshold, against the smallnesses of spirit – fear of seeming foolish, vanities, cowardice, or the greedy desire merely to possess – that make us deny the simplicities of being:

> Being here is magnificent. You knew it, girls, you also,
> sunk in your seeming lack – in evil
> city alleys suppurating with open rubbish.
> For each there was an hour, maybe not
> even an hour, one measure of time barely
> measurable between two whiles: there she had
> being. All. The vein-full being.
> But we forget so easily what the laughing neighbour
> neither confirms nor envies.

Yet, for all its insistence on simplicities, for all its arguments against petty human self-consciousness, there is nothing straightforward about the faith that Rilke describes. It knows itself as nothing more than faith in faith itself, a tautology like the lovers' ladders. Rilke is too intelligent to deceive himself, and too intelligent again not to see that his undeceived vision is as much a lie as the former illusion, and perhaps more misleading:

> Ah and around this
> centre, the rose of looking:
> blooms and defoliates. Around this
> pestle, the pistil, stricken
> by its own blooming pollen again
> conceiving illusory fruits of disgust, never
> aware of it, – bright with flimsy
> surfaces the frail smile-sheen of disgust.

At the furthest point from these flimsy surfaces, at the innermost depths or the dizziest heights, Rilke places his angel. Like everything else in the poems, the angel continuously transforms: perhaps, more than anything, the angel is transformation itself, a catalysing agent of perception and creation. At the beginning of the sequence, the angelic orders are everything that is beyond human finitude, summoning the gargantuan energies of galaxies: terrible, violent, indifferent, amoral, beyond questions of life or death, witnesses to truths beyond the fragmentation of human perception. The angel can seem to be the shape of unmediated desire, unmediated being, the world of the 'invisible' that inhabits yet is alienated from the material world. Yet it can stoop down from its airy dimension and take human form, like the angel at Tobias' door, seeming only to be a young man humbly at the domestic threshold, 'no longer terrible'; or, like a marionettist, animate a puppet with the essence of gesture, a distilled act that is generated from the sheer intensity of attention paid by the spectator.

There is something suspiciously human about Rilke's angels. Like Blake's gods, they reside in the human breast. 'Who are you?' Rilke asks the angel, and obliquely answers himself: 'Early blessings, you coddle creation's / mountain ranges, the red dawning edges / of all making...' Rilke's angel is crucially a poet's angel: a protean, visceral, impersonal, amoral energy closer to Lorca's idea of *duende* than to any Christian conception of cherubs or mediating messenger of God (Rilke himself said his angels were drawn from Islam more than Christianity, meaning that the angel was subordinate to the prophet rather than to the Divine). More than anything else, the angel is the force of *poeisis*.

We approach the angelic through a true, subjective recognition of life's beauty. Rilke explores a number of means towards this recognition in the *Elegies*. We come close in the radiant transfiguration of love, but our vision there is obscured by the image of the beloved, who steps before us and blocks the light. Rilke often speaks of lovers with the amazed wonder and envy of an outsider.

> Lovers, you, who fulfil yourselves in each other,
> I ask about us. You seize yourselves. Have you proofs?
> See, what happens to me is that my hands
> move within one another, or my used
> expression considers itself in them. That gives me a little
> sensation. Yet who would gamble existence on that?

Love also calls up the fraught darkness of sexuality, which coils within the smallest child: at once the place of ampleness, fertility and pleasure, and the source of bloody atrocity. In 'The Second Elegy', the poet remembers his childish dreams as he slept in his bourgeois bedroom:

He, new, fearful, how he was tangled
in the long vines of inner event
winding already to intricate patterns, to strangling growths, to bestial
predatory forms. How he gave himself up –. Loved.
Loved his innerness, his interior wilderness,
these ur-forests within him, on whose mute collapse
stood his greenlit heart. Loved. Left it, and went
down to his roots and out to immense beginning
where his small birth was already outlived. Lovingly
lifted down into older blood, the ravines
where horror lay, gorged with his fathers. And every
terror knew him, winking, was so understanding.
Yes, atrocity smiled . . . Seldom
have you smiled so tenderly, mother.

The angelic is also summoned within the human desire to make. Again
and again Rilke invokes simple objects, and celebrates their transformation
into expressiveness – music, architecture, language – through the medium
of feeling.

Yet the wanderer brings from the mountain edge
not a handful of speechless earth, but a word
hard-won, absolute, the yellow and blue
gentian. Perhaps we are here to say: house,
bridge, spring, gate, jug, fruit-tree, window –
at most: column, tower . . . But to say, you understand,
oh to say in such a way that these things never
meant so intensely to be.

Human perception, human love, invests itself in the things that we make,
the objects with which we mark our transitory traces on the world. In
the shaping of a pot, or the building of a pyramid, we breathe, like gods,
our animation into inanimate clay. The angel is the catalyst, the far light
that, while it is neither love nor creation itself, annunciates the human
desire to love or to make, and the angel, for all his transcendence, finds
the truly marvellous in our tender investment in the material.

Praise the world to the angel, not the unsayable, to him
you can't brag of magnificent beatitude: in the world
where he so feelingly feels, you are a novice. So show
him the simple, formed from generation to generation,
which lives as a part of ourselves near the hand and in looking.

150

Tell him the Things. He will stand astonished, as you stood
beside the roper in Rome or by the Egyptian potter.
Show him how happy a thing can be, how innocent and ours,
how even complaining grief purely decides on a form,
serves as a thing, or dies into a thing, – and beyond
approaches the bliss of a violin.

The animal, the coupling beast, is not simply placed, as might easily be
assumed, in polar opposition to the angel: that place of opposition is
reserved for the human. The 'clever animal' that perceives that we are
not 'trustingly at home / in our imagined world' is sometimes closer to
the angel than we are: the bird, like the angel, possesses flight; the
creaturely world perceives, without impediment, the 'open', the freedom
of being that the angel consciously inhabits. The animal, like a child
released into a moment of total absorption or a person on the point of
death, is unaware of its own belonging. Unlike animals, we are aware of
our own death; but like them, we wear the heaviness of our material
being. And even in animality, Rilke perceives an inarticulate sense of
exile that he construes as exile from the womb: the loneliness of singularity.

And yet in the wakeful warm animal
is the weight and sorrow of a huge dejection.
For it also clings to what often
overwhelms us, – a memory,
that what we thrust after, was formerly
nearer, truer and its connection
endlessly tender.

Rilke's conception of beauty is essentially tragic: beauty exists wholly in
the process of human perception, but that very perception makes us
agonisingly aware of our own finitude. More than anything else, the *Duino
Elegies* are an extended meditation on death. The poems move inevitably
towards a clarity that follows a felt understanding of mortality:

Each thing once,
only once. Once and no more. And we also
once. Never again. But this
once was real, even if only once:
earthly and real, shining beyond revocation.

The *Elegies* culminate in an extended encounter with sorrow. In 'The
Tenth Elegy', Rilke invokes sorrow as 'our enduring winter leaf, our dark

evergreen', a season that is also a place, a 'home'. He takes us on a tour of the land of pain, which moves ever outwards from an imagined city: first the streets and markets, full of brag and noise, past the church with its ready-made consolation, out to the suburbs, where a carnival distracts us with its noise and colour. There, unnoticed behind the advertising hoardings with their false promises of immortality, at last he finds the 'real': children, dogs and lovers, who tenderly 'follow nature' in the shabby grass.

From this humble, ordinary place, the poet might be briefly seduced by a Lament, a handmaiden to sorrow; but only the dead can go further. They alone can enter the fantastic hinterland of pain, which Rilke maps with its own mines, mountains, pastures, trees, valleys, stars: even its own aristocracies and economies. And having crossed this realm and witnessed its marvels, at the centre of them the 'source of joy', the dead must climb alone, in silence, the mountains of 'primal pain'.

The living, however, can only be where they are: we can only imagine the paths that the dead must tread. The final movement of the poem is not upwards to transcendence, but down, towards the earth. We fall, always, but the compassion wrung from pain graces us, at last, with happiness. No lines in this poem move me more than the penultimate stanza:

But if they awakened a likeness within us, the endlessly dead,
they'd show us perhaps the catkins hanging
from empty hazels, or
would mean rain falling on dark earth in the early year. –

The stark purity of these lines is hard won. They hold, as in an open hand, the meaning of the whole poem. These wintry miniatures – a glimpse of spring catkins, the sound of rain – are details that so often pass unnoticed and unrecorded, part of the trivial textures of our lives; and yet they are the very things the dead envy us. The maelstrom of Rilke's longing holds in its still centre the world of concrete, material reality. He leaves us in the middle of our ordinary lives, as human, mortal and full of yearning as we ever were, but momentarily transfigured by being able to see our world in all its fabulous poverty, banality and mystery, neither less nor more than it is.

Peter Robinson

Peter Robinson has recently published *Selected Poetry and Prose of Vittorio Sereni* (Chicago), *The Greener Meadow: Selected Poems of Luciano Erba* (Princeton), and *Talk about Poetry: Conversations on the Art* (Shearsman). He is Professor of English and American Literature at the University of Reading.

Rilke, thou art translated

'We usually think of the "poetic" as that which cannot fully translate, that which is uniquely embedded in its particular language', Marjorie Perloff observes in an essay about 'Wittgenstein on Translation' in *Differentials: Poetry, Poetics, Pedagogy* (2004), adding that 'The poetry of Rainer Marie Rilke is a case in point.' She then turns to William H. Gass's *Reading Rilke: Reflections on the Problems of Translation* (1999) and, using his gathered examples of attempts at line one of the *Duino Elegies*, concludes that not only is Gass's version of the line 'no better', but that the characteristics of German when contrasted with English usage intensified by Rilke's unique art 'create a dense sonic network that is inevitably lost in translation.' What she says is incontestably true: and 'inevitably lost' means that for her translations of poetry must, without exception and inescapably, at least partially fail. Yet when the pastoral-traditionalist Robert Frost and the postmodern-futurist Marjorie Perloff agree that the 'poetry is what gets lost in translation', it could just be that a self-evident truism is being used to defend an untenable position. Because the 'poetic' as she puts it, or 'poetry' as Frost does, won't exactly reproduce in another language, can it not be translated? Their truism conceals the likelihood that the word 'translate' is taking a vacation in Wittgenstein's sense ('philosophical problems arise when language *goes on holiday*'). If 'translate' doesn't mean perfectly reproduce, then could the poetry or the poetic prove as more or less translatable as anything else?

William Gass is in substantial agreement with Perloff and Frost: 'find an English song for these words, these phrases, from 'Die Spanische Trilogie,'' he urges; and, after a quotation spree including, with line-breaks suppressed, his 'favorite, ... *wie ein Meteor in seiner Schwere nur die Summe Flugs zusammennimmt*', he adds: 'You don't have to know German. Just look at it: *zusammennimmt*. A god can't do it.' T.S. Eliot's strange gods might well include the one referred to in Rilke's phrase from the third of *Die Sonette an Orpheus*, 'Ein Gott vermags' – A God does it. The same poet appears to support the 'lost in translation' faction when he remarks in 'Rudyard Kipling' (*On Poetry and Poets*, 1957) that 'the music of verse is inseparable from the meanings and associations of words'. Yes, like a divorce lawyer, the translator begins by separating what God, as you might say, hath joined together. Perloff reminds us that the original's fusion of auditory shape and significance cannot be exactly reproduced ('zusammennimmt' is rendered as 'concentrates' by Michael Hamburger and 'gathers within' by Stephen Mitchell). Not that translators will have wanted to reproduce it, mind you, because the noises would sound bizarre in English. My point, however, is that a God wouldn't need to do it, being linguistically all-knowing; but a living person might – and could, with luck and patience, find equivalent resources in the sonic contours of the receiver language.

Perloff's and Gass's instances of what cannot be fully conveyed are supported by observations on both the differences between German and English, and on details of Rilke's poetic techniques. If the former is the problem (and I'll get to Rilke later), then all translation across this language barrier – whether of poetry or prose – must face similar losses. Yet for Perloff, in the same essay, '*poetry* is that which deals with the connotative and tropical power of words and the rhythmic and sonic quality of phrases and sentences, whereas *philosophy* ... involves the conceptual and abstract language of making meaningful propositions.' These latter, she asserts, are translatable without significant loss; and by quoting English, German, and French versions of a Wittgenstein remark from *Philosophical Investigations* she illustrates to her own satisfaction that the differences of formulation and texture from language to language are incidental. But Perloff's distinction is, as Eliot's remark on the music of poetry indicates, the exaggeration of an emphasis to the point of plain falsehood. Philosophy has tropes and connotations, rhythms and sounds; poetry contains meaningful propositions. Her assertion also drastically underestimates the art of a prose translator conveying both the matter and style of a writer. Though Lichtenberg and Nietzsche both wrote aphoristically, and the later admired the former, their writings are hardly similar; *le style c'est l'homme même*, and to translate their ideas – whatever those might be shorn of exact formulation – so as to make both writers sound the same would not be to translate them. In 'Translation – For and Against' (1936) it was finding Nietzsche translated on a Paris bookstall that prompted Walter Benjamin to note: 'There is no world of thought which is not a world of language'; for, in that particular case, 'the horizon and the world around the translated text had itself been substituted, had become French.'

If critics or poets fall back on a distinction (which Perloff describes as 'perhaps so obvious ... we don't usually take it into account') that in poetry the figuratively musical, the 'connotative and tropical', the 'rhythmic and sonic' is essential, but in other texts, including Wittgenstein's philosophy, it's 'the *denotative* meanings' we're after, then they have reduced his writings, like those of Lichtenberg, Nietzsche, and many more besides, to the level of a user's manual – where I'm willing to grant that the tropical shouldn't be to the fore, though any clarity of style does have its auditory component. More challengingly, Hamburger suggests in his introduction to *An Unofficial Rilke* (1981), that it was the poet's fluency with the 'poetic' features of a text that helped precipitate the central crisis and dilemma of his creative life: 'Rilke's virtuosity of feeling encountered too little resistance from the hard real quiddity of things – and people'. 'This', Hamburger adds, 'was Rilke's peculiar danger – a facility most conspicuous in his multiple rhyming, alliteration, assonance – all of them linking devices that suggest semantic, as well as sonic, affinities'. Commenting on his 'dynamization and neologization of verbs and their prepositions', Hamburger observes that 'A typical instance is his use of 'ausgefühlt' in a letter of 1914 – 'felt through', by analogy with 'worked through' or 'thought through'. This 'feeling through' the most diverse material was Rilke's speciality and strength as a poet, his weakness and inadequacy as a man.' Not only does this likelihood produce a qualm about what we're enjoying if we like his poetry; it also draws attention to the fact that the 'poetic' features of his work most challenging to translators are embroiled with the least admirable aspects of his cultural example. It should remind us too that the 'figurative' and 'tropical' features of poems are not values in themselves. It doesn't automatically increase the 'poetry' in a work to turning up the volume on that side at the expense of its 'meaningful propositions'. The value of a poem also resides, inseparably from its meaning-music, in what it can be understood to say.

As a result of an unusual childhood including a dramatic departure from Austria for the United States in 1938, fascinatingly described in her memoir *The Vienna Paradox* (1994), Perloff is bilingual in English and German. She is well placed to experience the drawbacks of Rilke in the one, or, as she goes on to show, Robert Lowell in the other. Yet she's also in a position not to need a German Lowell or an English Rilke. Thus what Frost and Perloff appear to be defending when they emphasize the untranslatable nature of the 'poetry' is the special access granted to mother tongue speakers. Even if they don't actively promulgate it, poet and critic haplessly consort with a linguistic manifest destiny, 'The Gift Outright', as it were. There's nothing to touch an original; though this truism doesn't mean that in exceptional cases a translation may not prove a finer poem. Nor does it follow that native speakers are bound to fathom literary texts in their language better than 'foreigners'. To appreciate a poem you have to apply yourself, and being a native speaker is no guarantee you'll do that well enough. Moreover, while some of us through the chances of birth or life have multilingualism thrust upon us, many don't; nor are any of us so linguistically capable as to circumvent entirely the Babel of global tongues. If world poetry is to be more than a closed book, strictly speaking, to most of us, then there need to be translations, losses and all. We face another paradox: the untranslatable is not only in need of translation; it's forever being translated – a fact which Rilke's example amply illustrates, for, as Joseph Brodsky noted in 'Ninety Years After' (*On Grief and Reason*, 1996): 'in the past three decades translating Rilke has become practically a fad'.

Discussing the issue of work-preservation in his *Languages of Art* (1968), Nelson Goodman confronts a partially analogous problem that arises with the performance of scored music:

> Since complete compliance with the score is the only requirement for a genuine instance of a work, the most miserable performance without actual mistakes does count as such an instance, while the most brilliant performance with a single wrong note does not. Could we not bring our theoretical vocabulary into better agreement with common practice and common sense by allowing some limited degree of deviation in performances admitted as instances of a work?

Goodman answers his question in the negative because 'If we allow the least deviation, all assurance of work-preservation and score-preservation is lost; for by a series of one-note errors of omission, addition, and modification, we can go all the way from Beethoven's *Fifth Symphony* to *Three Blind Mice*.' This funny example only underlines the gulf between theoretical vocabulary and practice, for even a Portsmouth Sinfonia performance of the former work would not, I expect, be reduced to a rendition of the latter. Yet, in the gap between poetic original and translation, the like may have been not infrequently achieved. Fortunately, in translations exact preservation of the original work cannot be a criterion for success or failure.

Nevertheless, Gass touches a number of Goodman's bases when writing that some translators 'would rather be original than right; they insist on repainting the stolen horse; 'it's my translation,' they say as they sign it, as if their work were the work of art. How should we fare if printers did the same, putting out their own *Lost Paradise*, their personalized versions of *As You Prefer It*?' We should fare as people used to do in the days when Tottel rewrote Wyatt's 'They fle from me that sometyme did me seke' before anthologizing it in his *Miscellany*. Yet, equally, the apparent equivalent for Goodman's 'the most miserable performance without actual mistakes', namely the prose paraphrases at the page foot in those Penguin editions of poetry in other languages, turn out not to be, again strictly speaking, performances of the work at all – which may be why they have been so helpfully inspiring for poets doing versions of their own. The gulf between the poem and the prose begged for reparative revision. Let's try then to accept the inevitable, and make our theoretical vocabulary fit the common practice.

Translations, like performances of scores, are always interpretive variations; none of them can be perfect matches. The relative preservation of the work in performance is achieved by skills that respond imaginatively and creatively to the promptings of the score, or the original. Just as we can enjoy variant performances of a much-loved work, perhaps one whose score we are skilled enough to sight-read in our heads, so too different translations can be appreciated for their variant solutions to the same challenges. In this sense, translations are not competing to match their originals, because that's impossible; they are creating variants from it that may or may not please with their fidelity, subtlety of interpretation, and imaginativeness in rendering tricky passages. A poetry translation might aspire to be a convincing transposition for another instrument, with the inevitable losses entailed and fortunate gains finessed. If a poetic translation's equivalent to a performance of the *Fifth Symphony* sounds like *Three Blind Mice*, that's an implicit judgment on the playing. The 'poetry', or the 'poetic', is translatable when the word 'translation' is back from its holidays and properly understood as interpretive performance. The original cannot, by definition, be reproduced in the second language; but it can be variously imitated, and its loss can be complexly, and more or less faithfully, compensated for. Like Gass's objection to translators who would 'rather be original than right', with the proviso that 'right' means 'as accurate as practically possible', my long-held objection to Lowell's *Imitations* amounts to a revulsion at their not being sufficiently imitative of their originals.

However, for long stretches *Reading Rilke: Reflections on the Problems of Translation* is not about the problems of translation, but, rather, the problems of reading Rilke. I want to move now to some thoughts about how the practically false notion of poetry's not being translatable has equivalents in the equivocal example that Rilke's life and art offer for Gass's speculative retelling. His book contains many highly-wrought and well-meaning passages of what the Wittgenstein of the *Tractatus* might have included under the rubric of his final sentence '*Wovon man nicht sprechen kann, darüber muss man schweigen*', translated with debatable

157

inflections by C.K. Ogden, as 'Whereof one cannot speak, thereof one must be silent.' With Wittgenstein's famous remark, problems don't only arise from the fact that the German 'man' can't be simply Englished; they remain in the translated ambiguity of 'muß' in 'must', marking either logical or moral compulsions for 'muss man schweigen'. It is a complexity in a philosophical text not unlike Empson's conception of poetic language; and that area about which we either cannot do other than be silent, or must strive not to enter with our meaningless talk, contains (as in 6.421) all ethics and aesthetics. Gass writes his way right into it:

> Beauty, in Angels and elsewhere, is the revelation of a wholly inhuman perfection, for art, as Rilke wrote, goes against the grain of nature and transcends man. Just as, in Plato, any apprehension of the Forms is achieved through a deadly separation of the rational soul from the influence of the body, so in these *Elegies* a glimpse of such purity is possible only by means of a vertiginous breach in the self as might be made by a mighty quake of earth – one which can close as abruptly as it opened.

If beauty in art is 'the revelation of a wholly inhuman perfection' we need hardly be surprised that it prove untranslatable. As Gass describes poets at work, to be visited with this vision of beauty and perfection, they would evidently have to suffer the little death of inspiration. Yet if you need a definition of *Kitsch*, this flirtation with death as a source of absolute values, ones not so much discovered and tested in the vicissitudes of lived experience as fixedly authorized by some arbitrary higher power, this might be a place to start. Robert Hass noted in his introduction to the Mitchell *Selected Poems of Rainer Maria Rilke* (1982) that this poet's theme is 'the abandonment of ordinary life for the sake of a spiritual quest', and to this we might add Hamburger's point that for Rilke 'Music (rhythm) is the untrammelled superabundance of God, who has not exhausted himself in phenomena'. The poet also famously wrote that 'Gesang ist Dasein' – but he hardly intended by the slogan any old stroller in the park who hums a tune. Over and over, readers encounter Rilke's self-alienating tendency to attribute ordinary human capacities, in impossibly idealized form, to an evoked divinity of questionable provenance. We can see it happening towards the end of 'Liebes-Lied', from early in the *Neue Gedichte*, where, having described the two lovers as one chord produced by bowing two strings, the speaker asks 'Auf welches Instrument sind wir gespannt? / Und welcher Geiger hat uns in der Hand?' The poet finds himself projecting the two people's love as played not by themselves but by some mysterious spiritual fiddler. Rilke doesn't, of course, answer his questions, allowing the poem to expire in a sigh: 'O süßes Lied.'

Gass writes that 'art ... goes against the grain of nature and transcends man', inserting the words 'as Rilke wrote' to step away from affirming the absolute he seems to stand by, while, in effect, articulating just such a would-be truth. He thus asserts as a current verity what may rather be an exploded bundle of cruelly unhelpful contradictions and conundrums long past their sell-by-date. He had earlier written that with 'a romantic naiveté for which we may feel some nostalgia ... Rilke struggled his entire life to be a poet' and 'A high priest of the poet's art, he takes the European lyric to new levels of achievement – forming with Valéry and Yeats perhaps, a true triune god – and creates the texts of a worthy religion at last, one which we may wholeheartedly admire, in part because we are not required to believe in it or pay it tithes.' Sentimentality is having an emotion without being willing to pay for it; but Gass in effect believes and pays, writing in his Preface that the poet's 'work has taught me what real art ought to be; how it can matter to a life through its lifetime; how commitment can course like blood through the body of your words until the writing stirs, rises, opens its eyes'. As if in the footsteps of the Shelleys, good writing for Gass blinks awake like a Frankenstein's monster.

I am arguing for a different sense of how art can 'matter to a life through its lifetime'. Two of Gass's holy trinity had already belatedly advised us to look elsewhere for inspiration. 'We must try to live!' Valéry urges in the final verse of 'Le Cemetière Marin', an exclamation that springs from the sound of the preceding phase, 'The wind lifts!': 'Le vent se lève! ... Il faut tenter de vivre!' Rilke on his deathbed was, Gass tells us, translating Valéry's poem. Yeats's 'The Circus Animals' Desertion' familiarly concludes: 'I must lie down where all the ladders start, / In the foul rag-and-bone shop of the heart.' These writers are tiptoeing away from the consequences of what Wallace Stevens, himself announcing a nineteenth-century theme as if it were a new discovery, wrote in his 'Adagia': 'After one has abandoned a belief in God, poetry is that essence which takes its place as life's redemption.' Those of us who are religious believers do not need poetry as a substitute religion; and those who feel they must, or would prefer, to live without such beliefs, don't need one either. Art isn't even an alternative to religion; it is more like, as Richard Wollheim asserted in *Art and its Objects* (1980), borrowing his term from the later Wittgenstein, 'a form of life'. Discussing aesthetics with his Cambridge students in the 1930s, the philosopher discouraged attempts to find an essential definition for the 'beautiful', preferring to ask how the word is used, what role 'beauty' and the 'beautiful' play in life –

definitions that will vary and alter between cultures, large and local, as well as through time. You can only know it by looking at and reflecting upon specific cases in experience.

Gass is clear-eyed about how Rilke's life does not offer us any Jamesian self – or other – sacrificing Lesson of the Master. He announces this theme in the first half of the sentence from his Preface cited above: 'The poet himself is as close to me as any human being has ever been; not because he has allowed himself – now a shade – at last to be loved; and not because I have been able to obey the stern command from his archaic torso of Apollo to change my life, nor because his person was always so admirable it had to be imitated...' But, come on now, you can only be close to a 'poet himself' if he allows you to be so in his life. After reading *A Ringing Glass: The Life of Rainer Maria Rilke* by Donald Prater (1986), and now Gass's often all but repelled biographical sketches, I'd be tempted to suggest that Rilke's life shows exactly how not to do it for poets who aspire to be reasonably decent husbands, wives, parents, relatives, colleagues and friends. What Gass knows in detail is how Rilke had commitment-issues with regard to everything except his art, his life's central crisis occurring when he feared that it had abandoned *him*.

In a passage of, presumably, imaginative identification with his subject's emotional complexities, Gass offers a gloss on this familiar German phrase:

> *Ich liebe dich*. No sentence pronounced by a judge could be more threatening. It means that you are about to receive a gift you may not want. It means that someone is making it very easy for you to injure them – if they are not making it inevitable – and in that way controlling your behaviour.

But the words don't mean what Gass says they do; some people can mean that by using them selfishly. Perhaps Rilke was one of those people. Though in his 'Paris Diary' (1930), Benjamin reports Adrienne Monnier's saying 'very beautifully of him' that the poet 'seems to have given everyone who knew him the feeling that he was profoundly involved in everything they did', this must have been an effect of his social style, not an index of his actual involvements. The poet's brief attempt at fatherhood and domesticity quickly collapsed, or as Gass puts it: 'We need not describe the layer of boring chores, the clutter of mismated china, sticky pots, and soiled silver, annoying habits and nervous tics, which will cloud the rich cloth when reality arrives'. I'm not sure how reality would 'cloud' a 'cloth', unless it's one of Yeats's 'Cloths of Heaven'; but the china economically catches Clara and Rainer's ill-paired

160

state – while Gass effectively offers this vignette as one *Dinggedichte* that the poet never could have written.

Nonetheless, Rilke's prolonged crisis was to be of real significance for the art of poetry. His sense, as he asserts at the close of the 'Archäischer Torso Apollos', that 'Du mußt dein Leben ändern', his alter-ego's 'learning to see' in *The Notebooks of Malte Laurids Brigge*, his attempts to get beyond the work of seeing to that of the heart in 'Wendung', whether he succeeded or failed, produced staying examples and enduring influences. Still, the great improvement in concreteness and occasioned utterance that occurred in his poetry at the time of the justly famous and widely influential *Neue Gedichte* shouldn't encourage us to exaggerate their 'thing-ness'. When reminded by Gass that Cézanne's paintings influenced these poems, there started again a youthful sense of disappointment. I do think his legacy has been the *Dinggedichte*, but those famous works, 'Der Panther', 'Römische Fontäne', 'Orpheus. Eurydike. Hermes', 'Buddha in Glorie', they're *Kunstgedichte*. Their objects, as in 'Der Tod des Dichters', are so frequently art-objects – a Rodin sculpture, in that instance. Rilke finds occasions in things because confronted and startled or trapped by them; as in 'Der Panther', material objects and others form bars to his cage, and the world beyond this symbol for the poet's self is first nullified then annihilated by his look. Even his most world-embracing works sublime things before our eyes with the poetic techniques of his subjectivity; and in this they contribute to an aesthetic spiritualizing, one which simultaneously makes a fetish of the artwork's unique and 'untranslatable' perfection. Do we really feel some nostalgia now for this?

An indicator for such processes taking place in those crisis-ridden years was the assertion that artworks have, or had, because now they were losing it thanks to mechanical reproduction, an 'aura' – a term that Benjamin drew from the poet Stefan George and his circle. Yet engravings and etchings had been mechanically reproduced for centuries before the arrival of industrialized mass production, as had literary texts after the introduction of the printing press. Whatever clings, or clung, to works of art cannot be lost by translation either – manifestly a non-mechanical and inexact mode for reproducing a work in another medium. Might that 'aura' not be a 'jargon of authenticity' word for the specific value we attribute to individual artworks as they help us imaginatively live our lives? While those who can read and appreciate an original may collaborate with the text to produce such an aura of specific value (and will likely feel its loss in encountering a translation of the same work), those who cannot access the source poem can often find such specific value in a translation – while those able to read both texts need not make such a superior song and dance about the native language artwork.

Gass alludes to 'O sage, Dichter, was du tust?', when he suggests that 'on the page, in a poem, the contradictions which were his chief affliction could be reconciled.' Clive Wilmer's delicate version *'after Rilke'*, from *Of Earthly Paradise* (1992), is also skilfully half-rhymed:

> Say, poet, what it is you do. – *I praise.*
> How can you look into the monster's gaze
> And accept what has death in it? – *I praise.*
> But, poet, the anonymous and those
> With no name, how do you call on them? – *I praise.*
> What right have you though, in each changed disguise,
> In each new mask, to trust your truth? – *I praise.*
> Both calm and violent things know you for theirs,
> Both star and storm: how so? *Because I praise.*

In 'The Translator's Apology', a poem from the most recent *Agenda*, Wilmer alludes to Ernest Dowson's 'I have been faithful to thee, Cynara! in my fashion', typecasting the translator as a lovelorn decadent poet ('I have been faithful to the text, after my own fashion'). This translating poet's pursuit of 'some other dusky beauty' is then said temporarily to mislead him from 'Truth', or 'that perfect form' to which he would attempt to stay 'in perfect constancy', re-enacting thus the terms of Rilke's own *fin-de-siècle* yearnings for and fallings from ideal realms of gods and angels. But there is, I'm afraid, no perfect constancy in life. It's because translation, of poetry or anything else for that matter, can never generate exact reproductions that it requires exacting art and is such an art; it's because it cannot be exact that, like the playing of scored music, the variable fidelity of a performance may be evaluated, and so valued. Wilmer's version, to pause on it a moment, appears to be moving finely until that 'know you for theirs'. *The Penguin Book of German Verse* (1957) by Leonard Forster, a likely source for Wilmer's wording, has 'And how is it that both calm and violent things, like star and storm, know you for their own?' Gass's more direct, paraphrasing version has 'And the calm as well as the crazed / know you like star and storm?' Wilmer's slightly odd wording, close to the original's sense, loses touch with usage momentarily, all but throwing me; still, hanging on, I get to 'how so?' and am once again felicitously in the land of the living. Such translations occasion understanding and gratitude.

But is Rilke's 'O sage, Dichter, was du tust?' the kind of poem Helen Vendler in *The Art of Shakespeare's Sonnets* (1997) says cannot exist, a dialogic lyric? There are two contrasting reasons why it just might not be: because the poet, though not exactly 'represented as alone with his

162

thoughts' as Vendler describes all lyrics, did write both sides to shape his complex statement; and because the responding phrases, which Wilmer prints in italics above, can't help sounding (and may in the original have been meant to sound), not so much Gass's 'contradictions ... reconciled' as someone reiterating his point in the face of the other's implications. It's certainly possible to feel that 'Ich rühme' is a confidently evasive response to an interviewer's questioning. Confronted with the thoroughly implied grim vicissitudes of life, to praise appears a grandly accepting affirmation, but it is also a choice among other possibilities for what poets can, and this poet did, do – evoke, satirize, comfort, or lament, for instance; and it is an unresponsively slogan-like one, a way, curiously enough, of refusing life by converting it into another of this poet's distant gods. Hamburger has suggested that his 'becoming a little human' would have required Rilke's 'ceasing to write'. He couldn't or didn't want to do it; but, more importantly, his example has encouraged many who came after him to try and integrate the practice of the art with the living of an ordinarily responsible life.

'Il faut tenter de vivre'; and if we are to change our lives for the better, it will be by hard practice amongst our own 'mismated china', our equivalents for Yeats's 'mound of refuse or the sweepings of the street, / Old kettles, old bottles, and a broken can, / Old iron, old bones, old rags...' There are poets who have so lived and who offer a humanly useful version of how poetry can 'matter to a life through its lifetime'. Take Roy Fisher, one example among many, whose prose sections from *City* show knowledge of the Paris rendered with a neurasthenia-driven intensity in *The Notebooks of Malte Laurids Brigge*. In the fourth of his 'Handsworth Liberties', we can encounter a locally improvisational 'cottage garden with hostas / in a chimney pot' where, perhaps acknowledging Rilke's archaic torso, 'in the crowd of exchanges / we can change.' If you want to change your life, then, you might best do it by interacting attentively and reciprocally with what's immediately around you, using poems and translations as guides to, examples of, and analogies for that constructive process. Good poems and translated versions can help us to work at this not least because, as Goethe put it in his 'Dreistigkeit' from the *West-östlicher Divan*, before he sings and before he stops – 'Eh er singt und eh er aufhört, / Muß der Dichter leben' – the poet has to live.

W.S. Milne

Sam Milne, poet and critic, lives and works in Surrey, although his heart resides in Aberdeen. He has retired from teaching, and is now putting together his forthcoming book of collected essays, as well as updating his critical study on the poetry of Geoffrey Hill.

Celan and Rilke

We know from Celan's finest and most meticulous critic, John Felstiner, that Celan prized Hölderlin and Rilke above all other German poets, and that as a schoolboy he knew by heart, and recited regularly, Rilke's 'The Olive Garden' and 'Jar of Tears' (John Felstiner, *Paul Celan: Poet, Survivor, Jew*, Yale University Press, 1995). Already, by the year 1964, the critic Hans Holthuse was comparing (it must be said, somewhat disparagingly) Celan with Rilke. We also know from Felstiner that Celan started, but did not finish, a German translation of the considerable French correspondence between Rilke and André Gide, and that 'For his poems Celan borrowed a definition from Rilke: 'Enclosures around the limitlessly wordless"; that 'Celan ... greeted Rilke's ideas about 'The Open' as that unbounded realm where the human self can set itself free and Rilke's sense of death as the richly present other side of life'; that Celan believed that influences must be deeply respected, and felt, indeed, that Rilke was one of those influences on his own work. In a speech made in Tel Aviv in 1969 Celan, in fact, stated quite categorically that 'Rilke was very important to me'. (When friends visited him in Paris he was fond of pointing out to them the hotel where Rilke had written *Malte Laurids Brigge*.) Perhaps more significantly, however, is Felstiner's astute insight that Celan read Rilke only to contradict him, as in 'Corona', for example, where the later poet 'invokes – while revoking – Rilke's marvellous "Autumn Day"'. Felstiner analyses this tense but creative relationship in other poems. He regards 'Stretto', for example, as responding to Rilke's tenth *Duino Elegy*, and that Celan's famous lines, 'there are/still songs to sing beyond/humankind [*jenseits der Menschen*]' rely on the opening to the *Sonnets to Orpheus*: 'Oh Orpheus sings! Oh high tree in the ear!', but not endorsingly, sceptically rather. Celan has no fundamental faith in the Orphic power of poetry, or the afterlife. Felstiner sums up this feeling by arguing that 'The drive to transcendence feels stronger in Rilke', and that '"praise" does not enter Celan's lexicon'; rather, for the later poet, 'everywhere the doors are shutting, and outside, 'in the open' (*im Freien*, the closing words of 'Blume'), hands go silent'. Poetry by now (especially in German) for Celan had become a very dubious enterprise indeed. Felstiner notes other traces: the symbols of the stone and the rose in his 1963 collection, *Die Niemandsrose* ('The No One's Rose'), owing something to Rilke's 'Archaic Torso of Apollo' and also to his 'Set no memorial stone. Just let the rose/come into bloom for his sake year by year' in *Sonnets to Orpheus*; and, indeed, to Rilke's own epitaph: 'Rose, oh pure contradiction, desire/to be no one's sleep under so many/ Lids'. One of the keywords in Celan's poetry, 'Zeitgehöft' (defined by Felstiner as a compound of 'Time', 'homestead', and 'farmyard') may owe something also to the 'one last farmstead of feeling' in Rilke's 'Exposed on the mountains of the heart'. Felstiner is in no doubt that Rilke's 'praising' (in 'Die Winzer' for example) 'rings bolder than Celan could afford'.

What follows is a short analysis of Rilkean influences in Celan's poetry not mentioned by Felstiner in his book, vestiges or traces that I, as a reader, over the years, have sensed or inferred. (The English translations from Celan are by Michael Hamburger, from his *Poems of Paul Celan*, Anvil Press, 2007). I will look at fourteen poems in a little detail.

'Talglicht'('*Tallow Lamp*'). Celan's image of 'Haar', 'hair', recurrent throughout his poems, is reminiscent of 'She was already loosened like long hair/and given far and wide like fallen rain' in Rilke's great elegy, 'Orpheus. Eurydice. Hermes', though the lamentation here is rooted in recent history, the hair of women made into cloth after execution in the death-camps, and the 'tallow' possibly made from their fat. The Symbolist tradition is de-aestheticised and turned to horror and terror, much as Romanticism is undermined by Goethe's oak preserved in the grounds of Buchenwald concentration camp (an image used in Alan Resnais' film *Nuit et Brouillard* – Celan translated Jean Cayrol's French script for this film on The Holocaust into German).

'Die Hand Voller Stunden' ('*Your Hand Full of Hours*'). One is reminded of Rilke's *Book of Hours* and of his 'Autumn Day' ('*Herbsttag*', of the *Elegies*); '*Bläther*' (leaves), '*Zeit*' (time), '*uhren*' (hours), and '*Tage*' (days) from the *Duino Elegies*; and also '*fluge*', flight, time passing, from the same sequence. 'The markets of lust': see Rilke's '*Gewerbe*' (trade) in the *Elegies*. 'The scales of grief' here seem weightier than the weeping and lamentation of the Mothers in Rilke's poem.

'Espenbaum' ('*Aspen Tree*'). See Rilke's poem 'Autumn', and '*Früchten*' (fruits) in the *Elegies*. Celan inherits the elegiac tone from Rilke, but renews and remakes it. Rilke's comforting *lares,* his praise of domesticity, is torn apart here through the themes of exile, murder and suffering.

'Der Sand Aus Den Urnen' ('*Sand from the Urns*'). Rilke's '*Haus*' in the *Elegies* becomes the image of death here: 'Green as mould is the house of oblivion' (*Schimmelgrün ist das Haus des Vergessens*).

'Ein Knirschen Von Eisernen' ('*In the Cherry-Tree's Branches*'). The poet, Orpheus, is now the 'beheaded minstrel' (*enthaupteter Spielmann*; in some cases, in the Third Reich, quite literally), and Hell is not the underworld of 'Orpheus. Eurydice. Hermes' but here-and-now, the times 'a crunching of iron shoes', the poet 'unshod', 'bareheaded', 'iron shoes buckled on to his delicate hands', lost in the post-Romantic 'garden of dreamers' (*der Garten der Träumer*). I take Rilke to be one of these 'dreamers'. This landscape is certainly not that of '*der dunkle Eingang in die Underwelt*' (the sombre entrance to the underworld) of the *Elegies*. There is nothing classical about it.

'Chanson Einer Dame Im Schatten' ('*Chanson of a Lady in the Shade*'). 'The silent one' owes something to '*stiller Mittelpunt*' of the *Elegies* (something akin to Eliot's 'still centre-point'), '*stille*' (stillness), '*Gestillen*', the quietened ones. (One begins to get an impression that Celan's work is, at times, almost a prolonged commentary on Rilke's verse, especially on his *Duineser Elegien*.) There is a greater sense, however, that Celan is calling into question the whole tradition of *Lieder*, of Schubert, Schumann, Richard Strauss, Schiller, Goethe, and Mahler, and possibly even his German-Jewish predecessor Heine's *Buch Der Lieder*. 'From threshold to threshold': see Rilke's '*Markstein*' in the *Elegies*, a boundary-stone, a crossing-point.

'Die Jahre Von Dir Zu Mir' ('*The Years from You to Me*'). 'We drink what somebody brewed' (tradition) is rooted, of course, in the German drinking-song, but especially perhaps in Rilke's '*Krug*' (jug) and '*Trank*' (drink); 'We lap up some empty and last thing' also, with the added emphasis on the bankruptcy, the inefficacy of poetry to deal with contemporary reality; laying 'the table of love: a bed between summer and autumn' reminds me of Rilke's 'garment', or 'mantle' ('*Gewand*', or '*Mantel*') and of '*bedecken*' (clothe), a sense of concealment that is both beautiful ('*Schönheit*') and terrible ('*Schrecken*'); for 'the deep sea's mirrors' see also Rilke's '*Spiegel*'.

'Corona'. We have already touched on this poem, but I also hear Rilke's '*Stimmen*' (voices) here, voices of despair in this case: 'Our mouths speak the truth', 'We exchange dark words' (Rilke's 'deep-dark sobbing', '*dunkelen Schluchzens*') far removed from the homely '*dich Worte, nah und warm*' ('words, near and warm') of the *Duino Elegies*, the '*Herz*'.

'Todesfugue'('*Death Fugue*'). This is probably Celan's most celebrated poem. It calls into question the whole German tradition, 'we are digging a grave in the sky', 'death's music comes as a master from Germany' (that indeed could be Rilke himself, or Goethe, or Hölderlin or, of course,

Bach). The traditional poetic images, or figures (hair, house, stars, sky, daybreak, nightfall, drink, milk, song, the dance, strings of the harp, or the lute) are all countermanded, compromised, the phrase 'your ashen hair Shulamith' particularly destroying any possible sentimental response. We have entered the nightmare world of extermination where a word is only 'a bullet of lead'. Any covenant with Rilke's *'Vergangenen'*(the past) is now broken, and his *'Verlassenen'* (the forsaken ones) are more than 'forsaken' here— they are tortured, killed, experimented upon, made eradicable. They are quite literally *'Gestillen'*, the silenced ones.

'Sprich Auch Du' (*'Speak, you Also'*). Here we are close to the voices of Rilke's *Elegies*, the *'Stimmen'*, and to the *'Weltraum'* (world-space) of that sequence, life's openness, its meaning (Rilke's *'deinen Sinn'*), but belittled, dwarfed: 'But now shrinks the place where you stand', the German language now his 'alien homeland' (see Celan's poem 'Schibboleth'). We are now in the realm of 'wandering words' (what Rilke called *'diese wolkigen Worte'*), loosened from all ethics and morality it would seem, lost in the shades and shadows (Rilke's *'Schatten'*).

'Heimkehr' (*'Homecoming'*). Although the title deliberately echoes Heine's *Der Heimkehr,* Celan's 'dumbness' clearly contradicts Rilke's *'Vollendung'* (Perfection), 'the ice wind' of the age turning all speechless – the poet feels he is being overindulgent in 'the too much of my speaking', a position very far removed from the articulation of Rilke's *'Engelen'*, his angels, their purported *'starkeren Dasein'*, their 'stronger existence'.

'Tenebrae'. 'Our eyes and our mouths are open and empty, Lord' sounds to me like an antiphon to Rilke's 'Lord, it is time', the opening to 'Autumn Day'.

'Blume' (*'Flower'*). The poet is now 'baling the darkness empty'. This is a far cry from Rilke's *'Wesen'*, or *'Dasein'* (the latter of course a word Heidegger thought he could make his own), ultimate essence, or being. It is closer to his

Nah ist das Land
Das sie das Leben nemmen.

Du wirst es erkennen
An seinen Ernste.

(Close by is the land/called life./ Thou wilt recognise it/
By its seriousness.)

Poetry is now 'a shard note, thin' (of 'Nacht'), an 'oath which silence annulled' (of 'Allerseelen', *'All Souls'*). Life is more serious now than it was for Rilke, less hospitable, more terrible. There is no place here for *'der Held'*, the hero, as there was in Wagner for instance. We are now in the realm of murder and butchery: 'the rifle-range near/the buried wall' of that fine long poem 'Engführung'.

'Engführung' (*'The Straitening'*). 'Nowhere/does anyone ask after you', the tone of abandonment echoed also in 'Psalm' from *Die Niemandsrose*, and in 'Es War Erde In Ihnen', *'There was Earth Inside Them'*, from the same volume: 'Where did the way lead when it led nowhere?' the poet asks. What is broken here is Rilke's covenant of the *'Liebenden'*, the lovers (they are all dead, murdered), their *'verdecken'*, togetherness, or *'die ununterbrochere Nachwicht'* (the uninterrupted message) of the angels. *'Denn Bleiken ist nirgends'* (For staying is nowhere) Rilke said, but this exile seems more terrible than any envisaged by the earlier poet. In Celan's terms

> A nothing
> we were, are, shall
> remain, flowering;
> the nothing-, the
> no one's rose.

> (from 'Psalm')

So, for Celan, tradition is both an upholding and a destroying, in a time when words and love are 'near like all that is lost... All the names, all those names burnt with the rest... 'Silence ... in/charred, charred/ hands./Fingers, insubstantial as smoke' (in 'Chymisch', *'Alchemical'*), 'my words being crippled/together with me' (in '... Rauscht Der Brunnen', '... *Plashes The Fountain'*), poetry only now a 'late word' (in 'Schaltjahrhunderte...', *'Leap-centuries...'*) in a world in which 'Ich höre, die axt hat geblüht', 'I hear that the axe has flowered' (the opening line of perhaps the most famous poem from his 1971 collection, *Schneepart*), murder now the only fruit, it seems, in the *'Fluren'* (meadows).

So it would seem that the influence of Rilke on Celan is substantial and lasting. Rilke's words sound like a largo, broad and slow, throughout the later poet's work, a threnody of dissonance and grief, of something gone terribly wrong. The tradition (Rilke's *'Vergangenen'*) is now 'treeless', barely a leaf left (see his poem, 'Ein Blatt, baumlos/für Bertolt Brecht') having been vitiated, attenuated by historical circumstances – circumstances which one can barely bear to think about it, let alone write of. Rilke's lyrics, it seems, were a good punch-bag for Celan to practice upon. Their 'patient heaviness' gave him the solid resistance his sensibility required in order to write learned and passionate verse in an age of unprecedented darkness. All of Europe might have benefited if Rilke's words had been heeded: 'Nothing must be vilified or degraded' he had written to his Polish translator, Witold von Hulewicz, in November 1925, explaining the meaning of the *Elegies*. His '*Klage*' (lament) seems somewhat muted, however, when pitched against Celan's bitter strings. Rilke, in recognising 'the perpetual refractoriness and dividedness' of the world (the phrase is J.B. Leishman's, commenting on the fourth Duino Elegy, in the Leishman and Spender translation of the *Elegies*, surely the finest in English), like most of his generation, had no idea just how deep and prejudiced that refractoriness and dividedness were. I'll leave the last word to Celan who, in his darkest hours, could still write within the tradition, 'The gate to justice is learning' (from his published speech of October 22, 1960, *Der Meridien*, on accepting the Georg Buechner Prize awarded by the German Academy of Languages). It is clear that he learned much from the German tradition, especially from Rilke; although he was gradually losing the ability to hope, in the end the German language did not abandon him.

Luke Fischer

See his biography in the Translations/Versions section.

Perception as Inspiration; Rilke and the *New Poems*

Few poets have denied the necessity of inspiration for the creation of poetry, even if modern poets speak more seldomly of the muse. Although inspiration is as important as skill or craftsmanship for the composition of poetry, in contrast, it seems to evade the will. We do not speak of learning inspiration as we speak of learning a craft. The poet, moreover, appears to be at a greater loss than other artists. The sculptor can study models and find inspiration in attending to the gestural language of the body. The painter can set up a canvas before a landscape and seek to transpose it onto the canvas, discovering inspiration in the process. The poet, meanwhile, seated in a study with only a white sheet of paper, seems condemned to await idly the arrival of the muse. A close look at the Rilke of the middle period (1902–1910) and his greatest poetic achievement of this time, the *New Poems* (*Neue Gedichte*), offers, however, a different view.[1]

The most significant impulses for Rilke's poetic endeavours in the middle period arose out of his intensive engagement with *visual* artists and their work. The fact that precisely *visual* artists were of such import is far from arbitrary. The sense of sight, or vision, was so central to Rilke's own way of being in the world, that Rudolf Kassner (a philosopher and friend of Rilke), chose the epithet 'Augenmensch' ('eye-person') to describe him.[2] Rilke's interest and study of visual art spanned his whole creative development. As a university student he studied art history; around the turn of the century he involved himself with the colony of artists in Worpswede where he met the sculptor Clara Westhoff, whom he married in 1901.[3] Rilke's keen interest continued into the late period and his often critical evaluation of the developments in visual art over this time was significant in the formulation of his own artistic values.[4] However, it was Rodin and Cézanne, the two artists with whom Rilke engaged intensively in the middle period, who played the most important role in his creative development.

The *New Poems*, one of Rilke's great works alongside the *Duino Elegies* and *Sonnets to Orpheus*, are inconceivable without Rodin. The project of the *New Poems* was formulated while Rilke was living in Rodin's presence and owes its original impetus to Rodin's example and encouragement to work like a visual artist.[5] Although Rilke had almost finished writing the first part of the *New Poems* when he began his profound study of Cézanne, Cézanne served to reinforce much that he had learned through Rodin, and gradually eclipsed Rodin in significance.[6] In a late letter (1924) Rilke claims that Cézanne was not only of great importance to him at the time of writing the *New Poems* but that he remained his single most important example.[7]

Through his engagement with these artists Rilke learned to work like them, in two senses of the word 'work'. In the first sense, he trained his vision, practised a way of seeing things, akin to the visual artist. He learned that through schooling his perception he could find poetic inspiration. In the second sense, he discovered that language could be crafted, in ways analogous to Rodin's sculpting of stone, and Cézanne's composition of colour. It is the first sense that I wish to shed light on here.

Rilke was very impressed by the way Rodin worked from models. What most struck him was Rodin's attentive, participative, and exact way of perceiving the models, and the way in which this manner of perceiving facilitated insights central to Rodin's creative process. In the 1903 monograph on Rodin, Rilke states the following about Rodin's practice of drawing models:

> Rodin had the theory that if inapparent movements made by the model, when the latter believes him/herself/itself to be unobserved, were caught rapidly, they would contain a vividness of expression which we do not surmise because we are not accustomed to follow them with keen, alert attention...[8]

Rodin followed the movements of his models with an attentiveness far more concentrated than our everyday habits of perception and in this way, Rodin discovered an expressivity, a gestural significance, which he immediately sought to translate onto the page. These studies of models were crucial to his sculptural work. A little later in the same monograph Rilke writes:

> He catches his model unawares ... seizing every incipient expression. He knows every transitory expression of feature, knows whence comes the smile and whither it departs. He lives through a human face as through the scene of a drama in which he himself takes part; his place is in the midst of it, and nothing that occurs is indifferent to him or escapes him. He refuses to be told anything about the person, he wants to know only what he sees. But he sees everything.[9]

171

Rodin's seeing is radically selfless, completely given over to the model before him, registering the smallest details. This seeing has the character of *participating* in what is before it, in the way in which an audience member becomes involved in a dramatic performance. It is a gaze that forgets itself in order to identify with its object. This seeing enables a certain knowledge or insight into the thing seen; Rodin 'wants to know only what he sees.'

This kind of insight is not attained in an abstract manner. In his effort to describe Rodin's seeing, Rilke poses a rhetorical question: 'what we call mind and soul and love: are these things not only a slight transformation on the small surface of our neighbour's face?'[10] Rilke was not a reductionist; he did not ask this question in order to put forth the view that the spiritual (mind and soul) is reducible to the physical. Rather, he was of the view that through attending to the visible, one becomes aware of the invisible. We might synoptically formulate the character of this seeing in calling it a 'dynamic, exact, *physiognomic vision*.' The term 'physiognomic' is apt insofar as it suggests a perception of inner qualities through their outer expression. It is 'dynamic' in that, in contrast to the historical science of physiognomy, it does not begin with a system of correlations between outer features and inner characteristics. Rather, it discovers the expressive meaning of certain features *in the moment*.

Rilke characterises Cézanne's way of seeing similarly to Rodin's, only more emphatically. In the *Letters on Cézanne*, a self-portrait serves as a point of departure for one of Rilke's characterisations.

> The strong structure of this skull which seems hammered and sculpted from within is reinforced by the ridges of the eyebrows; but from there, pushed forward toward the bottom, shoed out, as it were, by the closely bearded chin, hangs the face, hangs as if every feature had been suspended individually, unbelievably intensified and yet reduced to utter primitivity, yielding that expression of uncontrolled amazement in which children and country people can lose themselves, – except that the gazeless stupor of their absorption has been replaced by an animal alertness which entertains an untiring, objective wakefulness in the unblinking eyes. How this watching of his was and how unimpeachably accurate, is almost touchingly confirmed by the fact that, without even remotely interpreting his expression or presuming himself superior to it, he reproduced himself with so much humble objectivity, with the unquestioning, matter-of-fact interest of a dog who sees himself in a mirror and thinks: there's another dog.[11]

The painting reveals Cézanne's amazing capacity of seeing, both in terms of *what* it presents (the author) and *how* it presents (its compositional structure). We witness a repetition here of themes already noted in relation to Rodin. Cézanne's way of seeing is exceptionally *attentive* and *alert*. His seeing registers the properties of things right into their details; it is 'unimpeachably accurate'. Rilke employs a metaphor, which strikes one as slightly exaggerated and comical, in order to emphasise the *participational* character of Cézanne's seeing: he compares the artist's gaze to the gaze of a dog. The metaphor serves to convey a type of vision that is completely turned away from itself, wholly given over to the things before it, analogous to the manner in which a dog, devoid of self-consciousness, delivers its gaze to things without reserve. It is what Rilke elsewhere refers to as the 'anonymity' of this participational vision of things, which grants it a particular 'objectivity'.[12] This vision does not subjectively project attributes onto the object before it, rather it has the gesture of a self-forgetting, an attentiveness to the thing itself, which allows the thing, as it were, to reveal its own meaning.

Rilke does not hesitate to use the word 'objective', but this can be misleading. The word often implies a cold and reductive way of looking at things, a scientific gaze which limits things to their purely physical properties. It is wrong to interpret Rilke's ascription of the adjective 'objective' to Cézanne in a reductive sense. As with Rodin Rilke attributes a participational character to Cézanne's seeing. Rilke also ascribes an epiphanic and religious significance to Cézanne's vision which is incommensurable with such a notion of objectivity. Upon considering one of Cézanne's many paintings of Mont Sainte-Victoire, Rilke claims that 'not since Moses has anyone seen a mountain so greatly', and elsewhere speaks of Cézanne's 'being before the landscape and drawing religion from it'.[13] It is illuminating to consider these two statements alongside the following:

> ... I also noticed yesterday how unselfconsciously different they are [the paintings], how unconcerned with being original, confident of not getting lost with each approach toward one of nature's thousand faces; confident, rather, of discovering the inexhaustible within by seriously and conscientiously studying her manifold presence outside.14

Artistic vision includes an invisible or spiritual dimension. If it is to be regarded as 'objective', then it is due to the fact that this invisible has more than a subjective status; it is part of the revelation of things themselves. This seeing is 'objective' in a non-reductive and non-dualistic sense.

173

In these characterisations of Rodin and Cézanne, one of Rilke's most determining aspirations is revealed, namely, his desire to overcome the opposition between the visible and the invisible, the physical and the spiritual. Rilke (in the middle period) did not seek to overcome the problem of dualism through a philosophical theory concerning the 'oneness of being', or through retreating into his self. Dualism was an existential problem for Rilke and he sought to overcome it through cultivating a non-dualistic vision of things, which meant diligently attending to the visible and, thereby, discovering the invisible.[15] In both his letters and poems, it is clear that Rilke strove to attain a non-dualistic perception of things analogous to that of Rodin and Cézanne.

In many of the letters having a bearing on the middle period, Rilke speaks of the ideal he came to formulate and realise under the auspices of Rodin and through his study of Cézanne. This ideal was to stand 'before nature [vor der Natur]' – a formulation Rilke repeatedly employs – like a painter or sculptor and draw inspiration for his poetry in this way. Harry Graf Kessler, in a journal entry of 16th November 1908, records a conversation where Rilke went so far as to use the expression 'vor der Natur dichten' ('poetising before nature').[16] The expression 'vor der Natur dichten' suggests that Rilke conceived his creative process as corresponding to the way in which a painter paints his or her *vision* of a landscape. He had come to identify his own manner of working, in the most intrinsic sense, with the practice of visual artists.

In a letter of 1926 Rilke speaks of having written the first (and most famous) of the *New Poems*, 'The Panther', upon following Rodin's advice to work like a painter or sculptor 'before nature'.[17] Encouraged by his engagement with Rodin and Cézanne, Rilke became an attentive and diligent observer, in a way not true of his earlier self.[18] In this regard it is significant to note that Rilke came to employ the word 'model' in a manner that relates to his understanding of Rodin's use of models. Rilke, however, employs the word in a sense wider than its common usage (to which we have thus far adhered in our discussion of Rodin). Ordinarily, when we speak of an artist's 'model' we think of a human being whose appearance is drawn upon for a work of art. Rilke, in contrast, refers to landscapes, plants, animals and other things in addition to human beings as his 'models'.[19]

One particularly significant 'model' for Rilke was the animal. A number of 'animal poems' feature in the *New Poems*. Throughout Rilke's letters one finds numerous descriptions of encounters with animals, encounters in which the animals assumed a particular symbolic or spiritual significance. Though animals continued to hold a special place in Rilke's world-view into the late period (surely one of the most memorable lines of the *Duino*

Elegies is 'What *is* outside, we know from the animal's/countenance alone'[20]), it was, without a doubt, the practice of seeing undertaken in the middle period, which enabled animals to acquire such a unique meaning for him.[21] For these reasons I have chosen to focus on Rilke's perception of animals (one of his 'models') as an exemplification of the manner in which he saw his 'models'.

In the letter of 13th June 1907 to Clara Rilke we are offered an amazing record of one of Rilke's attempts to enter the world of an animal. Rilke recounts,

> Yesterday, by the way, I was in the Jardin des Plantes for the whole morning, before the Gazelles. Gazella Dorcas, Linné. There are two there and another by itself. They lay a few steps away from one another, ruminating, restful, looking. As women gaze out of pictures, so they gaze out from something with a soundless, definitive turn. And as a horse neighed, the one by itself listened, and I saw the radiating of ears and horns around her slim neck. Were the ears of those in Al Hayat also so grey (like tin to gold standing to the hue of the other hair), with a soft, dark, branched marking inside? I saw only the one stand up for a moment, she lay down again shortly after; but I saw, while they stretched and examined themselves, the marvellous work of their legs [Läufe]22: (they are like rifles, out of which leaps are shot). I couldn't depart, so beautiful were they, and I felt exactly as I did before your delicate photography: as if they had been transformed just a moment ago into this Gestalt.23

At the beginning of the passage Rilke uses his characteristic formulation, in speaking of being 'before the Gazelles', as a painter stands before a scene to be painted. It was not the mere passing glance of a tourist that he offered to the Gazelles, rather he spent the whole morning observing them. The descriptions which follow testify to Rilke's attentive, participational, and precise way of seeing. Despite its precision, Rilke's gaze is far from being cold and analytic; it is a gaze steeped in wonder before the sight of the animals. Correlatively, all the sensible aspects of the creatures are disclosed gesturally, expressively, in a living way; we might speak of a 'dynamic, exact, physiognomic vision' of the animals.

Prior to his concrete descriptions, Rilke names the exact species of the Gazelles – 'Gazella Dorcas'. He proceeds to recount the way in which, while sitting down, they ruminated and peacefully looked out – two Gazelles lying close to one another, with a third by itself. Their manner of looking is compared to the way in which women in portraits silently gaze out of the space of the painting. The quiet, motionless, gaze of the

Gazelles is thereby evocatively conveyed. This suggestive analogy already indicates that the Gazelles did not reveal themselves to Rilke's perception as merely indifferent objects. What strikes us about a great portrait is that the more we consider it the more we feel like we are being looked at and addressed by the figure in the painting; it doesn't remain indifferent to us. Rilke felt addressed by the Gazelles' presence in an analogous manner. In this analogy we also see that Rilke sought to enter the space of the animals themselves – to intuit their way of being, the space out of which they gaze.

Rilke concludes the passage by drawing upon his understanding of the work of art as the transformation of things into a higher form of existence.[24] He writes that before the Gazelles he felt as he did before Clara's photography. What amazes Rilke about the Gazelles is that they already seem to present the finality and perfection of a work of art; they already seem to be 'transformed beings'.

There are more than just loose correspondences between Rilke's and Rodin's way of seeing. Rilke observed his 'models', in this case Gazelles, with great attentiveness, participation, and exactness. We can appropriately say of him that he lived through the Gazelle's expressions as 'through the scene of a drama in which he himself' took part.

Approximately a month after (17th July 1907) this encounter Rilke wrote the poem, included in the *New Poems*, 'The Gazelle'. We will now turn to this poem and in so doing illustrate points of connection between Rilke's account of his perception of the Gazelles in the Jardin des Plantes and the poem.

The Gazelle

Gazella Dorcas

Enchanted one: how can the consonance of two
chosen words ever attain the rhyme,
that in you comes and goes, as if to a sign.
Out of your brow rise leaf and lyre,

and all that is yours passes already in simile
through love-songs, whose words, soft
as rose petals, to the one who no longer reads,
settle upon the eyes, which he closes:
in order to see you: carried, as though

176

each leg were a barrel loaded with leaps
and only held from firing, so long as the neck

inclines the head in listening: as when bathing
in the woods a woman halts:
the forest pool in her turned gaze.[25]

Although Rilke observed a number of Gazelles he gathered many of his observations to present the Gazelle in the poem. In the sub-title the precise species is given, Gazella Dorcas. The first line of the sonnet begins by naming the Gazelle the 'enchanted one'. This means not only that the Gazelle is itself enchanted but that, as the enchanted one, it is capable of enchant*ing*. We saw in the letter that Rilke found the Gazelles enchanting; he could only with difficulty leave them. To be enchanted by something means to be addressed by it in an indescribable ('unsayable') way. The vocation of poetry, in turn, is saying. What this poem seeks to say is the Gazelle. After naming the Gazelle the 'enchanted one' the poem poses the question as to whether it is possible to say what comes to expression in the Gazelle – the rhyme that 'comes and goes'.

In the last line of the first verse concrete aspects of the Gazelle are named for the first time, the 'leaf [Laub (foliage)] and lyre' that rise from the Gazelle's brow. 'Leaf and lyre' suggest the ears and horns of the Gazelle. The reference to these two features recalls the question concerning the 'consonance of two chosen words' and the unattainable rhyme that 'comes and goes' in the Gazelle. This rhyme, which follows some elusive sign, could be interpreted as one which sounds when 'leaf and lyre' come into view, like the 'radiating of ears and horns' described in the letter. The first three lines of the poem ask the question whether the Gazelle can be said in the poem, the fourth line suggests that the Gazelle's 'leaf and lyre' present an unsayable 'rhyme'.

The expression 'leaf and lyre' also involves mythological allusions. The 'leaf' suggests the laurel wreath, which, in connection to the 'lyre', leads one to the thought of Apollo, who wears the laurel and bears the lyre, attributes which signify him as the god – the inspirer – of poetry and music.[26] 'Leaf and lyre' imply the 'consonance' of word and music in Apollo, and Apollo's function as the god of these arts. This is significant to note with regard to the genesis of the poem; in inspiring the poem the Gazelle(s) literally played the role of Apollo.[27]

These lines remind us of the end of the passage quoted from the letter, in which Rilke refers to the Gazelles as transformed beings like the things in Clara's photography. If we substitute one art form for another, photography with poetry, then a correspondence between the letter and the poem can

177

be seen. If Rilke understands art and poetry as a transformation or transfiguration of things, then the difficulty regarding an artistic presentation of the Gazelles lies in the fact that this transformation seems to have been already accomplished by their sheer being. Like Apollo the Gazelle represents an insurpassable embodiment of poetry.

A slight shift occurs in the transition to the second verse. We are now told that everything that properly belongs to the Gazelle is present *already* in 'love-songs' in the form of similes. If the first verse asks whether it is possible at all to 'say the Gazelle', then the second verse begins by stating that the Gazelle already has its presence in poetry. The Gazelle has often been employed in the poetic tradition as a symbol of love, of gentleness or grace, and as such it already inhabits poems. (The mention of 'love-songs' and their 'words' also elaborates on the earlier reference to 'lyre' and 'leaf' – music and word.) The comparison of the words to 'rose-petals' further develops the presentation of the Gazelle as a manifestation of gentleness and delicateness. In the letter Rilke speaks of the Gazelles as reminding him of Clara's *delicate* photography. The presence of the Gazelle is so subtle and delicate that the reader of a love-poem must close his eyes in order to see it; it can only be seen in the subdued space of the imagination.[28]

Although the octet (the first two verses) of the sonnet introduces many elements which do not directly correlate to Rilke's perception of the Gazelles (as recorded in the letter), illuminating connections are discernible. The descriptions of the Gazelle in the sestet are more concrete and show clearer correspondences to Rilke's encounter with the animals in the Jardin des Plantes.

In the third verse Rilke found a way of directly adapting to the poem the simile he used to describe the Gazelle's legs in the letter; the line from the letter was transplanted almost without further ado into the poem. However, in the space of the poem it serves, in addition, to articulate a moment of suspense in the Gazelle's behaviour. This is presented in the transition to the final verse, where the Gazelle is portrayed as poised for a short while in a state of listening, capable of dashing off at any moment with its powerful legs. This image is a paradigmatic presentation of a 'dynamic, exact, physiognomic vision' or a non-dualistic perception – here inner and outer form an indissoluble whole. Although there is no mention of a neighing horse, this image also clearly recalls the description of the individual Gazelle in the Jardin des Plantes in its act of listening. Similarly, the final line of the poem, as Wolfgang Müller points out, is reminiscent of the characterisation of the Gazelles gazing out as 'women gaze out of pictures' with a 'soundless, definitive turn'.[29]

We will now turn to another letter in order to draw a similar connection between Rilke's perception and poetry. Although written after the middle period, the letter bears a clear relationship to Rilke's work at the time of writing the *New Poems*.

In the letter to Magda von Hattingberg of 17th February 1914 Rilke describes, as an exemplification of his way of seeing, an encounter with a dog. At the beginning of the letter Rilke states, 'I love 'in-seeing' [Einsehn]'.[30] Later in the letter he confesses that his greatest moments of happiness were found in 'indescribable, rapid, deep, timeless moments of divine "in-seeing"'.[31] If Rilke speaks of these moments as 'indescribable', it was nevertheless such moments that offered an irreplaceable source of inspiration for his poetry – the attempt to say and describe. Rilke begins his explication of this 'in-seeing' as follows:

> I love in-seeing [Einsehn]. Can you think with me, how marvellous it is, for instance, to see into a dog while walking by, in-seeing (I don't mean seeing-through, which is, in contrast, only a kind of human gymnastics and where one immediately comes out again on the other side of the dog, only, as it were, regarding it as a window into the human lying behind it, not this)...[32]

Rilke contrasts this 'in-seeing' to a more superficial perception of things which only regards things in narrowly anthropomorphic terms; he contrasts seeing *into* things with seeing *past* things.[33] The interior dimension of this '*in*-seeing' has more than a merely subjective status. Seeing into the dog involves,

> ... letting oneself into the dog, exactly into its centre, to the place where it starts being a dog, there, where God, as it were, would *have* positioned himself for a moment, when the dog was complete, in order to oversee its first embarrassments and incidents and to affirm that it was good, that nothing was lacking, that one could not make it better. For a while one can endure being in the centre of the dog, one must only watch out and be sure to leap out in due time, before its environment [Umwelt] wholly encloses one, because otherwise one would simply remain the dog in the dog and incapable of anything else [für alles übrige verloren].[34]

Rilke speaks of this seeing as finding itself at the very centre where the 'dog is a dog'. The characterisation of his own seeing or 'in-seeing' is as emphatic, or even more emphatic, than the earlier characterisation of Cézanne's participative and 'objective' vision. This participative perception is also much more radically described in the above passage than in the letter concerning the Gazelles. In the earlier letter Rilke describes the Gazelles as gazing out from something in the way women in portraits gaze out of paintings. In the above example, to continue with the analogy, we might speak of Rilke being transposed into the painting itself, uniting with the face, to gaze out with it from within the enframed space. Moreover, he does not only speak of being in the dog's own centre, but adds, no doubt exaggerating in order to emphasise the radicality of this participation, that in this state of identification one faces the danger of becoming so united with the animal that one risks never returning to one's ordinary self.

Although this letter was written as late as 1914, it is possible to find a direct link between it and the first 'new poem' Rilke wrote, 'The Panther'. The central verse of the poem seems to perform the magic of transposing the reader into the very centre of the panther. The panther's movements are likewise portrayed in a dynamic physiognomic (non-dualistic) manner.[35] Within the space of four lines much of what we have sought to articulate in this essay finds its concentrated expression.

> The supple gait of pliant strong steps,
> which in the very smallest circle turns,
> is like a dance of strength around a centre,
> within which numbed a great will stands.[36]

The exceptional kind of vision that Rilke seeks to characterise in his letters and which was integral to his poetry was clearly not something given to him without effort. This capacity of vision or 'in-seeing' was acquired on the basis of his practice of standing before things and devoting his attention to them like a visual artist, a practice which he diligently carried out in the middle period. Although we have limited our considerations to the example of the animal, a close look at the *New Poems* reveals that their author could take almost any thing as a 'model' – works of art, artefacts, people, places, animals and flowers. Just as Cézanne's paintings convinced Rilke of the painter's great capacity of vision, the *New Poems* testify to their author's precise and participative perception of things. It was this schooled capacity of perception, fostered through Rilke's engagement with Rodin and Cézanne, which served as a major source of inspiration for his poetry.

Notes

[1] Though the boundaries are, of course, blurry, the middle period of Rilke's work is generally marked by his arrival in Paris in 1902 to write a commissioned monograph on Rodin, and the completion of his novel *The Notebooks of Malte Laurids Brigge* (*Die Aufzeichnungen des Malte Laurids Brigge*) in 1910.

Whenever I refer to the *New Poems* without further specification I mean both parts considered as a whole – the *Neue Gedichte* (1907) and *Der neuen Gedichte anderer Teil* (1908).

[2] Rudolf Kassner, *Rilke; Gesammelte Erinnerungen 1926–1956*, ed. Klaus E. Bohnenkamp, Neske Verlag, Pfullingen, 1976, p. 13, p. 34. Kassner repeatedly emphasises the central significance of sight for Rilke.

[3] In 1902, in a time of financial need, Rilke was commissioned to write a monograph on the Worpswede artists. The painters featured in *Worpswede* are Fritz Mackensen, Otto Mondersohn, Fritz Overbeck, Hans am Ende, and Heinrich Vogeler. The monograph was written in 1902 and first published in 1903. It can be found in Rilke, *Sämtliche Werke*, vol. 5, edited by the Rilke archive in connection with Ruth Sieber-Rilke, overseen by Ernst Zinn, Insel Verlag, Frankfurt am Main, 1965.

[4] For a good explication of the significance of visual art for Rilke's late poetry, and in particular, Rilke's critical relationship to non-objective art, see the essay by Hermann Meyer, 'Die Verwandlung des Sichtbaren; Die Bedeutung der modernen bildenden Kunst für Rilkes späte Dichtung', in his book *Zarte Empirie; Studien zur Literaturgeschichte*, J. B. Metzlersche Verlagsbuchhandlung, Stuttgart, 1963.

[5] Rilke states this in the letter of 17th March 1926 addressed to a young female friend ('an eine junge Freundin'). Rilke, *Briefe*, vol. 2, 1914–1926, Insel-Verlag, Wiesbaden, 1950, p. 517.

Rilke was commissioned to write a monograph on Rodin in 1902. He arrived in Paris on 28th August 1902 and took up residence there in order to make a personal connection to the artist and see him at work. The monograph was published for the first time in 1903. On the basis of a lecture paper first given in 1905 a second part was added to the monograph and both parts appeared for the first time in a single volume in 1907. From the Autumn of 1905 to May 1906 Rilke was employed as Rodin's secretary. Though Rilke travelled frequently throughout the middle period Paris formed his residential and cultural centre over this time.

[6] Rilke attended the Cézanne retrospective at the 'Salon d'Automne' in Paris on an almost daily basis between 6.10.1907–22.10.1907. The most immediate document of his reflections and impressions are his letters to Clara Rilke written at this time. These letters were posthumously published as the *Briefe über Cézanne* (*Letters on Cézanne*). Rilke did not have the chance to establish a personal connection to Cézanne as he did to Rodin, as Cézanne had already passed away (1906) a year before the emergence of Rilke's serious interest in his work.

[7] Letter of 26th February 1924 to Alfred Schaer. Rilke, *Briefe*, vol. 2, p. 440.

[8] Rilke, *Sämtliche Werke*, vol. 5, pp. 177–178. Rilke, *Auguste Rodin*, transl. G. Craig Houston, Dover Publications, Mineola, New York, 2006, p. 26; translation altered.

[9] *Sämtliche Werke*, vol. 5, pp. 183–184. *Auguste Rodin*, p. 30.

[10] *Sämtliche Werke*, vol. 5, p. 212. *Auguste Rodin*, p. 46; translation altered.

[11] Rilke, *Briefe über Cézanne*, ed. Clara Rilke, Afterword by Heinrich Wiegand Petzet, Insel Verlag, Wiesbaden, 1952, pp. 40–41. Rilke, *Letters on Cézanne*, transl. Joel Agee, Foreword by Heinrich Wiegand Petzet, Fromm International Publishing Corporation, New York, 1985, pp. 84–85.

[12] Rilke speaks of the 'anonymity' of artistic vision and a meaning which is only born at the place of encounter between seer and seen in the letter to Clara Rilke of 8th March 1907. Rilke, *Briefe aus den Jahren 1906–1907*, Insel-Verlag, Leipzig, 1930, p. 214.

[13] *Briefe über Cézanne*, p. 89. *Letters on Cézanne*, xxiii–xxiv; translation altered. *Briefe über Cézanne*, p. 83. *Letters on Cézanne*, viii.

[14] *Briefe über Cézanne*, p. 26. *Letters on Cézanne*, p. 47.

[15] Rilke's radical monism, which he came to represent all the more strongly with time, is already articulated in *The Notebooks of Malte Laurids Brigge*. Certain passages explicitly present the view that life and death, the earthly and the heavenly, are two sides of a single whole. See for instance, *Sämtliche Werke*, vol. 6, 1966, p. 862, pp. 928–929.

[16] Rainer Maria Rilke/Auguste Rodin, *Der Briefwechsel und andere Dokumente zu Rilkes Begegnung mit Rodin*, Insel Verlag, Frankfurt am Main and Leipzig, 2001, pp. 249–250.

[17] See note 5.

[18] The main character of Rilke's novel (written in the middle period) claims, 'Ich lerne sehen' – 'I am learning to see'; Rilke also learnt to see at this time. *Sämtliche Werke*, vol. 6, 1966, p. 710–711. In the letter of 13th October 1907 to Clara Rilke, Rilke states: 'If I were to come and visit you, I would surely also see the splendour of moor and heath, the hovering bright greens of meadows, the birches, with new and different eyes; and though this transformation is something I've ... shared before, in part of the Book of Hours [Das Stundenbuch], nature was then still a general occasion for me ... I was not yet sitting before her ... How little I would have been able to learn from Cézanne, from van Gogh, then.' *Briefe über Cézanne*, p. 27. *Letters on Cézanne*, pp. 48–49.

[19] See, for instance, Rilke's letter to Clara Rilke of 24th June 1906. Rilke, *Briefe aus den Jahren 1907–1914*, vol. 3, Insel-Verlag, Leipzig, 1930, p. 282.

[20] *Sämtliche Werke*, vol. 2, 1957, p. 714; my translation.

[21] In this regard E.F.N. Jephcott speaks of Rilke's 'systematic attempt to enter' the world of the animal 'through empathy, or *Einfühlung*, an attempt which led to numerous poems on animals.' E.F.N. Jephcott, *Proust and Rilke; The Literature of Expanded Consciousness*, Chatto & Windus, London, 1972, p. 129.

[22] I have translated the word 'Läufe' with 'legs'. 'Läufe' means in this context both 'legs' and 'barrels' – in the sense of the barrels of a gun.

[23] Rilke, *Briefe aus den Jahren 1906–1907*, vol. 2, pp. 265–269; my translation.

[24] An exemplary expression of Rilke's view of the work of art as a transformation of reality into a higher form is contained in the following statement: 'The thing is defined, the "art-thing" ("Kunst-Ding") must be more defined; freed of all chance and indistinctness ... capable for eternity. The model seems, the "art-thing" is. So is the one the nameless development through the other and beyond it [der namenlose Fortscritt über das andere hinaus]'. Rainer Maria Rilke/Auguste Rodin, *Der Briefwechsel und andere Dokumente zu Rilkes Begegnung mit Rodin*, p. 78; my translation.

[25] *Sämtliche Werke*, vol. 1, 1955, p. 506; translation by Luke Fischer and Lutz Näfelt.

[26] Wolfgang Müller refers 'leaf and lyre' to attributes of Apollo in *Rainer Maria Rilkes 'Neue Gedichte'; Vielfältigkeit eines Gedichttypus*, Verlag Anton Hain, Meisenheim am Glan, 1971, 73n. 'Leaf and lyre' might also be regarded as an allusion to Orpheus. In any case, both Apollo and Orpheus share in common the fact that they represent a supreme embodiment of poetry. Connections between 'The Gazelle' and the later *Sonnets to Orpheus* have been made by a number of scholars. See, for instance, Kih – Seong Kuh, *Die Tiersymbolik bei Rainer Maria Rilke*, Berlin, 1967, pp. 68–77.

[27] 'Leaf and lyre' might also be regarded as an allusion to Orpheus. In any case, both Apollo and Orpheus share in common the fact that they represent a supreme embodiment

of poetry. Connections between 'The Gazelle' and the later *Sonnets to Orpheus* have been made by a number of scholars. See, for instance, Kih-Seong Kuh, *Die Tiersymbolik bei Rainer Maria Rilke*, Berlin, 1967, pp. 68–77.

[28] 'The Gazelle' appears before 'The Unicorn' (and after 'The Panther') in the *New Poems*. The Gazelle might be regarded as existing between the everyday world and that of the imagination; it already presences in poetry and has a magical quality but it is not a 'fictional' creature like the unicorn.

[29] Wolfgang Müller, *Rainer Maria Rilkes 'Neue Gedichte'; Vielfältigkeit eines Gedichttypus*, p. 195.

[30] Rilke, *Briefwechsel mit Magda von Hattingberg 'Benvenuta'*, ed. Ingeborg Schnack und Renate Scharffenberg, Insel Verlag, Frankfurt am Main and Leipzig, 2000, p. 114.

[31] ibid., p. 115.

[32] ibid., p. 114.

[33] One might see a connection here to the eighth of the *Duino Elegies*. There it is claimed that rather than letting the child see the 'open' in the animal's face we turn the child around so that it only sees things backwards, in terms of the human 'interpreted world' (The First Elegy), *Sämtliche Werke*, vol. 2, p. 714. Rilke makes almost precisely this point a little later in the same letter to Magda von Hattingberg, Rilke, *Briefwechsel mit Magda von Hattingberg 'Benvenuta'*, p. 116.

[34] ibid., p. 114.

[35] In his essay, '*Rilkes Partnerschaft mit der Natur*', Hans Mislin gives an excellent characterisation of Rilke's non-dualistic and physiognomic presentation of the panther. See Hans Mislin, '*Rilkes Parnterschaft mit der Natur*', *Blätter der Rilke-Gesellschaft*, 3/1974, p. 47f.

[30] *Sämtliche Werke*, vol. 1, p. 505; my translation.

Nicholas Jagger

Rilke in Paris

The butter-soft arms of the balustrades
encircle the park where he walks.
Gold brimming dusk; a flooding calm.
This city was born to him misshapen,
known mostly through the rideaux of winter dusks.

And scumbling over the strictures of pulse
are premonitions of another illness,
spotted in the dregs of summer's cup.
Dahlias gather their knots of frozen reds
against diluting light, holding fast
to what is already lost; a gift of black
the night's retreat, a hard November's theft.
Yet the tenebrous vigil passes
and goldfish still circle in the Luxembourg pools.

Today the bare-branch trees jostle for his attention,
and the deep angular bark of each lime
is picked out by this late though mid-day sun.
The strong blue shadows of fractured branch
coagulate with thoughts of cold:
the bed in which he cowered,
the room from which he now escapes to note
the cooling pinks that fail November's question.

This searing doubt is what is feared most, tinting the dusks
of his own broad skies; the néant of the muse's shadow,
her silence, itself a manner of presage:

oh this hope of being able to begin, and always obstacles
in the way...

Each nightfall, though seeming neutral, takes its stance
curtailing his presence,
yet still enough remains to stem the pen.

At the Frauenkirche, Dresden

– after 'Rilke's 'Spanische Tänzlerin'

As if in her hand an unstruck match
a moment before the dance ignited:

it began within a wall of spectators,
bursts of flashing flame extending in all directions,

and then it was fire completely; she only flame.

In a moment her hair was kindled,
the fiery torque of her dress a brand of self-combustion,

her serpentine arms boned by feeling
rose from the fire to rattle accusations.

Then as if dissatisfied, she gathered up the flame
and jettisoned what she had seemed to conjure and embody,

and though she stood quite still, the dancing light defied her,
until her stamping foot ground away the embers.

Angie Estes

Lilac Fugue

The tenth century invented a way
to depict the pitch of notes
by placing them vertically
on the page the way winter hangs
its zigzag ice and April's finches perch
and sing on every limb
like notes. Rilke believed
that repeated notes rising
from the organ for centuries
inside Notre Dame
had rounded the curves
of every arch – that there are strains
of music, musical sprains, contusions
and even a bruise or two in March
whenever lilac booms.
                              In that case,
What is the question? Stein asked
before dying after no one
responded to *What*
is the answer? Perhaps she was thinking
of phantom pain – how it remains
when the hand is gone but its home
in the brain is not – of the medieval
monks who drew elaborate bars
in illuminated books to fill
the space that remained on each line
when the text had come
to an end.
                    What winds up
the trunks of trees until there's nothing
but stars in sight? Wisteria, minding
all the way, mute
as the stars' insistence. And what
does the beech tree inscribe
on the sky with its flourish of copper
serifs? Each angle
of the conductor's baton

still holding its place
in air, the late evening sky
still lighted by its white
crossed scars of flight.

David Brooks

Boria

Winter
and the Boria come full force
clubbing and clubbing at the village
all night and into the morning,
shaking the doors and windows
like a man whose wife has locked him out
or a soldier come home to find no one,
only a lean, angry dog in the neighbours' yard
howling for no reason,
tearing at anything not tied down.

Note on 'Boria': The Boria comes directly down onto the northern Adriatic from the Julian Alps. A cold and often harsh, bitter wind, it can occur at any time of the year but is most oppressive – and powerful – in the Autumn and Winter, as often as not on bright, clear days such as that upon which Rilke, at Duino, directly in the Boria's path, received the first lines of the Elegies in January 1911, as a voice coming to him through the gale.

Language

We talk all night
peeling back the layers.
Later it seems
not even the skin comes between us.
In the morning
I watch you put it all on again,
the language,
the past,
the mind's clothes as well as the body's.
You step out onto the street
and the street catches you,
but the street knows only the half of it.
Pale, soft fruit. Odour of dusk.

John Burnside

Shape shifters

i.m. Edmund Cusick

It was more of an art than we thought;
not how we slipped from one form to the next,

but how we forgot, in an instant,
the shape we discarded,

the old self bundled away
to the kingdom of others.

Another sense of what we mean by grace
this leaving ourselves behind, like empty shirts

filling with light and wind, at the water's edge:
dusk in the trees, and the swimmers already gone,

their eyes and voices
hurried into darkness.

Meanwhile, a hedge fills with bees, or a meadow reveals
a changing map, precise as any

magic trick
                    while somewhere in the grass
a song emerges, or a silence blooms,

and, one by one, the bodies come to light:
this knot of gold, that skew of red and silver.

Note: 'Shape shifters' was written in memory of Edmund Cusick, who died recently. Edmund was a poet with whom I shared a number of interests, including the sub-Arctic, and the myths and stories of those who inhabit that region; he also had a fascination with angels, or those angelic forms whose capabilities included divine utterance and shape shifting. He once asked me if I had ever met a shape shifter, and I could see in his eyes that this was a serious question. For Edmund, I always felt, Rilke's angels were immediate and actual presences.

Edmund Cusick was a fine poet who had only just begun to overcome the diffidence that was so familiar to those who knew him. In July 2006, his only full-length collection, *Ice Maidens*, was published by Headland.

Elena Karina Byrne

A Concordance of Rilke in the Gallery

They pretend proximity the gold honeycomb's confines along the spine

       where a vice enters into it,
blood for blood.

It's everything that I can sadden or see
       from winter's bare inherited space of one eye

without any fixed abode or fog-blue barb of memory
left in the gut, *of an infinite loneliness* where
Everything is gestation

bait and switch, beauty-born
with all the other
       errors, desires and longings, – there

oh, downfall-force, the dark,

I recognized you in it, your grammarless face as if absent from the hours,

nevertheless, *necessary, irrepressible*

with the mirror's open bird cage, mind's closed fist, body,

our *necessary, irrepressible,*

       a pomegranate stain on the skin, or burnt violin
          in the ear,

something so permanent about you

       by not breaking.

Name Fable

... 'like a dark inscription above an entryway'
— Rilke

as in
this name unnaming, person's system of names
for things (piano floating the ocean), not nominal, nor the face
of a coin turned
         over,
or yes-name, to conjure, to evoke a spirit,
free-falling fork-dark, swallow tail and turn,
overture address that inverts redress,
moniker, nomen,

write them together; yours as fair a name
sound them, it doth become the mouth as well;
weigh them, it is as heavy; conjure with 'em...

to conjure with purpose, postmarking history
out of this, outing for

Nom de Guerre, assumed
name, 'war name', in the combat winter worn to find her,
      every entrant into the French
army to assume this name, especially
in the times of CHIVALRY, when knights were known by device
of their shields,
to shield the winds' one head when they are carrying her voice
        over

silence. His mouth means fiction; you can hear her
(singe, singe) singing and singing, there,
             in deep sleep...

191

Yield

'gone by without a letter'
                                        – Rilke

Like broken safety glass, stars
spread themselves out on the hood of

darkness. I pour sugar into a

spoon. I have to love the kind of stranger
I have become when you're near

me. Now, there are 9 hours of light left in

the day. I'm still living in the unlikelihood
of my own mind, exile of displaced numbers

in longing. I walk here without

shoes. I can hear the wind drag its dead body down
the dark closet of my ear where I press it to the wood picnic

table. There's a bonsai that grows in the brain.

A tipped mockingbird remains impossible in
twelve songs over the garden. Yes, I forgive the death

of my childhood.

Bird Talk

consider *yourself*
                    – Rilke

I am forever looking up,
unlucky habit

under the ceiling zero, the opened cage aviary
where no bird can be ill omen,

where if you get too high, the ice sings as it breaks
around your body.

Whether bird, foul out of custom, the beaten bush in sleep, birds
do dream, random

patterns'-worth, handed over in the augury like memory.

No Ra kingdom, no mariner's superstition
protected by Stormy Petrels, souls
of the dead ghosting
                    behind the wake's white afterlife, no
I am certain

speaking to us, from flecked heaven or hell-feathered, you decide,
where the landscape is hurtling upside down,
reams of rain,
through windfalls falling,
the dying man's walking where happiness is cruel,

there, the birds are.

Stephen Shields

Lapwings

To hatch them,
God might have planted
a peacock's feathers
then watched them multiply.

When it came to winter
and a groundmist
trapped the low field
in a fishing net,
they swarmed like eels,
as though they had forgotten
the grandeur in their genes.

Gothic

Singing like whales,
we float alongside
in a sea
of our own making.
My hand lands,
a gothic roof
over your finger of rings,
the jewel
a great choir of windows,
glowing below,
glowing above.

Patricia McCarthy

Word-Bells

(from Rilke's letters)

i

Epistles of light etched in the sky in your beautiful hand
from Muzot, Duino: vast insoluble questions wanting to expand

from jottings whose inner life anchored you to things:
Gothic cathedrals, pressed heather, portraits and paintings –

the Louvre, Jardin d'Acclimatation, Jardin des Plantes...
There you waited for secrets of statues, for streets to descant

to you a syntax wherein you would lose and find
yourself. Castles injected their turrets into your mind

until you could swing words like bells, and women, animals
and earth happened to you like events, important only if capable

of transformation into poetry. You didn't mind stunting your life
like an unplayable organ – for you clung to the belief

that what you commented upon was taking place elsewhere,
the nearby distancing itself as if painted on silk in an affair

of colours: pearl-grey houses, rainbows of booksellers' stalls,
brown bindings, green albums matching the green squares, walls

lime-washed with your lines. Standing always as if before
something great, like a painting by Cézanne, its musical score

fixing the vital ground hues, forever removing indecisions,
you invited the sea to impose the sway of its ellipses and elisions

upon whatever in you had become bewildered and confused:
bits of people like brush-strokes the Impressionists used,

the perished animated still, floating in a wind from nowhere,
falling and overtaking each other in a fountain, aware

you were a maker with the roots of centuries in you,
how all the time past and to come would happen anew.

Liebeund werte Gräfin, Dear Princess, Dearest Friend, Dear Lou,
Dear Clara, Liebe Gnädigste Frau, you wrote. 'I long to hear from you'.

ii

You must feel your emptiness, you said,
like a vacant room around you, like an arch
through which comes breath warm as bread,

scents and solitariness in bottles,
and autumn appearing in rust, gold and red
like a visitor out of season – to create

the wind, its accomplice, overhead,
piling sky upon rushing sky, decorating
lanes with vertebrae of the leaves it bled.

iii

No mourning for you – your task to use

the joys and splendours of life, your Muse,
while old selves enacted miniature deaths,

and your best selves remained at a remove
from the loved one who could not pass away –
possessed without possession
to encounter the infinite, breath by breath.

No mourning: grief for the vanished future

an immeasurable legacy without sutures,
Death not the banished stalker prepared

to pounce, but at home in fields of blossom,
seasoning life. Goethe calling for light,
Beethoven shaking his fist at thunder, like you,
in their final hours refused to be spared.

No mourning: your excuse for absolution
as you passed in, through and away from women
who gave themselves to you, while regularly

you gave them up, sidestepping precipices
of the Love you approached – to perfect it
in that Solitude which preserved you,
you claimed, from petty perils of the daily.

No mourning. No wake, no widows' weeds.
Yet, hand in hand with Death in your elegies
you remain the requiem-maker for our exequies.

                         iv

How the smallest bird voice
                         hit you and concerned you.
How a bird's nest appeared
                         to you an external womb
furnished and hidden exclusively
                         by the female who trusts
the universe like her own body
                         and sings in it as if singing
in her own inwardness, no distinction
                         between her heart and the world's.

                         v

What you wanted: long walks barefoot in the woods,
growing a beard day and night, lighting an evening lamp,
a fire flickering onto the ceiling your moods;

the moon to visit when it suited her; to be mobbed
by stars while you translated rain and storms
into gods; the company of books, hog-skin bound,

197

and of maîtres like Rodin, Jacobsen from whom
you could learn; trimmed box hedges, wild-flower-summers,
bowed rafters from some dark, remembered room

and the familial smell of old wardrobes heaped with things
into which you metamorphosed, given the gift of seeing
with your body, of breathing with the pen, renunciation

identical to fulfilment. And O the saying in every pass
you made at women, their glances blinding as the sun
while they stained themselves into cathedral glass.

Behind your stare, the blood of their colours
filled you with longings, with fantasies of security
which made you live, always, beyond yourself.

Russia, Paris, Vienna, Bremen: journeys
away from your life-sized life that wronged you –
and on to Munich, Pisa, Naples, Paris again, Capri,

never escaping the hinterland of your Self,
your solitude in bad hands, unless in your own.
Places, departed from, turning into bright hours:

of deep sleep in the open, each pavement stone
more familiar than a pillow cut from the slab laid
by Jacob under his head; angels grafting their bones

onto yours, changing the visible into the invisible
and back, excelling human action with velocities
of a higher reality. You, too, surpassed

mankind to look back with overtures
of compassion, radiating your presence, expecting
nothing, rinsed and run clean like Nature.

What you did not want: a worldly home,
an exercise book underlined in red by Life,
to arrive incomplete at the present;

the abyss over which you perched, psychoanalysis,
lost innocence, to be dragged up a mountain of pain,
a heart battered, embittered and formless;

the lighthouse sending out signals beyond you,
not meaning you, not knowing you,
its light a question mark threatening a crushing answer.

vi

In villas, hotels, rented rooms, castles, retreats
you wrote on our bodies with your heart's racing beats:

Lou, Clara, Elizabeth, Anna, Gertrud, Elena, Ninette,
Camille, Christiane, Hedwig, Erika, Marthe, Annette,

Elsa, Loulou, Claire, Marina, Aline, Imma, Sidie –
double and treble-barrel names as you courted nobility...

You took us and left us with our grief which you said
dies into a thing, Were we anonymous in bed?

Yours the cop-out of an aesthete, no Adonis at all.
You told Lou you were no good a lover despite us in thrall.

In villas, hotels, rented rooms, castles, retreats
you cosseted Solitude, spilled your seed on fresh sheets,

visions of us more provocative to you than our skin,
though your letters insisted you preserved us within.

Your correspondence contradicted you, would not let us go –
in German verse, French prose, like journals on public show

your words dressed us in feathers, silks, satins and lace,
yet never a long lease, nor commitment could you face.

Baronesses, Princesses, Countesses, Fraus and Fräuleins;
our breath only of statues ... such as Paula, Baladine.

As the skies play around you,
looping the world's loop,
dropping like stage curtains,
then lifting up, you borrow

thermals from your angels
to retrieve more than you manage
from memory so that what you receive
in your fullest being is consumed

without trace in your blood,
not a single fact in your head.
From cracks in your closed eyelids
you pull, still, endless yards

of daydreams. But, catching onto tabs,
purple, orange and grey, of ribbons
of sleep, you escape that net
tangling tighter with every effort

made to get free. And you endure
in the here and now, letting
things happen in your great gestation.
No matter if you deem women

better equipped for love, and,
in your most secret being, admit
that, like the troubadours and Dante,
you skirt merely around it,

masked in word, song and epic.
The standpoint of the angel you desire,
that workaday angel, steel-winged,
who can return to things

their *laric* value, and convert
for you the abstract into the concrete,
nomen into *numen*, furnishing
with the intimate this estranged world,

the annunciations woven
into your tone defining
their indefinableness and pointing
always just beyond the given.

As the skies play around you,
looping the world's loop,
you re-appear through stage curtains,
giving your life and death the slip.

viii

Was it nightingales your angels emulated:
calling in tremolos from a deserted garden
with their souls, glass-clear, like one soloist
exorcising a world long awaited?

Secretive, nocturnal, operatic composers,
their repertoire hinting at a beyond...
Did you feel – with their full-throated triplets
and arpeggios on speech's edge – a bond?

And your lines improvised to their music,
teasing new theories of phrasing and motifs
from pitches outside the harmonics
of a human ear? Did you take your pick

from pipings, carols and signature tunes,
schooled in long territorial recitals –
of Latin constructions and metrics –
sung, from deep cover, for their rivals

and each other? Lilacs by the orangery
quivered as choir-stalls of branches shook.
And in theatrical silences, you took out your book,
transposing, into ink, winged unnameable keys.

Your death-bed requirements: Valmont,
clean linen, night-shirts, soft white or beige
from a sales catalogue, books for the journey

to the South of France, possible now only
in your head, the straight talk of the sea,

no last sacraments, no clergy;
a nurse who does not know your poetry,
who reads to you the *Chronique Mondaine*

from *Le Figaro*, though you hated newspapers,
to append you to the trivia of the daily

which you repeatedly wrote was death
to a relationship in letters like homilies.
Nanny Wunderly in the afternoons

reciting from *Les Cahiers Verts* –
Proust, provoking remembrances,

French the last tongue in your ears –
the adopted rather than native
stressing your preference to become

invisible, alone in whatever Language
you built into a permanent home –

forbidding her to stop when she thinks you
asleep with your shout: 'Continuez!'
No medical diagnosis, sublimating

demons hidden in flowers of your anxiety.
No friends, lovers, no comforting words;

just the hand-squeeze of a doctor,
the wheeling outside of a bird
and your eyes fixed on someone near:

through shredded missives, Lou picking up
on you with her sixth sense from afar,

until you sit up, your blue eyes wide open,
stilled into those of a visionary.
And a cold wind blows over you

from across the sea that has travelled
to you, wave upon wave in a lullaby.

                              x

Your angels tap-dance with the rains,
clickety-click, nothing insubstantial
about their formal steps, metal on wood.

Borrowing plumes from horses
on carousels, they sashay with trees
across horizons, choreographed

by the breeze. Waltz, tango, foxtrot,
Charleston ... they know the moves –
and fling off corsets lacing them

into convention. Daredevils, they swing
from beaks of crows on telegraph wires
and nose-dive to sweep out,

with splayed wings, rats from drains.
Then, as if in Vaudeville, they stomp
on the hammers of pianos – ruining

concert pitch. Though they knock out
guardian angels, they give a singing
to the unheard that surpasses the heard,

to the ragtime movements in stillness.
Migrating flocks scatter at their approach.
Not many go near them.

Dottor Serafico, no wonder earth froze.
Grave-diggers battled with the thud
of clods that would not melt as you chose

deliberately the new year's cusp
on which to attempt to die, knowing
how ghosts then stalk the living

and in shades make clouds of their breath.
Nothing new – your life always full of death.

Serafico carissimo, a Catholic by birth,
did you revert to the little mountain church
for stone angels on tombs to borrow mirth

from your angels? And dance with the children
whose frozen-blue fingers held up your wreaths?
For you, there had always been above and beneath –

no ground-level for the horses and the sleigh
bearing your coffin to slide along. Only a way

for the harness bells' jingle and mercury
of the Rhône to carry you on and on over peaks,
in formation with birds, snaking through valleys

where whole woods genuflected to the Angelus.
As the children sang, you gave back the wreaths
for their deaths they would carry through life

and dug up your own. Serafico carissimo.
Organ and violin play Bach with accelerando

for you still, settling you in the house designed
by Rodin on the site of himself: a refuge over which
he is the sky that he numbered and signed;

he is the forest and stream from a world
without hunger, separateness or desire, where one
has no self, no boundaries. Just a carillon.

Beyond Raron, Dottor Serafico, Serafico Dottor,
our sight now is insight. No asking for more.

Notes:

Word-Bells, the title of this sequence is an attempt to evoke in English the lyrical genre, the *Dinggedicht* or 'thing/object poem' created by Rilke in the *Neue Gedichte*. The *Dinggedicht* obviates the lyrical I or relegates the 'I' to the edge of the poem, as in a Cézanne painting. As Jack Herbert explains (*The German Tradition*, Temenos Academy Papers No. 15, 2001): the empathy with the subject of the poem is so great that 'the writer disappears into his poem like a Chinese master into his hanging landscape scroll', resulting in 'lyrics that *are* things, like pieces of Rodinesque sculpture'.

V: Rilke described Rodin's 'The Thinker' as thinking with the whole body, alluded to here in the fourth stanza.

VI: The women chorusing here are those of real women named in Rilke's letters with whom he had affairs.

VIII: In his letter to Clara Rilke from Meudon-Val-Fleury, written on 3rd May, 1906, Rilke gives a detailed account of walking through the midst of some nightingales as if 'through a throng of singing angels' who chorused in 'a Buddha of voices'.

IX: In the last line, the sea itself actually travels to Rilke, instead of the other way around. There are several examples in Rilke's work where natural and manmade environments have their own strange unknown energies. For example in 'Vor der Sommerregen', the park seems to move closer to the windows of the house, and the walls in the hall and the pictures 'step away' or 'recede'.

X: Rilke's *Duino Elegies* appeared in 1923; hence the angels here are au fait with the dances of the 'Roaring Twenties'. (Eliot's *The Waste Land* appeared in 1922.)

XI: 'Dottor Serafico' and 'Serafico carissimo' were the words Princess Marie von Thurn und Taxis used to address Rilke in many of her letters to him.

The fourteenth line of the poem evokes the up/down movement in so much of Rilke's verse and relates him to the up/down gymnastic movements used by Milton in *Paradise Lost*, and by Gerard Manley Hopkins, even if for different purposes.

In the second to last couplet of XI, the vision of human existence when unshackled by our mortal coil echoes the thought of Meister Eckhart, the thirteenth century mystic often linked to Rilke.

In the last line, 'our sight now is insight' not only delineates the final epiphany that the reader experiences, it is also linked to the instances of 'The Erlebnis' experienced by Rilke, similar to the epiphanies defined by James Joyce: the world suddenly viewed in a different, universal light in a moment of heightened awareness. This kind of moment took Rilke into the realm of his albeit pagan angels, and is referred to again in V verses 10–11. Sight becoming insight, not only refers to Shakespeare's *King Lear*, but also to Rilke's own seminal statement: 'Ich lerne sehen' ('I am learning how to see'). This relates Rilke to Goethe; like the latter, Rilke was visually gifted and an 'Augenmensch' (eye-person).

Raron is the little mountain village in Switzerland where Rilke chose to be buried.

Lotte Kramer

Recorder

In a drawer it rests
Now unplayed,
Chestnut-grained wood;
Many years ago
In another life,
My first musical
Instrument
Evoking a simple tune
With lizard fingers,
The music teacher's
Patient imprint
On my receptive self,
Leading to the more ample
Sound of the piano.
Yet persisting in the lone
Flute-like lament,
Silently unheard
For her whose life
Was shattered.

Note: her career was ended as a musicologist by Nazi race laws. She committed suicide.

Friedrich Nietzsche

The Loneliest One

(a fragment)

Now that the day
Has tired of the day and all the longing brooks
Are splashing with new consolation,
And all the heavens hung with golden cobwebs
Are telling every tired one: 'Rest now' –
Why don't you rest, you darkest heart,
What stings you into footsore flight...
Whom are you waiting for?

Translated by **Lotte Kramer**

Roger Garfitt

Young Lester

He rolls the only dice
                at which he never loses
so quick and light the sixes
                fall beyond belief

The New Orleans Strutter
                the kid who had to Charleston
to his own horn has the room
                at his fingertips
all eyes on the freaks of touch
                that are conjuring notes
from the by-ways of the metal
                bluegrass leaps
back country blues
                and C-melodies
transposed for the tenor
                as if the paces
of the unicorn
                were to be found
in the horse

                All the accessories
are still to come
                the hieroglyphics
on his cuff-links
                the matching suede shoes
with every suit

                but already he has
his call – that little hoot
                as he goes up in the air –
and his calling
                the light tones the hipsters
will take into their cabbala
                and sing under their breath
as alive as the dust
                under the shaded lamps

of the pool room
      to the ascension
of the everyday

Note: Rilke and Lester Young were only just contemporaries. Lester started playing in the Twenties, as a young boy in the Young family band, but he made his reputation in the Thirties. Where there is an affinity with the Rilke of the Duino Elegies is in the inward, spiritual quality of Lester Young's playing. Rilke would have been very surprised to find himself in a Kansas City pool room but he would have understood the hipsters singing under their breath.

John Greening

Huntingdonshire Elegy

for Stuart Henson

The land dries. Cracks open amongst the stubble.
In the distance, there is a strawstack the size of an office block.
The radio mast, wanting to stir and dissolve this pastoral,

broadcasts its reminder: you are not in the Tate, late walkers,
though there could be a god, and there have been nymphs,
their underwear, look, on the hawthorn bleaching. Was it Bacchus

with his chariot drawn by pards? Our walk to the White Horse
marks the end of summer. Only one light across the field
towards the disused branch line: there, under his bushel, glows

Il Penseroso, when he's at home and not out here, lyrics
pushing from dust like seventeen syllable knotweed,
stanzas flocking, sonnets ripening, vine translating the bricks.

From that locust tree whose seeds I brought you and you planted
after a Black Forest holiday, we follow the middle way.
We want to survive, but we also want to be Dante

entering Huntingdonshire's dark wood. And although
you are radiating Italy and Rilke as we walk and you're sure
this is a new path, the right path, you must know

that last elm on the horizon is dying. No dragonflies are flying
as they were this time last year. No owl yet. No buzzard
so late, though you tell me they are to be seen there preying

on rabbits. But it is a hare starts up and wheels round
the field like the hand on a gameshow clockface; then stands
framed in the hedgegap, tonight's winner against the sun.

Stuart Henson

Rilke in Florence

(Part of a longer sequence)

Annunciation

'Beauty is only the first touch
of terror we can still bear'
(Duino Elegies 1)

She would be at prayer, naturally,
when he appeared –
out of the shaft of sunlight,
resolving gently into the visible

till she became aware
of fear like birdsong in her womb
and he was there
attendant, as thought waits, in the still air.

He would be near yet somehow far,
that way we apprehend
the promise of rainbows
inflected through their hazy arcs.

Then he would speak at first or seem to speak
and she would dare
to raise her eyes, slowly, to knowledge,
feeling the soft wings pulse in the crib of her heart.

Angels

'My desires run riot
and out of all paintings
the angels follow me'

Rilke: *Florence Diary*

The masters of the *Quattrocento*
were well-schooled
in gesture.
How else present
the ineffable to the ignorant?
And to paint like this
you must believe
in the body of angels.

There cannot be as many in Heaven
as here in the Uffizi,
attendant upon their offices
with the patience of centuries.

I am at ease in their company:
in mute acknowledgement
they have seemed to say
Noli me tangere
but I have felt the breath
of their wings' longing.

When God is dead
where else will they go –
unless it were
to flit behind me, unseen
in the dark corners of the world,
seeking another way
back to eternity?

Viareggio triptych

(Based on an incident recorded in Rilke's *Florence Diary*, and the poet is Rilke himself)

The Poet

He must work and he must wait,
knowing the world, his capricious master,
is generous and cruel in equal measure.
At this turn of the year, the spring sunlight
wears satin gloves: it buffs the waves to white
whispers beyond the dunes, and blends a mistier
lapis tint into a sky that will mature
to a noon clarity, promising insight.

On the balcony, his notebook open,
the poet, caught up in meditation,
has begun to discover the garden's
mystery, the secret of the seasons'
deaths and beginnings: the flux of creation
spellbound in a perfect equilibrium.

The Black Monk

A shadow on the gravel, inaudible
footfall, silencing the chatter of birdsong.
Darkness become material among
the shades of the garden: the yews, the tall
conifers, the ivy on the house-wall.
Alms for the poor – given in obligation;
but something about this apparition
shudders the soul with a sudden chill.

It is time, he seems to say, for someone
to leave the house and go with him, to follow
slowly down the path and out of the garden.
Whoever comes must walk with him alone
along the soft shore; leaving a window
ajar, the table laid, the gate open.

The Girl

To be so young and yet be tired of love!
Its disappointments and denials age us.
We, who as children gave ourselves in trust,
soon learn to keep our distances with life.
But she, trying to hold her eyes aloof
from the world, she, surely, should embrace it most,
not hasten to this last and darkest tryst
in the garden that she cannot bear to leave.

Her white feet on the steps will hesitate
before the point of no return. The sun
is warm on the stone; the poppies' red mouths
tremble like kisses taken long and late.
Even the bees are murmuring her doubts.
Her torn heart beats in her breast like a drum.

Will Stone

Angelic Intervention

For Stephen Romer

Like the sail silhouette
which stymies the vacant horizon,
or the person
who half enters my room
to stand late-flowering, vulnerable
by the open door,
she wells up from the grey
weather of people.
We choose the same moment.
Our feet touch.
Only once the frail rendezvous.
Just in time she comes to.
Gone.
As the current pulls
the crowd stamps out all evidence
of our affair.
How long could I remain there?
An uncertain image on her eyelids,
given up in a shop window
so cursorily.
I turned round then
and they shielded me.
The overworked angels raised
their matted wings.

The Swifts

Powered by screams
and the black bat twist of their wings,
they slice through the insect cloud.
Heavenly dogfight, no quarter given,
the plunder ravished unseen.
Round they come again,
cyclists on a bend
clinging to their manic carousel.
The air cannot hold them.
The sun slips from their sleek
gunmetal backs.
They are gods.

June English

The Violin Maker

For my uncle James Dooley

Year after year he sat cross legged,
pen-knife in raw-boned sailor's hands,
(roughened by years of cable laying),
whittling away at the wood, slowly
shaving and shaping a block of pine.

> She got the gist: forty one pieces
> glued together, book-matched pine
> for back and Sycamore to curve
> the breast, Canadian Maple bridge -
> ready made pegs and catgut strings.

He camped out in the basement, studied
Stradivarius, 'His Life and Works'.
Using resin from the Tung Tree,
and mineral mixes – high in silica –
he made and exploded varnishes!

> She lived with the smell of lacquer,
> 'in white violins' resting on sideboards,
> wood shavings and Sea Shanties –
> the catacoustics of strained strings
> that scratched her home grown melodies.

Sometimes, when his children called,
he'd swing the baby shoulder high
and dance a jig, till one by one
they all joined in and she would smile,
aware his work would call him back –

> *it's time to birth a Dooley Violin,*
> a masterpiece of hand and eye,
> he's tuning notes, exploring scales,
> she's found the resin for his bow,
> his eyes are closed – his spirit soars –

> in a song of four birds – *The Lark Ascending...*

Luis Benitez

Joy and Fall

First harmony there I saw you, it wasn't necessary
to look about parts of your entire kingdom but there I saw you
and I didn't want to pause at your border, your border
that is in simple things full of your waving shadow.
How delicately, light in light, core of the day,
you become corporeal or choose a candid shape
when you lend us your eyes
and how an eternal love takes us by the hand
towards your creature, there where you are indeed,
alive, the infinite dance,
the very complaint of what exists.
All high serenity is your vase and each one
declares a new colour yours. It's April
of a year that doesn't count for you and however
a sweet warmth led you here by my side. I was only
a certainty this morning and the foam of sleep
and the sides of the day were cancelled in me.
I only asked, ran to your contagion,
so that a breath on the cinders that powdered things
lighted a world of carbuncles again,
amethysts in the air ... the many features
of your bright glass windows, where do they come from?
from what deep abyss or public abyss and exposed,
from what other time hardly visited,
hardly glanced in the fire of fire?

There is no worse fasting than that within you.

Rimbaud's Eyes

Blue, barbaric. Today soft trills
sing for you and in the literary workshops
the voice of the parrot gets thinner: moved
it sweetens the Great Glances, their confectioner's lesson.
On this side we pray for you kneeling before a wolf:
how beautiful a science is a room looking onto darkness
and man, that inconstant scholar,
is only a few steps that come along and go.
Today when teachers of letters have forgotten everything
the convicted know about you
and the vagabond who, at the risk of being smashed by cars,
stops the metaphor of this tread to pick up the miracle
of a leaf, without reaching an explanation,
today when the lift-men scarcely
rise above the others,
today when this mad substance appears smothered and defeated,
as it always was, as it is always going to be,
floating on the waters of numbers;
today when casinos have settled in your virgin forests
and disco music sounds in all thundering Africas,
today when on 88th street and Broadway a horrid so and so shows you
printed on the T-shirt, smiling at all the American Glory,
today when you, bound in leather with golden letters
are exhibited by dentists in their libraries
and the swift drug-dealers honour you their way, distributing poison
along the streets of the world,
today when walls fall and all posterities collapse,
today when History, that old foe,
laughs at us saying it doesn't exist,
as in your time the Devil repeated;
today when the soft muscles of the representatives
can throw thousands of sturdy foreigners,
if they want, into the sea,
today when the shy democracy proved to be
more effective than kings,
today when finally we all become good
and the pink, black, yellow and copper-coloured
banquet of life lifts its radiant glass, beyond
the charitable groups attempting the sonnet,

through the bookshelves swept by dust and secretaries,
without typing or voice or hope or reason,
geographies go across two thick and powerful lights
surrounding the Earth like a ring.
Not because of the symbol but for the glance
you are like the plastic god which the scared one
hangs from the wall so that those Eyes follow him
around the house. For us
the minimal ones, for us the few, for us the weak,
who only want to remain idle, your eyelids are
always open, disdainful brother,
Jesus Christ the Terrible,
today when it's shameful to be hungry
they keep on looking at your wild lanterns *all the same*.

David Cooke

Night and Rilke

> *How like an angel*
>
> Hamlet 2–2

Lute music most lachrymal – *night* not far,
Not far – the cosmos a wheel turning and tuning
A vast and soundless city and voices singing
Each to each. Yet starlit still, almost as
A constellation, a wanderer, a pilgrim in
The *great night* he would pace – would tread
And tread his battlement, as Hamlet before him,
Listening for inner voices, communing
With the sad-joyous *night* inward and starry still,
Where world balanced at the tipping point moves
Most slow, where – as in some tremulous after
Life the transformations begin, where
The *lamentations* and *wanderer*
Might meet another – and view
On the endless plain, the cities of *Loss*
And *Grief* and see, behind the ruined
And empty façade of this world, creation
As an abstract pattern weave and unweave,
Ravel then unravel its surface ease.
        The moment of the *angel*.
The intense moment when the interpreted
World falls and shifts – and the abstract pattern
Moves and slides and almost are seen *things-in*
Themselves which become as they always are,
Will be. The *angels* who hear yet do not hear,
Who live their own existence, who keep their
Ambiguities and are mainly indifferent
To the human situation.
        Our plight is to summon them,
To see the difference between those who by their
Slow sad patient presence and gaze uphold us
Who wait in the shadow-fed world. Yet should
Their gaze meet ours we would surely gash
Gold, fold and fall as if rain to earthen soil.

Their existence is before and after our all
Brief existence, and bears the pain of lovers
Parting at dawn, or at dusk the pain of children
Who have lost their childhood, to whom the world
No longer is delight nor discovery – these figures
With their wreathed smiles and unspoken words,
Not more fleeting nor desolate than my own,
Who in the dark seek consolation, the world
Unravels and disinherits. Yet that music which
In the night revives – lingers and wanders lost
For a time where the watery Thames moves
To and fro, where time's lutenist plays
That slow sad ravelling, unravelling
Music, lachrymose and still.

The Night Half-open

Doch der Tote muß fort

– Rilke, *Duino Elegies* – The Tenth Elegy – line 96

I

You who are not at home in the received world
With its interpreted language and opinion –
Who have forgotten your journey's journey,
Who must again become a wanderer over
The Earth's moving surface.
        You who were placed, set down here
In the young time of the year – how the world
Awaited you. Yet all its levels of interpretation
Weighed you down, so that one night taking
Nothing with you, not even your own self,
You slipped from the skein of your old life
And took off as a wanderer where
The soul coils and ascends
A small mountain path.
                Night never far away –
Inward and starlit still, yet peopled by delicate
Precise presences which found the dark

222

Unyielding, the angel indifferent.
                    Only through language
Could you speak to them – only through words,
And your own self a wanderer, already a pilgrim
Estranged from the received world. Night held
You there – that night internal yet external,
Of the world yet not the world.
                    You would invoke and bring
The angel's gaze upon your self, for world is
Not light enough – the night not dark enough,
Our knowledge, set against *things-that-are*,
Not great but small, leaving each attempt
Echoing *a different kind of failure*,
For who will attune their
Consciousness to a world within world.

II

You who are not at home in the interpreted world,
Who are yet out there in the star-flung night,
Or in that world breathing within
World where the laurel grows...

The wanderer who through the night
Has been on the wild hillside, scrambling
Through darkness, listening to foxes
Bark in the still quiet –
Until hushed among owl-calls he
Searches some rare gift hiding
In forest from the immense
Breathing that was following.

Then he came down sudden
From the tall hillside, in a slide
Of earth and stone, to this under
Place, to find a cottage standing,
Lights in the window – a home
He had once known, whose missing
Inhabitants or family had once been
His – but now transformed, and he
Also transformed into someone other.

223

He knocked but no-one answered,
Yet found at the threshold the door
Half-open, and on an oaken table
Food and wine in an earthen jug
And a wreath of laurel laid out
In a circlet – and set down there,
A lute and a book which
Contained his own true name.

III

The lutenist in the tall constellation
Of his calling, like Orpheus before him,
Tunes his lute and does not look back nor
Directly at us – but face turned away
Plays a rare rhythmical breathing,
A sound that wakes the invisible ones –
The shades and memories that cluster
Around, who extol the night and bring
Transformation – until he leaves the world
Unsolved and attends his own destiny,
And *look look* – how his lute points
Beyond this mortal residue.

Alexander Small

Her Hour Come Round

'Surely some revelation is at hand'
'The Second Coming' by W.B. Yeats

Like a stone Her coming weighs on me, like rain
is graining me, as the stonier waters stun
dull rock when seas in their seasons run. A pain.
More kith than kind, with soundings She's begun
to factor in, enacts the paradigm.
At one with tides, and to that sullen moon
blood-bonded, whose signings chime dumb time,
yields me merely grace-note to her tune.

But mine is the Changing! She manifests with me,
invests with me her flowerings, in this wound,
that other days and woundings might presume
an earth for seeding, clay where their dreams display:
no rocking cradle, nor roughest best unbound,
but has its roots within my teeming womb.

Graveyard on the Shore

To walk with dark-drawn waters, and to hear
dark sounds, wrung from the sea, though seas seem clear
enough, that gulls entrance, that glintings crave
what their silver darlings hint, where hintings wave
white flags of supplication to the year.

Whose wider eyes won't see, men, though near
encounter, still refuse to act their fear,
to know an hour can shuffle death, or rave
of cause and consequence. Too prized, they'd save
shelved lives, that guilt's manurings fruit the year.

But all field the questions here! None find dear
what a siren-song would tell – hard-edged, sincere,
of pretence spare – how weirdings wake the brave.
To hold this ground, who lie around are grave,
who graft as walls must lichen year by year.

Peter Robinson

Unheimlich Leben

Seeing that far-fetched look of yours,
again I have you coming home
from Valparaíso, as it might be,
to the Isle of Ely.

Maltings, greens, a sunken lane
seen then on a daily basis
turn aside, as if withdrawn,
at your coming home –
home to hear how the natives complain
and with so little reason,
to find its quiet brick streets and walks
grating on you all the more.

I see them as though through your eyes,
those drowned lands with their roundabouts,
industrial parks, estates
now high and dry
when a local bus fails to materialize...
but what would these glimpses be for
if not to make peace with our places and times?
Leafage is thick like the summers before,
your guess, as good as mine.

Raubkunst

It would have been better to ask permission
before stealing a glimpse of suburbs
on Vienna's furthest outskirts with the woods,
and woodland paths for taking a stroll
one autumn afternoon, my words
taken into quiet air but still not quite
enough coming back to set me at my ease –
which is why there was yet more to tell
like a confession, a therapy session,
though no one would be paid for the time
and as if it were making the slightest difference
to dead wood crackling underfoot,
the creak in high branches, a rummaging breeze
that stirred perpetually tops of trees...
It would have been better to ask permission.

226

Poplar, walnut, birch, diseased
chestnut leaves are motionless
and, for garden statuary,
take this draped, reclining figure
held up by two wicker chairs
who's talking to me here.

But caught up in an over-crowded dream
like the thick mist filling sunlit fields
from Innsbruck to Salzburg, its luminous gleam
populous with things you were to see
in moments intervening, I hear him say,
'Now we're all for the freedom of art
in its own time, though painted with opprobrium,
become common property,' and I'm
not even missing the closed Belvedere,
its glimpses of expropriated Klimts
with their gilt frames, gold showers, touched-up displays
like drowned lives that flashed before the eyes
of gallery-goers moving through silence
filled with the dispossessed, burned, the lost.

Equally ours, more ideas
start as conversations slow,
framing landscapes for the ears
in a light of near departure –
although there's barely a shadow
of that cast on each feature;

and perspectives extend beyond the garden
to take in flea markets, maples, a shrine
with misunderstandings or taken offence,
as at those earlier attempts of mine –
bungling not supposed to happen
that did, the more-than-bargained-for
lingering still in every consequence
like visits unmade, a fast stain from the things
you didn't do or, done, you can't undo.
But now the mown lawn's taken an imprint;
train timetables must play their part,
hushed leaves stirring memories to the last.
Taking my leave ... he saw what I meant.
It would have been better to ask permission
before stealing away with that past.

Clive Wilmer

Gregoire, 60

For Gabriel

Jane Goodall met him in Brazzaville zoo – a living skeleton, every bone in his body visible, almost hairless from malnutrition. Born 1944. Believed to be the oldest chimpanzee in the world.

Note from *James and Other Apes*:
photographs by James Mollison

Shakespeare. Imagine him
Granted a further decade as God's spy –
He might have looked like this:
                                    blanched white
The patchy beard, and parched the mottled skin.

Or Rembrandt, older still, and with an eye
As dim,
A will as faint,
A hand too frail to lift a brush and paint
His own nobility exposed to light.

Fragment

                    And then
The end of consciousness begins to seem
Like a great woman, splayed across her bed
In shadow, curtains drawn against the day.
She summons you. She shows her darkness to you.
She draws you to her whispering, 'My darling.
Come home to me, my sweet one, stay with me.
Forget success and failure. Fuck, and sleep.'

W.S. Milne

'Night-Lines'

i.m. John McGahern (1934–2006)

Ice hardens to armour and polishes the laurel.
Your gentle face and gentler voice are gone.
John, winter has thinned the trees out now
and the wind is singing your right, discerning style.
Ice hardens to armour and polishes the laurel.
If only, like you, I could find the *exact* syllable.

Sappho's New Poem

(In Scots)

Quines!
Be kind
ti music and poetrie.

Hinnie-sweet
your breists.
Whit fine!

The hairp
tak, and mak it play
cleir and sweet

in tune
wi luve and poetrie.

Me?
A'm auld and scunnert nou,
the hairp A barely tak in haund.

Ma locks, that aince were maidly-derk,
are whicht nou, and straigglie.
Ma saule o its mort is seck and wearie:

ma jynts are cracked, and sair;
cauld dirls ma banes;

ti think that aince, like you,
ma quines, like a hind
A dunced. Nae mair!

Anerlie poems, nou, and miserie.

Life spills, and whit is warse,
quines, you lose your luiks, your hair.

Think on Eos, goddess o the daan,
and her luve o Tithonus
catched in her lair:

nae mindin him mortal,
a man, and that auld and grey
he'd turn, and nae immortal like her.

Antoinette Fawcett

Three Statues

We had a metal model
of a statue by Zadkine,
Jan Gat or John with a Hole:
tortured limbs, a great big gap

where heart and guts should be,
face of despair, strong
but futile hands trying to hold
the sky back which was raining

fire, deafness, pressure, blood,
800 deaths and 80,000 homeless –
The clock ticked black, its bronze
weights pulling time away, another

mini-giant perched upon its top,
stoic grimace, muscles rippling
down the torso, a world, a universe
held on the shoulders – Atlas

in patience bearing what seemed
impossible. On his cross
above the mantelpiece I watched
Jesus calmly watch my mother

cry out loud for her *verwoeste stad.*
Woest I knew meant angry, savage,
wild, mad, desolate. I laughed
in shock. You told me recently

about my mother's nightmares –
troops marching through the wasteland
like grey machines night after night
for twenty years, at least, of marriage.

But those statues made no comment
as you set me across your knee,
smacked my bottom, at her request –
protecting her, teaching me.

Zadkine's statue *De Verwoeste Stad*, known in English as *City without a Heart*, commemorates the aerial bombardment by the German Luftwaffe of Rotterdam on 14th May 1940 and the almost total destruction of the city centre.

Listening to Your Sweet Speech

who really listens
to every single mote
of pollen

whoever really listens
to the nectar
in the beanflower

who ever listens and listens
to the gathering hum
from end to beginning

listens to your sweet speech,
honey dripping from the tongue,
muse queen

Judith Kazantzis

Eternal and cigar

for PP 8.6.2005

You were the life and soul, how could
        you leave so soon? Paddy dear,
    no more crowing? Just a sister clucking
for a gone beyond recall old cock?
        Left with this nightly tipple of not -
till I burn the same hole in zero.

Paddy, it's so easy, in drab sadness,
        to take your best wit in vain.
    Don't mind me, and I won't mind me.
I'm looking and looking: sugar and heaven
        deprived, with my unbelief's
worn out gnashers. Only hard fudge

left for the old bag ... stones on the stomach.
        Didn't I crave the same perfect glory,
    the enchanted tiers, the overhead lightning –
and of course the very best pork pies to come –
        Heart and soul on a pure drift,
your rich traditional bellow the best speeches

we ever had (in ever-heckled congratulations
        of big birthdays of special saints,
    mother, father, lost too, darling and dear) –
which soon so crack up all your greeting saints,
        they flap off their fluffy banquettes
and in a rustling rush flip-flop feet together

back to chaos, back into shoes, into their own
        sitting-rooms, bedrooms, bathrooms,
    into traffic jams, bars, pubs, betting-shops,
and the last time I saw you, a June Friday,
        cutting an enormous cigar,
tenderly, behind the door, as I said goodbye.

Paul Groves

This Poem Is Not About My Granddad

much as I would like it to be
nor about how he took me to the park
or balanced me on his knee
when I was three.

Granted, it's about his funeral
but in the most oblique of ways.
I would hate, on his account, to bore you
on this the saddest of days
with even one mawkish phrase.

So when the sombre cortège
threads through the suburbs think
of what it passes: a Threshers,
a laundry, a pink
shop called The Kitchen Sink.

Visualise traffic lights,
pedestrians who do not mourn,
having never known the eighty-year-old
(spry as a leprechaun
until the end). He'd been born

yet hardly anyone knew.
A lifetime has flitted by
almost invisibly. Look
at that factory,
at the faintly mottled sky.

Here is the crematorium
though I shall not tell you about it
except to say that the grounds
are perfectly kept. I doubt it
would interest you.

Jean Cassou: Timothy Adès

Jean Cassou (1897–1986), a distinguished art historian, intellectual, novelist and poet, created the Musée National d'Art Moderne. He had composed the *33 Sonnets of the Resistance* in his head in a Vichy prison. These are published by Arc Publications alongside the award-winning translation by **Timothy Adès**, who has more Cassou poems including *The Madness of Amadis*, with facing translation and background material, forthcoming from **Agenda Editions**.

Timothy Adès is a translator-poet who tends to work with rhyme and metre. His awards include the John Dryden Prize and the Premio Valle-Inclán. His other book to date is Victor Hugo's *How to be a Grandfather*, from Hearing Eye. A volume of Robert Desnos' poetry is forthcoming.

Farewell To Rilke

(December 1926)

To change into himself, he did not wait for eternity. His gaze, his voice, his handwriting already signalled certain patterns of thought and feeling that the normal mind can hardly imagine, except in its very last moments when making ready to depart: patterns that, for him, had long since become habitual. A subtle mysterious discretion, heavy with allusions: that was Rilke, and this discretion carried on into the simple actions of his last hours, dreading lest his face be seen in its final rictus, and refusing injections because he wanted his own death, he said, not that of the doctors. This notion of death as inalienable haunts all his work. Its melancholy presence helped him to live, to be sure of his own existence; it tempered the light that he cast with its element of shade. And in that death, at last acknowledged, in its strong integrity, accepted and embraced, he reverted gracefully to himself, always infinitely refined and alone, and irrationally modest like his Prodigal Child, who fled and vanished so as not to be loved too much.

This perpetual meditation, this deepened knowledge of the secret that grows in us gradually like a wound, that widens and finally opens out in the supreme moment when it seems all is finished, gave to whatever he weighed up an inestimable, marvellously doubled value. He would fix on something, not absently toying with it as one might in the knowledge that one has to move on, but enfolding it in the strange tenderness, the secret passionate sensuality of one who sees, beyond outward forms, the hidden reasons for its presence, and perhaps the laws that govern its sorry fate. No-one loves life and beauty more than the lover of death: one who knows how to love and live passionately is led to admire death, to cherish death. Are not the finest dirges prior to Rilke's those of Whitman, the great lover of life?

Only recently, in his full European glory and at the point of his deepest awareness, he had added to French poetry these *Orchards* that overflow with goodness of heart. A vibrant emotion reigns there which caresses the humblest object, needing no more than a line, or a sigh. All is loved, understood, exalted: fruits, flowers, a landscape, the flash of a thought. And that music is the more seductive for all the intense awkward grace born of the poet's struggle with an unforgiving language. That spirit which measured itself against angels liked to imbue all its actions with a charming coquetry, a sense of honour and danger, even a little sorcery.

The perceptible universe, the seasons and cities and human beings and their depressing aspects, whatever around us we think of as useful or dependable: all these have rarely seen themselves loved with such attention, knowledge, and fervour. Sometimes there comes an intercessor, an intermediary, by whom we feel ourselves linked to what is beyond our grasp. Edgar Poe and Novalis were of their number; so too was their brother, Rainer Maria Rilke. While in our midst, they are our guarantors, our sole witnesses; they answer for us; they are almost unknown to us; they know us, and they know things above and beyond us. We may remember the Abyssinian prince's words on the death of Arthur Rimbaud: 'Those whom the earth is not worthy to carry, God calls back to himself.' Yet they love this earth, and weep for it with the clear, fierce, disturbing pity that the Mad Virgin found in the Accursed Husband. Rilke has left us. The world is desolate!

From *Pour la Poésie*, Editions R. A. Corrêa, Paris, 1935.
© Buchet Chastel.

From *Three Poets* (1954)

I was of course very young when I met Rainer Maria Rilke during his last stay in Paris: it was Edmond Jaloux, to whom I owe so much, who bestowed that invaluable gift. I shall always see him as on that first evening, his frail form wrapped in a half-belted coat, as worn in central Europe. At that tender and impulsive age, when I still knew only fragments of his work, he embodied for me the dreamy German romantic world that bewitched me; he was indeed Malte Laurids Brigge, the exile, *der Wanderer*, peopling the lonely uncertainty of Paris with mysteries, harmonies and ghosts. I was close to believing in ghosts myself: and I saw a sign in a later meeting with Rilke, one night as I crossed the precinct of Notre-Dame. It was a troubled time of my youth, and I took this sudden apparition as a mark of heavenly favour. Life is prosaic and serious, and I had no right to its free gifts; and Rilke sprang from my dark side, which was neither serious nor settled, nor amenable to help from anyone.

Everything disposed me to an intimate, poetic affection, just as he himself had probably loved Jens-Peter Jacobsen through his writings, and with that part of our being that yearns for foreign literature of any kind.

What struck me, during the less transient but still infrequent encounters he granted me, was his power of attention. He followed conversations, he weighed up entities, with a rare courtesy and regard. He brought to all his friendly dealings a refined care, whether presenting his writings or carefully choosing a ribbon for a package. Once, when he summoned up for me the look and speech and ideas of the philosopher Simmel, I saw his face contorted as if to convey how this professor strained his whole being to position words in his hearers' ears, as if they were smooth solid particles. Rilke's strange Slavic face, sharp and mobile, could take on these intense expressions to convey an idea; the accompaniment was a whole expansive movement of hand and fingers. I shall never forget how he looked at a sick bird, found on my mother's window-sill in the Île-St-Louis; a look of curiosity more than compassion, an intrigued look. The world intrigued him and he received it with a respectful and solicitous frankness. There was a Chinese politeness, but it was based on no social order, just the order of the heart.

Such a capacity for sympathy extends beyond our own limits, to beings innocent of our weaknesses and contradictions: angels, animals, women, the dead...

The invisible is not transcendent. Rilke insisted on this. He says in a letter to his Polish publisher Witold von Hulewicz: 'My consciousness is purely, deeply, joyously terrestrial... [My work] is to bring what we see and touch here into a greater sphere, the greatest sphere of all.' What we see and touch assumes its fullness in the light of death, which is itself something 'here'. For all this he takes responsibility. He is not the owner of things, but the person responsible, as is Rimbaud: 'responsible for mankind, even for the animals'.

Of the flower between the rails, the flower in the gardens, the offered fruit, the perpetual jet of water in the fountain; of ripenings and happenings, of hidden and silent attractions, of bruised loves, chaste intentions, and stifled accords, of relationships – those *Bezüge* that keep recurring in his poetry – of all manifestations of the life-force, of cosmic spirituality – of all this, he was the worker bee. 'Our compulsion is to plunder', he says in the same letter, 'the honey of the Visible, to hoard it in the golden hives of the Invisible.' And the Seventh Elegy – *hiersein ist herrlich* [to be here is magnificent] – raises, as a supreme monument beyond all man's monuments, the protest of the outstretched open, hand, like Rodin's hand, 'as a defence and a warning', *wie Abwehr und Warnung.*

Responsible for everything, death included. Death, which in his final throes he possessed so jealously, his own and not the doctors', just as he refused that of the priests. For there could be no intermediary between him and that which is so deeply and intimately his own: death, earthly dénouement and justification; death, immanent and permanent. All those around Malte Laurids Brigge, male and female, beloved family and chance acquaintances, revered geniuses and obsessing figures of secular legend, all are laid bare in the aspect of being dead, that is in the truth of their character. From that vantage-point, he can speak with them of earthly joys and sorrows, life's troubles and delights, for they have gained a vision of that which is exact and complete.

Through them he can enter the realm of the sublime Tenth and last Elegy, which is not in the beyond, but is still among our own domains. It is closed off to the pale blind beings of our common run, open only to the poets and to those who by violent and splendid effort have brought death back into our midst: for example Eurydice, our friend before and after and for ever. And in that strange but again familiar country, what does he rediscover, under the branching foliage, the sweet and gentle shade, if not the Lamentations, those young women, our loyal sisters? They receive the youthful departed and give him instruction. They do it again and for ever and to the same, unchanging, universal sorrow and song and reconciliation. For on this earth we are what we are, in all fullness, namely we are the dead who suffer, who, in this thoughtful intimacy with our own suffering, breathe out our melody of consolation.

Rainer Maria Rilke, before he left us, made a last stay in Paris during which we got to know him, to recognise him. He was then at the peak of his glory: no doubt he knew he had completed his work and could take time off to enjoy talk, whimsy and fashion. That friendly and smiling Paris was certainly no longer the Paris of Malte Laurids Brigge, of the stranger lost and penniless, the Paris we loved through him, knowing ourselves steeped in his romantic nostalgia, a Paris whose traditional places, the Luxembourg, the Bibliothèque Nationale, take on a slightly fabulous aspect because they are the scenes of a haggard, lowly, vagrant solitude. Strindberg's Paris is not much different, its cheap, family-run private hotels haunted by witchery. For all its kindness that is grateful in its turn for being so kindly celebrated, it is the image of this older Paris of Rilke, the Paris of his deepest memory, that I was delighted to rediscover in his eyes.

After that, thanks to a friend's generosity, he lived out his last months in a corner of the oppressive Alps: Valéry called on him and was shocked by their dreariness: as a splendid Mediterranean man he could hardly appreciate what pleasure one can take in such surroundings. No doubt for Rilke it was one of those places where the good things of earth ascend to the most exalted offertory. He said one day that for him this bleak terrain mysteriously united aspects of two lands he had loved, Spain and Provence – two of the loveliest parts of the world! Poets imagine these things, and we do not clearly see on what basis. In this last phase, it must be said, there was not only the search for a Thebaïd but the choice of a tomb, in short a pattern of intention that implies a heavy and morose sadness. The pilgrim was no longer content to have passionately adored his times of passage in places of sunshine, rich in history and luxury and inheritance, palaces inhabited by precious friendships, a subtle princely comfort that revolutions and wars must by now have wrecked for ever. Equally, through the successes of his late career, the poor Paris of Malte Laurids Brigge had become unrecognisable. He could only accept his retreat into a landscape of slow and melancholy austerity, and there await the gathering shade.

As for the correspondences and analogies he drew from them, once again they were his business. And that is precisely the business of poets. The business of philosophers is to create rationally and systematically, and does not call for their close personal involvement. They put aside their life-story, childhood and gradual development: they forget all that, and objectify themselves in the object of their studies, whose existence is all the more validated by being seen as independent of their own. Poetic creation, by contrast, comes entirely from the poet's being, from the traces that accumulate from the vicissitudes of his life. This is why a poet's work can only be understood in the long term. Only then can the reader, the generations of readers, indeed the poet himself, recognise the themes and symbols that impel him and hold his work together. Only gradually has the poet assembled his repertoire of familiar objects and meaningful repetitions. Here's something he says: why does he do so? He himself scarcely knows from what chance meeting or incommunicable memory it sprang, for what subconscious reason it occurred to him, what compelling affinity raised it from the undifferentiated morass into his line of vision. Then it recurs, insistent, and now seemingly certain that its insistence is well-founded; it has become his accomplice, and knows, better and more clearly than he, what till now he has only sensed; a leitmotif, combining with other motifs that are lodged in the poet's flesh and blood, in the irreducible of his character and his destiny, and these motifs illuminate each other and finally form the stuff of what will be this poet's system, his peculiar universe.

So we possess and study the peculiar universe of every poet, and that of Rainer Maria Rilke. His was formed by a prodigiously painstaking art, during the most profound human existence. Rilke's faculty of attention, his urbanity, reveal the dialectic of things: it's all a subtle game, a dance in which they appear and disappear, chase and dissolve, and in that very act establish an existence at a higher level. Words lend it their refinement; art compels them. Rilke's poetry, then, is tinged with preciosity. But all great poetry is precious, Rilke's and Shakespeare's, the English Metaphysicals and the Spanish *Conceptistas*, Petrarch, Mallarmé and the mystics. Preciosity is poetry's very essence: the necessary expression of the poet's intelligent love for the soul of the world.

All fervour is precious and relies on moments of delicacy...

...The interlacing of preciosity, or simply of poetry: the blend of themes, motifs, symbols which the poet's mind has finally grasped and mastered and which he now works to the limits of ingenuity: all that mathematics finally becomes plastic, as thought, music, and words all assume a form. It is in the constraint of a genre like the sonnet that we taste the joy of it at its best. My inspiration, observation, memory, dreams have supplied to me this image, this harmony, this strange line of poetry with its particular weight, its potency, its one or many meanings, its colours and rhythm, its secret known only to me, or to some other more deeply hidden inside me; and then this second line, and all this construction of lines. But it is unfinished, and there is a wiser and thus more fertile construction of lines to produce, the demand made of me by the squaring of the sonnet. The composed parts will be concentrated, will reduce to one last cipher; so many scattered associations will settle and not stir again, shrinking to the rigour of a point. And all that will make a whole. A creation will be created. The soul will become a face. For poems are soul, of the soul. But a sonnet is a face.

Rilke had a need to know faces. So his perfected art offered up to his master Orpheus fifty-five Sonnets which are one of the finest monuments of the German language and of world poetry, finishing in the supreme synthesis, and there is no expression beyond it, of the passing and the permanent, of being and becoming.

> *Und wenn dich das Irdische vergass,*
> *zu der stillen Erde sag: Ich rinne.*
> *Zu dem raschen Wasser sprich: Ich bin.*
>
> *(And if the earthly has forgotten you,*
> *to the quiet earth say: I flow.*
> *To the swift water speak: I am.)*

(Sonnets to Orpheus, 2.29.)

Form says: I am; form allows the poet to say: I am. This volition of form, impassioned and unexpected, can be felt in all Rilke's images and all along his spiritual course. In each major upheaval, at every encounter that he knew would be decisive, be it with a living contemporary like Valéry or a dead giant like Maurice Guérin, he felt the pressing need to wrestle with translation. Other encounters, no less illuminating and enriching, were like thunderstrokes of possession: Cézanne and Rodin. Here was this poet of a barbarian and Cimmerian tongue: we cannot avoid a certain pride, if it was our greatest painter and our greatest sculptor, through whom the French genius asserted its inalienable, essential character of plasticity, who most crucially compelled him, taught him, gave him his own self, raised him to the summit of his power. Someone no doubt, kindly and patiently distinguishing the nuances of Germanic culture, will remind us that Rilke was Austrian, of that same strain that produced Mozart and Schubert, and Vienna too, one of the permanent capitals of civilisation, a crossroads of peoples, cultures, aspirations: so much so, that Rilke's yearning for form and light was more than a German's melancholy, it was the effect of the natural civilised capacity that drew him into his travels and friendships, drew him to discover ideal homelands, be it an imaginary Denmark or a Russia steeped in Tolstoyan pity. Looking more closely at his origins, and plunging with him into the tangle of pasts and messages which he perceived as his inheritance, we realise that among so many claims on our recognition we must acknowledge him as one of the last Europeans.

Yet this European speaks German, and for an artist ravished by form and light, that is a hazard to be overcome. We French may be glad that in this battle he called to his aid these two figures who symbolise our nation's genius: the Painter and the Sculptor. The first, because his element is the light, he is all light; with him, objects strive in their own light and in his for that incomparable degree of scrupulous clarity; none more so than apples, their roundness, colour, delight: those apples which Rilke in his earthly myth-making sanctified equally with roses. As for the second, the Sculptor: his company, his example, the awesome sight of him, his beaming friendship – sadly blurred by a misunderstanding at the last – were perhaps the most invigorating Hippocrene from which Rilke's genius ever drank. The book he devoted to Rodin is not just about Rodin's art: it is about Rilke's poetic art. Rilke had discovered a dialectic of things, a De Natura Rerum: to this, he adds a whole study of a no less lively and subtle class, namely of forms. Forms at their birth, forms taking shape in space under the demiurge's hand, marrying their secret and vibrant wills to his. For in the flow of connexions and remarks that he makes on the adventures of things, as much as on the adventures of his

241

own destiny, the poet constructs his world of symbols: but the signs themselves, lines, colours, volumes, sounds and words, take on life and he must understand and assist them, and by close attention judge if their intentions match his own as a poet, and the demands of his creative spirit.

* * *

Is what is lost, lost for ever? In art, man's greatest effort against the void, there is a huge element of the 'unknown masterpiece' which will be for ever unknown, not just to the public, but to the artist himself, chafing that he cannot include his frustrations, his blank spaces, all the unsaid and unsayable. And in his debate with emergent forms he must admit to errors and misconceptions. What possibilities are suspended or cut off! What blunders and dramas, such as leave scars for ever on lovers' hearts! I imagine forms too could have their afterlife in the Tenth Elegy, where they would wander like the Lamentations, reaching in a sweet melancholy their delayed perfection.

They too have this paradise; and, like that other one, it is here. The artist's self-belief makes good the lover's disappointed and uncertain dream; gives the heart, overcome by it all, a reassurance and a guarantee; promises him the prize, the outcome, the welcome, that which is personal, alive, and unchallengeable: that shining apparition, the finished work.

Modest and mysterious are the intentions of the infant form. If they merge into a higher and stronger resolution, their demise is not in vain, but has all the fruitful value of a sacrifice, just like the docile, submissive, passionately resigned sacrifice of a poor darling sweetheart, a sacrifice to the artist's creative freedom. Pitting himself and his art against death, pushing it to the limits of his vigour, destiny and presence, the artist willingly and with rough joyous confidence accepts all that is submerged, incomplete, impossible, even absent and denied; and his acceptance is matched by that of whatever vanishes in the work's resplendent nuptial knot. Out of it all, he creates something positive.

Malte, straying among ghosts and their ghostly gibberings, among all that detritus, that march-past of palpable misery and unheard lamentations, became a workman and a maker. Nothing is lost, all is there. All, even unto death the signer and signifier, illuminator and celebrator, death which is life and which makes life alive. What power and strength were in this frail passer-by, so delicate, so sickly, so anxious about not seeing and hearing enough, not sharing enough, not saying enough, not saying it better! His whole work, a catafalque in an orchard of eternal blossom, sets up a solemn revelation of Being.

These passages are selected from Cassou's book *Three Poets: Rilke, Milosz, Machado*, Librairie Plon, Paris, 1954. © Mme Isabelle Jan.

Jean Cassou

Sonnet XVIII – the Rilke Sonnet

from '33 Sonnets Composés au Secret'

Stars, do not mind his going, since at him
you aimed your troubled shouts, your hue and cry.
Self-exiled, self-concealing, secretly
he wanders now at the enflamed world's rim,

a mere malignant ghost you cannot grasp.
Rainer Maria makes his Prodigal
Child run away just so, you may recall,
not to be cherished in that fearsome clasp.

Turn from him, friendly glances that confide,
heartfelt demands diffusing in the night.
And you, weighed down with pardons, you the dead,

cut out his barren sandbank from your flight.
He is the weeping stag that bows its head
and in its dreams comes nightly to your side.

Translated by **Timothy Adès**

Reprinted from '33 Sonnets of the Resistance and Other Poems', Arc Publications, 2002. © Editions Gallimard.

Yves Bonnefoy: Kieran Higgins

Yves Bonnefoy, born 1923, is a highly acclaimed French poet, essayist, critic, translator and art historian. He has been frequently mentioned as a candidate for the Nobel Prize for Literature. He was born in Tours, moved to Paris to take his degree in Philosophy, with further studies at the universities of Poitiers and the Sorbonne. After the war, he studied Art History in Europe and the U.S. In Paris he was closely associated with the Surrealists. Like Rilke, his central themes are existence, nature, death and the role of poetry. Like Rilke, too, he has said: 'I think, and in fact I have always thought, that poetry is an experience of what goes beyond words'.

Kieran Higgins is a professional translator living in Paris.

No-one's Sleep

(an extract)

> *Rose, oh reiner Widerspruch, Lust,*
> *Niemandes Schlaf zu sein unter soviel Lidern.*
>
> R.M. Rilke

i

We were at Raron, on a tree-lined track that climbs up to the church. Then, once there, where our eyes came up against the light, we took one of the lower paths with a view over the whole valley, and there it was: Rilke's grave. A wide but bare tombstone, like a blank page. Two verses were written on it, however. They could be translated into English as follows:

> *Rose, oh pure contradiction, joy*
> *of being No-one's sleep, under so*
> *many lids,*

but I am aware that much of the essence of words, even those that refer to the most simple concepts of existence, gets lost in translation. *Lust*, for example, sheds part of its meaning in the word *joy*, which might be better expressed as *sensuality*.

We stopped for some time in front of this grave to decipher the inscription, our senses overwhelmed by the shine off the stone. Then we looked up towards the sky and saw that it encompassed here an immense space, a whole region of the Valais stretched out along its river, among its vines: this is the wealthy 'lower country', behind which loom the high, deserted mountains. And finally we walked back down to the streets and small squares, amazed that our French language, the only one spoken a few miles from here, is already a barely known idiom in Raron, at least at the bakery or the hotel. A small observation, but one that reflects another level of the attention that up above was required more intensely.

The memory of the grave does not disappear, however. We were not struck dumb by the sight of it, despite the grandeur of the setting and the charm of the epitaph. Indeed, it was perhaps those beautiful verses that quelled the emotion normally aroused by places where a memory lingers. All the same, we are still close to it in our thoughts, and personally I feel that something is deepening within me – a sort of reticence or source of trouble – probably the work of the reflective unconscious that is as vigilant as a dream. I leave Rilke's grave, and I will soon leave the Valais, with the impression that I have been spoken to and I have listened, but perhaps inadequately, to the extent that I now need to try and listen better.

And today, some twenty years later, far from Raron, I will attempt to do so, picking up an essay I wrote at the time that makes little sense to me now – in other words, by taking up writing again, since no reflection can be properly pursued without putting pen to paper. Why should the people who accompany us during the moments that most mark us – to whom we will secretly dedicate the pages we write much later, never doubting that they share our thoughts – why should they not be just as present when we decide to understand an experience we shared with them? Why is it almost necessary to shy away from this game of questions and responses, from this vigorous exchange of voices that was so common among the Greeks, for example, and which Platonic dialogues have shown to be just as capable in going straight to the truth as any other form of thought?

There are certainly many reasons for this need for solitude, at least in our Western countries at this moment in history. This is something I have felt, often with some sadness, since the first day I set out to be a writer. I learnt, as we had all learnt by the end of the last century, that the notions we have, the ideas we form, be they true or false, cannot be attached to any defined signifiers that are easily explainable – cannot, in other words, be spelt out in a single word that is instantly understandable by the person we are addressing. We now know that the representations constructed by our intellect are networks, which extend deep into our internal thought processes, requiring the input of other ideas, sometimes unknown or dormant, to give them sense and shape. In this way, the many meanings contained in our words only become clear to listeners when they learn to interpret these networks, or at least some of the relations between them – a necessarily long process that cannot be accomplished in a heated and soon forgotten conversation. Each of us are texts that require deciphering even by those closest to us, and it is thus essential when addressing others to start in front of a blank page.

But there is another cause for this inward withdrawal, a cause that I understand or feel more acutely today than on that day many years ago, as I think back to the friend with whom we experienced it.

In our modern world of conceptual thought, we have lost the art of deciphering meaning from aspects of natural reality, as humans once knew how to do with such skill. We are no longer interested in learning from the setting sun, from the water that streams through a meadow or from the seemingly infinite layers of petals that make up a rose. Instead, we confine our astonishment or our worries to notions that have long become detached from these nonetheless evident external facts. In these conditions, it is hard to conduct a dialogue outside, in the presence of nature, with the friend with whom this anxiety is the shared core of both our thoughts, using simple everyday words to express our ruminations. It is better in these circumstances to turn to the written word, where the lost immediacy that we are so keen to recover can come back to life at any moment in the form of poetry, the fruit of our work with words.

Indeed, while our words are abstract on first hearing, this is less true of the phrases we form. Bringing together two words does not necessarily produce an idea, but it can take our conceptual reasoning by surprise, peeling back its logic to let the underlying notion through. And it is by writing in this manner, knowing that we have to slip between these walls of conceptual thought that determine to a great degree who we are, that we can hope to penetrate these walls with the light shed by a few phrases. Stretched over a whole page, these phrases can give substance to a life that has gone unexpressed in conventional words, and illuminate in the space our thoughts occupy the bright red of a bay or a shadow passing over the grass. In this way, we may be guided towards a horizon where, in the form of consciousness that draws directly upon the senses, the symbol will take shape among the colourless formulations.

This, in any case, would be a better way of asking what a symbol is and how it expresses meaning and reality. And this brings me back to Rilke's grave and the verses inscribed on it that seem to express, or so I believe, his most intimate thoughts. Let me return to the anxiety I felt when I returned to this low country.

What do I still retain of Rilke's epitaph, so boldly offered up to visitors to his grave, be they perplexed or understanding, and many of whom love his work? A sense of anxiety, yes, and even, as I have already hinted at, a feeling of unease, the impression that in deciding to place these words in this place something essential was neither understood nor felt, but which in this particular instance – a tombstone – should have been submitted to rigorous examination. A path was open but was not taken at the risk of suggesting Rilke himself would have eternally misunderstood it or even censured it. Yet it is in the experience of the greatest poets that its need can appear with the greatest evidence.

And so I return to these verses, or rather to their inscription, since their author expressly wanted them to figure on this stone. What is the meaning of these words, which are first and foremost an evocation of roses as they appear at the height of their bloom? Rilke wrote these words in the form of an analogy. The petals nestling tight against each other, with curves that for a few days are turned inwards towards the interior of the flower, so closed in on themselves although the light slips in through the porosity of their pale colours, making one think of the eyelashes that sleepers also keep shut, on what is intimate as much as invisible, but not without the day visiting these depths when the summer dawn invades their space, or during the peaceful siesta hours in Mediterranean countries that poets dream of. And a whole chain of thought was spawned by this poet, at least in these verses. The petals of the rose that has just flowered crowded in without flinching on this inexplicit interiority; one can even make out the corners of their lips which, like the lips of a Buddha, are gentle smiles, and in the sleep of which the rose is a metaphor, one can imagine the happy state of being at peace with oneself, at the simplest level of physical sensation, and one wishes to persuade oneself that this immediate and fully sensorial perception is a complete world in itself, and an accessible one: all one has to do is to abandon oneself to it without reservations, for example in the light sleep of an afternoon.

Such a thought is thus at the limit of thought itself and has abandoned its chimeras. In the untroubled breath of the sleeper unfurl the illusions that perturb the intellect, offering it vain hopes, troubling it with the fantasies that arise at the borders of the unconsciousness they create: it is this unconsciousness itself that dissolves, in the way that under the petal there is, amidst a yet more intense perfume, only another petal. And it is this idea of the individual, this invention of the Christian West, that breaks down in one's mind, giving way to the joy – or should I say the sensuality – of entering the fullness that has for too long blocked the dream of wanting to be. Is it thus a contradiction, to be 'no-one's sleep' under eyelids that remain human? In any case, this contradiction is 'pure', dismissively summing up all those that have escaped the human spirit throughout history, the last but unforgettable trace of the inadequate and dangerous logic of facts and events.

Moreover, the eyelids that Rilke believed he identified in the roses of his garden are numerous, even infinite, and this idea of a human existence free of personal chimeras draws on this aspect of a flower to create an analogy for the rest of society – this multitude that is a cause of anxiety because of its disorder – and to dream of a return by the whole of humanity to a form of existence that would be serenely natural, in a sleep comparable to that which the spirit – in this respect more original than human language – may seem to wish to pursue in the consciousness of animals, which attend to their needs without any intuition of a reality beyond that of their evident surroundings. The 'joy' expressed in these two verses is that of not existing with the non-existence of everything. And there are indeed other passages in Rilke's work where this idea can be found.

I open a French translation of his poems and read the rest of 'The roses'. I realise that Rilke clearly does not overlook another aspect of roses, one which, in the Middle Ages, or even during the Renaissance, recognised their cosmic structure, with spheres all stemming from the same centre, but still gave the human person a reality, and even an absolute one, since this cosmos was conceived and created specifically for him or her. Rilke was familiar with the rose that ancient theology considered a memory of finiteness and time as much as an image of the eternal. However, while the third poem ponders this dual aspect of the rose, the fourth decries this interpretation. Rilke writes at the end:

Summer: to be for a few days
The contemporary of roses

which expresses the desire for all consciousness to be suspended in the light. In other words, the 'no-one's sleep', even if this happiness can only last, in our Western countries, for a few days.

An even better indication of the indulgence given to this dream is to be found on the grave itself, on the terrace where Rilke wished it to be located. On this ledge one can see the whole of this lower valley, which is the meeting point of two languages and two civilisations. On the left, there are German-speaking regions, and on the right, there are French-speaking regions. And precisely at this point, at Raron, is where the line divides. These are two ways of being in the world and, because of their closeness, each are placed in perspective. In the Middle Ages, the unity of the word God surmounted such differences, denoting as it did, in both German and French, a fundamental truth whose universal obviousness overshadowed linguistic differences But today? What remains of this unity centred on a personal God, guaranteed as much as demonstrated by Him, after the collapse of the 'glorious lies' of his word?

Rilke's command of French was almost as good as that of his German mother tongue. He liked the look of it as much as if not more than the image he had kept, intense but troubling, perhaps painful, of his childhood years. He admired the languid forms of the 'no-one's' rose itself with its sensuality reminiscent of a Rodin sketch. And I am thus prepared to wager that he chose this terrace in Raron less for the beauty of its site than because it lies at the frontier of two languages, where their contrasts stand out, where their meanings and the actions they require appear illusory, leaving the rose in its summer bloom as the sole reality.

Was this really what Rilke was thinking in his late works, those written in the small garden at Muzot full of roses? In any case, it cannot be denied that this dream has given to what it desires between existence and the world such a beautiful face that some visitors to the grave consider that this rose with closed eyelids is not just one expression of Rilke's poetry, at least at the end of his life, but its perfect expression: they would even go so far as to call it a symbol. In their view, the rose of Raron is a symbol, and this symbol is the representation of an idea by a physical object, in this case a precise conception of life by one of the features of this place, which suggests a certain view of what poetry is. It should be understood that poetry is a thought that finds a figurative formula of this sort, in which some aspects of perception play a role of incitement or proof, enhanced by the appeal they exert on the poet's intellect.

iii

However, I am not prepared to recognise the rose on Rilke's grave as a symbol, at least in the sense that I think should be given to this word. And I even fear that the rose's predominance in this place overshadows an idea of what a true symbol would be, thereby stifling knowledge of the human condition that perception can, on the contrary, open up.

The first remark I would make is that when he speaks of the rose as he does, with this suggestion of a flowering at its peak moment, and with intense beauty, Rilke is aiming for much more than what is said in ordinary words, namely this supposed apex of colours, perfumes and forms that gives the flower for a few days a presence that the poet surely feels beyond the words with which he attempts to describe it. But the fact remains that in this fascinated contemplation, the author of these two verses has only focused on a few aspects of roses as he finds them. This implies that his apparent designation of a reality at its most intense is a lost contact with what, at the most profound level, it really is.

Loved for its eyelids and other charms that are almost carnal in nature, it is clear that the rose of the Rilkean summer does not offer up to its transfixed witness the thorn that swells its stem, the worm that already eats away at its corolla, the mark that spoils one of its petals, a forewarning of its withering. Rilke did not wish to see the rose of the botanist, nor the rose that the gardener clips, nor the rose that hurt him in Muzot or will hurt him. Of the flower he imagines, he has only focused on a few characteristics at the expense of many others, and of these, which principally appeal to the eyes, he has constructed a montage that is a substitute for his memories of reality as it is. And this is to forget what I have just called fundamental, and which I think should therefore be borne in mind even when, climbing up to the poet's grave in the light of a beautiful day, one is tempted to listen to the voice which, from its other side, attests to the absolute value of the experience of the senses. What is this other viewpoint that takes a step back from so much pleasure, and perhaps so much evidence? Clearly a finite form of thinking, the sentiment that reality is not what is apparent or the happiness one can derive from some of these agreeable aspects, but rather people and things, and in them the time in which they are born and to which they will one day fall victim. This admittedly makes them an efflorescence of nothingness, but it also makes them unique, each among the infinite number of existences: unique and, as such, absolute.

This reality – what I would call another way of looking at events or phenomena – is ignored, or pretends to be ignored, by these verses of Rilke. And remembering this other dimension of self-consciousness, the recognition of the individual being in his present state and location, it can easily be concluded that since these few verses, profoundly conceptual, have drawn into their abstraction everything they have borrowed from empirical reality, this epitaph is simply a linguistic trick, a mirage within another mirage despite the sensuality that runs through it. Conceptual thought: in short, a denial of the existence of death, a dream.

By kind permission of Yves Bonnefoy.

Philippe Jaccottet: Judith Bishop

Philippe Jaccottet, born in 1925 in Moudon, Switzerland, is a very well-known, award-winning French poet and translator. He studied in Lausanne, moved to Paris for several years and in 1953 went to live in Grignan in Provence. He has had visiting professorships in many universities in the U.S. including Princeton and Yale; and also in Europe at the universities of Geneva, Nice, Provence – Aix and Paris. His poems have been translated into English by Stephen Romer and Derek Mahon (*Selected Poems of Philippe Jaccottet*, Viking 1988), both of whom have featured in *Agenda*. Apart from his poetry, he is well-known for his own translations into French of, for example Goethe, Hölderlin, Leopardi, Musil, Ungaretti, Homer's Odyssey and Rilke. His translations of Shakespeare into French are held in high regard.

Judith Bishop, born 1972, lives in Sydney, Australia and is a poet, linguist and translator. Her first book of poetry, *Event*, is forthcoming in June from Salt Publishing, UK. She is working on a full length manuscript of translations of Jaccottet.

Fulfilment

> We are only mouth. Who sings the distant heart
> that dwells, intact, at the centre of everything?

To this wandering life without a nominated homeland, a life, in reality, subjected to laws no weaker for being less visible; to this life in which Rilke broke, one by one, all the inessential ties in order to resituate himself relentlessly – at the cost of efforts cruel to others and painful to himself – in a constellation of pure relationships; to this life that was deeply unified; and to the handful of places that played a determining role in it – Russia, Paris, Capri, Provence, Duino, Egypt and Toledo – was about to be added another, the Valais, which would enable its fulfilment.

Even before he has installed himself at Muzot, Rilke writes to Marie de La Tour et Taxis: '... *But what holds me back, that aside, is this marvellous Valais: I was imprudent enough to come down into this valley, as far as Sierre and Sion; I'd told you about the quite singular magic these places exerted on me when I saw them for the first time last year, during the grape harvest. The fact that Spain and Provence interpenetrate the physiognomy of this landscape in such a strange fashion had already deeply moved me, then – those two countries having given me a language more powerful and decisive than all others during the years leading up to the war: imagine, then, hearing their voices reunited in a vast valley in the mountains of Switzerland! [. . .] [T]hus the spirit of a great river (and the Rhône always seemed to me one of the most admirable!) carries through its countries its affinities and gifts. Its valley is so wide, so grandiose, filled with foothills in the context of the great mountain chains, that it offers to one's sight the most ravishing game of variations, akin to a chessboard composed of hills. A game in which these hills would be distributed, displaced–that's the effect (one worthy of Creation) caused by the rhythm with which the contemplated objects are ordered, an ordering which renews itself astoundingly each time one's vantage changes. The old dwellings, the old strong castles, move in this optical game with all the more charm for the fact that typically these dwellings have as their backdrop the slope of a vineyard, the forest, a meadow, or greyish rocks; and that they integrate with this backdrop as if they were images in a tapestry; with the most indescribable sky (almost rainless) taking part in these perspectives from on high and bringing them to life in an atmosphere so spiritual that the reciprocal positioning of things (just as in Spain) seems, at certain times of day, to manifest the very tension we feel we perceive between the stars in a constellation'.* So the great word is spoken. Enclosed, sheltered, in the centre of a landscape that's ordered like a poem – in which, at last, and once again, earth and sky are in harmony, in a world which seems appeased – Rilke can at last hope to rejoin (it's here or never) the heart of his inner universe.

In order to arrive there, he sets about updating a correspondence that has grown more expansive with every year, determined to interrupt it thereafter for whatever length of time might prove necessary. On the 26th November 1921, having hardly settled in, he writes to Gertrude Ouckama-Knoop, a friend from Munich whose daughter Vera – a girl who was very gifted at dance and music, but sickly – had died at the age of nineteen, asking her to send *some small object that Vera loved; something, if possible, that had been truly close to her.* On the 1st of January 1922 he receives, no doubt in response to that request, the notebooks in which Gertrude Ouckama-Knoop told about her daughter's illness, and thanks her for them: *What a unique and incomparable marvel is a human being! There appeared – at the very moment when everything which might, ordinarily, have sufficed for a long 'being-there' (being-where?) could have dried up in an instant – there appeared this excess of light in the heart of a young girl, in which, thanks to that infinite illumination, the two extreme limits of her pure intuition became visible: that is, that suffering is an error, a dumb misunderstanding which springs up in the body and wedges itself, a wedge of stone, between a unified heaven and earth – and, on the other hand, her open heart's complete accord with everything, with the unity of the world which is and remains, this yes to life, this emotional assent, given, up to the very last moment of her life, to the Here – but only to the Here? No (although she couldn't know it herself, under the first assaults of rupture and farewell) – to the All, something far greater than the Here...*

The unity of heaven and earth, already signified by the Valais landscape, was thus confirmed by the destiny of a girl who died in her youth. Throughout the month of January, Rilke still writes numerous letters, all open to the problems of others; but this sign which had come to him, signalling a destiny akin to those in which he'd always seen the evidence of Being–this sign which touched the closed and all but dead centre of his heart–brought it back to its most singular truth. Between the 2nd and the 5th of February, Rilke composes twenty-six sonnets, which he announces on the 7th to Madame Knoop: *In a few, gripping days, during which time I thought I'd be attacking other things, these sonnets were given to me.*

You'll understand at first glance why you have to be the first to possess them. In actual fact, however scattered the connection might appear (a single sonnet, the second to last, the 25th, inscribes the figure of Vera herself through the emotion that's consecrated to her), it animates and dominates the movement of the whole, and hasn't ceased to deepen the impression – but so secretly that I only recognized it bit by bit – of this irresistible birth that's shaking me.

Then it happens: more generous, violent and sudden than he'd ever imagined: after ten days' wait, the flood of poetry that never ceases to astonish us, either. That same day, the 7th of February, he writes the *Seventh Elegy*; the *Eighth* between the 7th and the 8th. On the 9th, the last verses of the *Sixth* (begun in 1913), and the *Ninth*. On the 11th, he finishes the *Tenth*. Immediately, he announces the completion of the whole to Marie de la Tour et Taxis:

At last,
> *Princess,*
>> *at last the blessèd day has come,*
– o how blessèd, given that I can announce to you the conclusion, as far as I can tell, – of the
> *ELEGIES*
> *numbered:*
> *TEN*
About the great and final one, whose beginning was set down, long ago, at Duino:

253

Dass ich dereinst, an dem Ausgang der grimmigen Einsicht, Jubel und
Ruhm aufsinge zustimmenden Engeln...;
this final one, which in actual fact, it was already understood some
time ago would be the last – about this one – I say – my hand still
trembles! – at this very moment, Saturday the 11th, at around 6 in the
evening,
it has just been finished!
    The whole of it in just a few days; it was a storm without name,
a hurricane through the spirit – as BEFORE *at* DUINO*; everything*
which is 'fibre and tissue' in me has cracked; as for eating during
this time, it was not to be dreamt of; God knows what nourished
me.
    But henceforth it exists. Exists. Exists.

Amen.

    So this is what I subsisted for, against all odds! And this was
really what was lacking. Only this.

But the surge continues: on the 14th, Rilke composes a new *Elegy*, called
the Acrobats, which he uses to replace the *Antistrophes* in fifth position,
at the centre of the cycle. This time, the composition is closed off.
Nonetheless, between the 15th and the 23rd, a new series of twenty-five
sonnets arrives to constitute the second part of the *Sonnets to Orpheus*.
Add to these two books – two mountain summits – a dozen important
drafts and *The Young Workman's Letter*, and all of that in less than a
month: there you have the quantitative measure of the miracle which had
come to reward the poet's long and patient wait. To take a measure of
the works themselves is another matter.

    For the reader of Rilke who remembers certain pages of the *Notebooks*
of Malte or his meditations on poetry; for the one who has breathed the
subtle essence of some of the *New Poems*, and still hears the inflections
of the voice rising from the 1908 *Requiem*, as if from the border of life
and death; if she has known how to listen to the *Elegies* and *Sonnets*, or
any poem from the final year, cast out in appeal to the gods of origin:
for that reader who has welcomed these successive proofs that Beauty
has *not* yet revealed her each and every face to us, and for the one who
knows, above all, that if this Beauty is a luxury or a lie, then light itself
must also be: for this reader, the assaults on Rilke by the doctrinaires
can only seem quite beside the point.

    No doubt the elements of doctrine that some have tried to deduce from his
work – and Rilke himself contributed in no small part to these deductions –
are, in the true sense of the word, arguable. Rilke replied to the pastor Rudolf
Zimmermann, who had probably questioned him on his religious position, on

the 10th March 1922: *As for the other part of your good letter, I can't respond to it today, other than simply to thank you for it. – Regarding the theme which you raise there again, I'm more and more inclined these days, anyhow, to allow it to be expressed, not by me, but inside my work, where it's to be found metamorphosed and remodelled, at its most intimate source. In discussions I would be too exposed, by temperament, to expressing myself in too hasty a fashion...* Far from avoiding the question there, Rilke was pointing out to his audience, ourselves included, that totality which we must read for: for no poem can be translated into prose as if it were nothing more than ornamented thought.

The *First Elegy*, which was written at Duino in January 1912, had begun with a question and a supposition:

Who, if I cried out, would hear me among the angels'
hierarchies? and even if...

At the same time, Rilke had noted down the beginning of what he foresaw becoming the final *Elegy*, and this beginning was formulated as a vow:

Someday, emerging at last from the violent insight,
let me sing out jubilation and praise to assenting angels.

And those *Elegies* which had been written last, in order to occupy a central place in the work, finish on a supposition which implies at once a vow and a question:

Angel! If there were a place that we didn't know of, and there,
on some unsayable carpet, lovers displayed
what they could never bring to mastery here – the bold
exploits of their high-flying hearts,
their towers of pleasure, their ladders
that have long since been standing where there was no ground, leaning
just on each other, trembling, – and could master *all this,*
before the surrounding spectators, the innumerable soundless dead:
*   Would these, then, throw down their final, forever saved-up,*
forever hidden, unknown to us, eternally valid
coins of happiness before the at last
genuinely smiling pair on the gratified
carpet?

[transl. Stephen Mitchell]

Even the beginning of the *Seventh Elegy* – which seems to celebrate

the drunk jubilation of spring and of summer, ushered in by the skylarks'
song – remains subdued by the reserve implied in the conditional mood
which introduces it:

Not wooing, no longer shall wooing, voice that has outgrown it,
be the nature of your cry; but instead, you would cry out as purely as
a bird
when the quickly ascending season lifts him up...

... Just like him
you would be wooing...

Oh and springtime would hold it...
                    [transl. Stephen Mitchell]

Questions, vows, suppositions, doubts: throughout the whole of the
Elegies the predominant mood is subjunctive, the mood of what is *possible*:
that's to say, at once uncertainty and opening. Even the firmest assertions,
the kinds of sentences one occasionally comes across (*To remain is to be*
nowhere – To be here is splendour – Conflict is second nature to us
[transl. Stephen.Mitchell]) must be understood as akin to knots, brief stops
amid this movement, this drifting, which the fundamental uncertainty
requires.

This movement began – the voice of the *Elegies* arose–because a painful
distance was experienced, on the one hand, between man and angel, and
because, on the other, that distance, however great, did not prevent the
angel's being glimpsed, from time to time, in its unbearable brightness;
thus, because of that *almost* which returns so often to the poet's pen, not
as a mannerism, but as what expresses and reserves the final chance for
human existence. A distance *almost* impossible to cross.

Thus, the doubts about our reality, and the hope of affirming it, which
are so tightly intertwined, underpin the ambiguous (and sometimes even
evasive or contradictory) form of this work which, were it any clearer,
would have been less true to experience. It's important therefore not to
look for the kind of sustained discourse, centred on a feeling, a scene, a
history, which characterises the ancient elegy, or even works such as
Hölderlin's *Return Home* or *Stuttgart*. Envisaged as paintings, the *Duino*
Elegies offers horizons that are unconstrained, changeable and often b
roken; but it would be less of a betrayal to compare them, instead, with
'fantasies', in the musical sense of the word (and excluding all frivolity
from its meaning), since each has its own tonality, its rhythm, its mood;
some of them developing almost all the themes which carry the movement

of the whole, others focused on a single one; some, such as the *Eighth*, playing on a single register, others, in particular the *Ninth*, embracing large intervals.

The great images of true and false ways of life that had haunted Rilke since *The Book of Hours,* though they, too, are subdued by initial ambiguity, return in this movement caused by the distance between man and angel, the tension between hope and doubt. Images of the void dominate the *Fourth,* the *Fifth* and the beginning of the *Tenth Elegy.* Their achievement in these poems justifies Rilke's assertion that each verse had to be a sum of lived experiences. Thus, the memory of the famous Munich Octoberfest, which in 1899 had already nurtured one of the *Visions of Christ* (*As I slipped through the crowd/suddenly I found myself at the prairie's edge/in front of a hut. Above the door /in poor and timid letters read: /The Life of the Passion of Jesus Christ...*) – combined, perhaps, with impressions of the Paris suburbs, and deepened by meditation, and deformed and magnified by dream–now springs up again in the landscape of the *City of Grief* in the *Tenth Elegy,* with its *huts for every bizarre thing,* in one of which you see *how money multiplies, anatomically,* and, *behind the last board,* begins *the meagre grass* where lovers, dogs and children loiter.

In the same way, a roadside scene mentioned by Rilke in his notebook on the 14th July, 1907, the spectacle of the saltimbanques put on by the Rollin family in front of the Luxembourg Gardens, is revived in 1915 by his long contemplation of a painting by Picasso on the same theme, and then becomes, in 1922, the singular image – bordering on real and imaginary – of the hard fate of a man whose work is likened to these pyramids of acrobats: that is, no sooner raised, at great risk, than destroyed: a tree from which there only falls unripened fruit.

These bitter and sometimes grating images, the complaints, and lines about the fragility and transience of man, in confrontation with the world – a distant echo of Job's complaint – interlace with, rather than oppose, the new and ancient images which exude a lesson of plenitude: like the fig-tree, disdaining to flower in order to fruit in secret (and what voluptuousness this dream reveals):

> *... and from sleep he plunges*
> *almost without waking into his sweetest work,*
> *as did the god, entering the swan...;*

or like those human figures to whom Malte became attached in his slow drift: lovers, saints, the youthful dead, or simple artisans, a pot- or rope-maker.

But these beings and things are no longer those he rendered so concretely in *New Poems*. The first movement, smooth or violent, which carries the poet of the abyss toward the angel (whose matrix, says a late poem, is *nothing other than the abyss*), leads his vision deeper and deeper into the inner space of the world (imaginary space or highest degree of reality). In this flux, things are merely signs, effaced as soon as they appear: designating not so much entities as directions. And as for the beings... If they are born out of real encounters, like the saltimbanques, then the song carries them over into that other dimension, where memory and desire tend to converge in glimpses set in unknown landscapes; but sometimes, the imagination's share increases further, and the interiorisation is amplified. Female figures, still intensely feminine in pose, voice, attractiveness (... *She says: / Far away. We live over there... Where? The boy/ follows. He is moved by her manner. Her neck, her shoulder... She's / perhaps of noble blood...*) are hardly more than emotions anymore, heart-dwellers: women, shadows or grievances; every thing and all beings have gone into the inner world, and the world becomes the heart: that place where angels can't be said to be real or imaginary, but are both at once, by some magic (and here it's timely to recall that none have recognized better than Rudolf Kassner that the space Rilke dreamt of was in fact a *magic* space, a space of *metamorphoses*, chronologically prior to the world of Christ and Logos, and therefore, necessarily hostile to it; and Rilke could not have read such passages as these from Kassner's *Zahl und Gesicht* without being profoundly moved: 'If there was no death, the lineaments and features of our face, our hands, our body would certainly be found in the orbits of the planets and the stars. In the very faces of angels and blessed spirits, the harmony of numbers and of faces are the same...' or: 'Angels are just such living forms or essential circles, miracles of face and number, children born of the marriage of absolute space with absolute time...')

Notably, Rilke writes this in a letter dated 13th November, 1925, in which he comments on the *Elegies*: *The affirmation of life and that of death turn out to be the same. To recognize one without the other would be–such is the experience celebrated here–a limitation which would end up excluding any sense of infinity. Death is the face of life turned away from us, unilluminated by us: we must try to attain the greatest consciousness of our existence, which is in its element in the two unlimited domains, and is inexhaustibly nourished by both... The true figure of life extends over the two domains, the blood of the supreme circulation passes into both: there is neither Before nor Beyond, nothing but the great Unity in which these beings which surpass us, the 'angels', are in their element.*

This is one of the statements – solemn-sounding and almost triumphant – in which Rilke seeks to define the ultimate meaning of his work after the fact. But how could the distance between man and angel have become so reduced, to the point where the poet, haunted from the outset by his anguish over death and love's failures, could have arrived at this positive affirmation? By what road could he have come? There was certainly the road of pure love, sanctity and heroism—which he knew he was incapable of following to the end. But beyond that was the road, celebrated by the *Seventh* and *Ninth* elegies, the one on which he had started out one day and from which he never parted: the world's transfiguration, the progressive interiorisation of perishable things through words:

> *Earth, isn't that what you want: to rise again*
> *in us, invisible? Isn't that your dream,*
> *to be invisible one day? Earth, invisible ...*

(here the juxtaposition of the two terms summarises the poetic aim).

It is important to understand what this means; and it will be better understood where the task of poetry isn't merely stated, but realised. Thus in the last verses of the *Eighth Elegy*, the most beautiful perhaps, completely consecrated to denouncing the difficulty of the human condition:

> *Who has turned us around, such that we*
> *have, in each act, the attitude*
> *of one who's leaving? As if*
> *from the last hilltop that displays for him, one final time,*
> *his valley all laid out, he turns and hesitates –*
> *we live this way, with each step taking leave.*

If Rilke never fell apart, though he could have done so often; if he never had to look for a remedy outside himself, in psychoanalysis, morality, politics or religion, it's because he was able to write lines such as these. He was able to observe such an evident truth as would seem enough to make life impossible to live, or else in vain; and *at the same time*, by means of the *image* with which he grasped that truth, he was able to inscribe it – without effacement or distortion—into an immensity which changes it, and into a metaphor which softens it; and by this means, to keep man and world *safe*. This experience cannot be proved, nor formulated: it can only be re-lived, intimately, by the reader. Poetry, finally, is that possibility of placing grievances in a totality that is able to absorb them.

What represents *victory* in the *Elegies* – what's able to answer to the anguish, and allows Rilke to say (at least for an instant, within a more uncertain movement), *To be here is splendour* – is the fact that poetic speech (this song which is, in essence, the inscription of lived experience within a foreshadowed totality) has remained possible, or become so once again, through all the trials.

Is the poet then the *only* one to be saved? Is Rilke's way nothing other than a pure aestheticism? Nothing of the sort. Rather, through all the doubts, the poet's role finds its justification as the one who maintains and recalls, while remaining, to a variable extent, outside of life and action: not living (or *half-living*) but only writing this possibility, apprehension, this chance at equilibrium and wholeness, which he sets against the powers of the void. It is admirably defined in the 1912 'Egyptian' parable, where the poet becomes the singer who gives rhythm to the movement of the rowers on the Nile: *In him the rush of our embarkation and the force of those who came to meet us were endlessly balanced, and if sometimes there was an excess, then he sang. The boat overcame the resistance; but he, the magician, he transformed what was insurmountable into a series of long and floating notes, which sounded neither here nor elsewhere, and which everyone welcomed. While his entourage kept taking on what was most immediate and palpable and overcoming it, his voice undertook to build a relationship with what was most distant, and we attached ourselves to it until we were carried along...*

And:

> *Between the hammers our heart*
> *persists, like the tongue*
> *between the teeth, which yet*
> *remains no less praise-giving.*

It's not much; and it's inestimable.

In this variable suite, whose register extends from long sighs to the most bitter dissonances and bursts of jubilation – this sensitive meditation, rich with deep insights into the risks and opportunities of man (of anyone, that is, not just the poet) – the vision is never farther-reaching than when it settles on the shadow cast by the youthful dead. It's as though Rilke's voice accorded, then, with an extreme note – a note heard by none before him – and his voice sounds truest at this range.

The ineffably tranquil verses which conclude the *First Elegy* with an evocation of the youthful dead –

> *No doubt it's strange, no longer living on the earth,*
> *no longer practising the customs just acquired,*
> *and roses, and so many other promising things,*
> *can no longer mean for you a human future...*

– open out at the end of the cycle into this limitless landscape, starred with unknown constellations: the Cradle, the Path, the blazing Book, the Doll, the Window, and the *M* meaning Mothers (those we always desired) – as far as that source which shimmers under the moon, the *spring of joy*, which is said to become a *river which carries all before it*, in the land of men; until, penetrating on his own *the mountains of the first Grief,* the young person who has died feels the silence and the space extending all around him – whom no-one, now, can follow:

And his footsteps sound no longer on the monotone path

If only we could recognize that pain is a ground of our being as much as pleasure is, then, instead of turning away from it, perhaps we would realize that even what *falls* is good, as is the rain in Spring.

The *Sonnets to Orpheus* come out of this same feeling of infinite calm made possible by the acceptance of death; and because they're all written at the same time, in the same happy and mysterious proximity which, twenty years before, the 'monk' in the *Book of Hours* had experienced when the tension of a long wait was finally released, they have a kind of serenity, a tranquil firmness (sometimes even a sort of childish gaiety), which the *Elegies* do not. But perhaps what had made this calm possible, finally, was the apparent luck of having read, a month before, the *Notebooks* written by Gertrude Ouckama-Knoop. A sensitive place in the poet's being, perhaps even the most sensitive, had been touched once again: the one which *young girls* and *death* had occupied together for a very long time (as a brief lyric drama begun in 1898 at Viareggio, in particular, demonstrates). Despite Rilke's dream of seeing some phallic god return in triumph over death in the Etruscan manner, the conjunction of death and the virgin (an object of horror for Germanic art, but one which acceptance of Vera had metamorphosed into a source of light) held a much deeper fascination.

Under the sign of the god who, like the angel, but in his role of singer, inhabits the two kingdoms without distinguishing too much between the living and the dead, and who brings a sense of order to fate, the sonnets are a tomb for the dead girl, this Eurydice who had made her goodbye into a dance – who'd accomplished the transformation that must be pursued always and everywhere:

Dancer: o transformation
of every passing thing into steps...

In a letter cited earlier, Rilke had mysteriously intuited a relationship

261

between the image of weighing scales and the idea of an epitaph. Thus while the *Elegies* are dominated by movement and are carried by it through all sorts of change and rupture, most of the *Sonnets* realize this magical sense of *balance* in their themes, images and form. They themselves are these very sensitive scales in which the weight of grief and that of praise, very slowly over time, are miraculously balanced by one another:

> *Only in the realm of Praising should Lament*
> *walk, the naiad of the wept-for fountain,*
> *watching over the stream of our complaint,*
> *to keep it clear upon the very stone*
>
> *that bears the arch of triumph and the altar. –*
> *Look: around her shoulders dawns the bright*
> *sense that she may be the youngest sister*
> *among the deities hidden in our heart.*
>
> *Joy knows, and Longing has accepted–*
> *only Lament still learns; upon her beads,*
> *night after night, she counts the ancient curse.*
>
> *Yet awkward as she is, she suddenly*
> *lifts a constellation of our voice,*
> *glittering, into the pure nocturnal sky.*
> [transl. S. Mitchell]

Underpinned by a (possibly ephemeral) serenity, the *Sonnets* can begin to accomplish what the *Elegies* hope for, and describe as a task. With uneven success, the *Sonnets* try to integrate into the desired whole not only what's most readily encompassed: apples, oranges, flowers, young girls, this or that memory of Russia or Spain; but also what seems to refuse incorporation: the machine (which must limit itself to being used), even the aeroplane (*The one who approaches from a distance/ will not be what he flies over, solitary/except in that moment where pure direction/wins out over the childish pride/of bigger and bigger machines*); the cruelty of the hunter or executioner: these multiply the correspondences and either enlarge or tighten their network, adding to the already sizable booty of images drawn from the visible and transferred to the invisible, including sometimes quite prodigious images, like this one, in the sonnet dedicated to mirrors:

You who waste even the empty room –
when the light dims, like woods on the horizon...
And the chandelier advances like a stag, great-antlered,
through your insuperable space...

Finally, the *Sonnets* approach the close-held secret of song itself. To say (as does the third sonnet of Part I) *Song is being*, doesn't mean that there is no authentic life other than the poet's, but rather, that there can be no song outside of true being; and moreover, as the preceding verses clarify, such song could never be covetous, greedy or demanding. Whoever sings, breathes (breathing being the primal form of exchange between the inside and the outside); but he breathes *in God*, and that breath is *for nothing*, like the wind, outside of any intention, in the forgetfulness proper to song:

To sing, in truth, is another kind of breath,
a breath for nothing. A gust of wind in God. The wind.

Conversely, to breathe is an *invisible poem*:

Do you recognise me, air, you, still full of my old haunts?
You were once the smooth bark,
curve and foliage of my words.

To sing while forgetting one sings, as this sonnet demands: this is what the first poem written in the wake of the storm of February 1922 had already posed as the condition of the authentic work, which it compares to the ball one throws into space, toward an *eternal partner* who is the world (the gender of which is feminine in German):

... It's
only by this risk that you can really play the game...
[...]

... out of your hands
the meteor flees toward its spaces...

As for this risk, taken in launching ourselves outside, toward the world: in a 1924 dedication to Helmuth Lucius von Stötden, Rilke will make this both the characteristic of human being in general, and paradoxically, our means of finding shelter in the All.

Philippe Jaccottet, *Rilke*, Éditions du Seuil, 1970: «L'accomplissement», pp. 143–165 (ISBN: 2–02–000087–3)

Edward Ragg

No Ideas but in Things:
Clive Wilmer's *The Mystery of Things*

Carcanet, 2006, £8.95

Clive Wilmer's *The Mystery of Things* establishes a relationship with Rilke in its very title; for Rilke is very much aware of the 'mystery' at the heart of human existence (not least how humanity connects, or fails to connect, with what Wallace Stevens calls 'things as they are'). In the Ninth Duino Elegy, for example, Rilke questions what we can take over with us into that 'other dimension' ('Ach, in den andern Bezug, / wehe, was nimmt man hinüber?'). For Rilke, this mysterious 'Bezug' implies a different mode of existence, another world which cannot quite be pinned down. In this collection, Wilmer is aware of a similar dimension, combining the particular with its nominal source: 'the invisible things // each frill and fibre / eternal power'.

However, where Rilke is more existentialist than Christian, Wilmer more frequently invokes Christian mythology to produce what is a devotional, literary and inspiring book. It is devotional because it scrutinizes the nature of faith and divinity; and because it reflects implicitly upon poetry's place in a tradition of devotional literature. For this reason it is also literary: the Bible and George Herbert are important presences. But, perhaps unsurprisingly, other literary forces come to bear on Wilmer's art: Dante, Shakespeare, Ruskin, William Morris and Wallace Stevens. These figures are not plundered for their 'mysterious' connotations: they appear, perhaps symbolically, because they have straddled the concerns of the secular and divine before (or have at least pondered what it might mean to have faith in something). For Wilmer is as interested as Rilke and Joyce in the notion of epiphany; and, like Blake, he knows that divinity resides in the human breast (particularly if that residence is a troubled one). What is ultimately inspiring about this poetry is that the poet's interaction with these major figures is on intimate terms with the reader, again reminiscent of Rilke who includes the reader confidentially in several of his major poems. Importantly, there is an impressive range of tones to the book that saves the devotional matter from sounding doctrinal.

Wilmer is keen, moreover, to explore the relationship between his own language and that of past literature: not as an explicit theme, as such, but as a realization of craft. This is apparent in 'To George Herbert':

Time and again I turn to you, to poems
In which you turn from vanity to God
Time and again, as I at the line's turn
Turn through the blank space that modulates –
And so resolves – the something that you say.

On a superficial reading, the self-conscious and self-reflexive quality of this poem might seem overplayed: the explicitly constructed enjambment of 'at the line's turn / Turn', the troubled or at least paradoxical relationship that exists between Herbert and Wilmer himself (that, for all the middle ground this poem wants to occupy, Wilmer is the echo of Herbert here whilst Herbert can only perhaps find new voice through Wilmer). But the poet would like us to go further: 'time and again' Herbert turns from vanity to God, just as 'time and again' Wilmer turns to Herbert but finds not a satisfied relationship with God, but a 'blank space' (just as, in an important sense, Wilmer does not necessarily find a satisfied relationship with Herbert). That space becomes a site for imaginative struggle: nothingness and doubt vie with faith and plenitude. As for Kierkegaard and Auden (who turned to Kierkegaard in the middle of his career), an apophatic relationship proves resourceful. Faith in poetry comes about by negative capabilities and Wilmer asks us to consider how a 'blank space', a potential place for inscription, can be a resolving force.

Wilmer can also cast a wry look at the desire to make literary allusions, as in a humorous piece like 'Much Ado about Nothing'. The poem's first line immediately follows on from its title, 'nothing' carrying also its Elizabethan connotation of 'noting':

signifying
a lot of fuss about fucking
or even about that primal quantity
known in those days as *naught*, as naughty,
As NO THING.

In fact, the poem almost spirals out of control in its desire to turn allusion, serpent-like, on itself:

For nothing doing. Since nothing
Shall come of nothing.
              Yea,
do on then this nought
else that thou do it for God's love and
nothing have these nothings if this be nothing

that is not there;
                 and the Nothing that is
our inner man clepeth All.

Here the allusion to *The Winter's Tale* (Leontes's jealous troping of 'nothing') and the end of Stevens's 'The Snow Man' coalesce, sparring with so many other allusions that it would be hard to discover Wilmer's poem were it not for the wit underpinning the desire to allude. What makes this a compelling book to read, in fact, is the poet's attention to the nature of allusion as an instructive force. Wilmer reminds us that there is much outside literary allusion that actually gives allusiveness its vitality (the opening poem 'Bottom's Dream' is a playful reminder of the 'bottomless' nature of association both as inspiring and bewildering phenomenon). As Stevens makes clear in his 'Adagia': 'Literature is the better part of life [...] provided life is the better part of literature'. In poems such as 'For my Daughter's Wedding', 'Wonderwoman', 'Chutney' and 'W. S. Graham Reading' Wilmer makes good Stevens's adage to an impressive degree.

Such a dialectic hinges, in this book, on Wilmer's scrutiny of 'mystery'. Certainly, the word proves etymologically compelling (perhaps not surprising given Wilmer's attention to such loaded words and concepts as 'visitation', 'stigmata', or ghostliness). The Greek origins of 'mystery' imply one who is initiated; also the act of closing ones eyes or making sounds with closed lips. To reveal mysteries is perhaps always to risk disclosing too much (or too little) about a treasured, if elusive, essence. This is a precipice upon which Wilmer's poetic pivots. The word 'initiation' implies beginning (Shakespeare uses 'initiate' as an adjective, as in 'the initiate fear that wants hard use') as well as instruction. But Wilmer is careful not to look for an ephebe or pupil, perhaps because he wants his readers simply to begin to look carefully at the contours of things, hence the book's attention both to various painters and the mere attractiveness of objects in a vibrant world.

As 'The Falls' asks:

Did Jackson Pollock
                 when he painted *One*
know the Lord's beauty by it?
                 What we call
randomness –
                 the white stream
lashed over brown and purple
                 sprayed and flecked –

266

                    not at all
                        deep canyons of the underself
        but the order in which things fall
                        or what intelligence will make of them.

I like the mimetic movement in Wilmer's lines here (seemingly matching
Pollock's flecks and sprays); and the enjambment is cunning: 'not at all'
rejects the notion that Pollock's work amounts to nothing but randomness,
but it also describes that work as comprising 'not at all / deep canyons
of the underself'. There is even an attractive elasticity in the title *One*.
Wilmer probably refers to Pollock's 'One: Number 31, 1950', but he may
also have an earlier painting 'Number 1, 1948' in mind. Such a poem
certainly prepares one for the book's later concentration on Piero della
Franscesca's painting *Resurrection* (part of which also adorns the volume's
front cover).

   If there is an intersection between people and things, it partly resides in
the marks and noises humans make (as a naturalist or pragmatist might say).
Let me turn to Wilmer's 'Stigmata' because this series says much about
how *The Mystery of Things* labours to make noises and scratches (a 'stigma'
is, after all, a mark), to sing somewhere between mystery and physical
reality, as Rilke sings between the realm of his angels and natural phenomena;
and, in fact, to show that the physical is always already mysterious.

   Wilmer suggests there is a spiritual economy in linguistic labour, as
the two poems that comprise section XIII of the 'Stigmata' series, 'The
Names of Flowers' and 'The Desert', demonstrate. In 'The Names of
Flowers', whose first two lines could well have been spoken by Rilke
who had learned about sculptural qualities from Rodin, we read:

                    We are
        Sculptors of air and what we make is speech,

        The given world as moulded to our needs
        In our design. So coursing through our frames
        The matter of our speech is briefly molten,

        Soon to be set in grammar, prosody
        And vocables. And so, in naming flowers,
        Your beauty makes a beauty that knows theirs –

        Teaches that what I name cannot be mine,
        Who, living in my words as in the world,
        Work to give utterance to that which is.

Paradoxically, it is precisely because 'the great world' is replete in 'all its rich redundancy' that marks, stigmas and stigmata matter. They must not only be invested with human meaning: that meaning must be earned in what, for Louis MacNeice, is an 'incorrigibly plural' universe. As if to reinforce the point, Wilmer adds 'The Desert' to section XIII (all other sections of the sequence being allotted single poems), to which I will turn in a moment. It is as though the poet emphasizes the extra work human language must always expend as an evolving, adapting tool, responsive to practical and spiritual preoccupations.

But are these tightly wrought poems themselves emblematic of 'the mystery of things'? If these poems labour, they are hardly laboured. I think Wilmer is attempting to find a diction that can only ever have a vital connection with 'things': in that idealist loop in which palpable physical objects are brought to life not merely by the senses but by the mind's activity (what, after all, the senses amount to). The mind continually reconstructs the world, but only really knows the pressure imagination bears when the world threatens to disappear before us: to become imaginatively stale and thus invisible. As Wilmer observes in 'The Desert':

> But when the richness leaves us, you leave it,
> And stone, sand, thorn and the stigmatic flesh
> Become the matter of the universe.
> Here is the proper place for meditation.

Note how it is '*the* stigmatic flesh' that takes on a similar substance to stone, sand and thorn – each with their Biblical connotations. The latter group are objects already capable of marking and changing the human body; but Wilmer enables us to consider also how flesh is stigmatic (not merely a recipient for bodily marks but an agent that marks the souls and lives of others). Looking back at the book's front cover – with its detail of bleeding flesh from *The Resurrection* – one is reminded of the dual signification of Christ's suffering: we imagine bodily pain, but we are also alerted to *the* stigmatic flesh as symbol.

All in all, Wilmer writes tightly and expansively: a combination that is hard to pull off. And there is mystery indeed in the turns and twists of these engaging poems.

In 'The Need for Angels', the epilogue to 'Stigmata', Dante draws a picture of his lost Beatrice having imagined her visitation as an angel. Drawing becomes a complex, if unwilling, prelude to writing:

> he went on drawing, drawing
> not yet writing.

You draw what you see,
but at times
not with the eye.
Dante, drawing,
knew her alive and,
knowing it,
wrote his poem.
Wounded,
writing it.

Where this collection attends to poetry's relationship with the visible made invisible and the invisible revealed, it collaborates with Rilke in showing fidelity to the mystery of things.

Paul Stubbs

To The Silenced – Selected Poems of Georg Trakl
translated by **Will Stone**

Arc Publications, 2005, £10.95

The task set themselves by most major European poets of expressing what it feels like to be alive in any one epoch does not, on the whole, apply to the poetry of Georg Trakl. The world outside was always something seemingly out of joint, screened off from his conscious awareness of it. His human existence appears to us now like a fragment of unearthly phenomena, which never could consist of the sum of its parts. Instead, he lived his life inside the body of a self already lost. His poems on the other hand are so acute, so memorable, that they seem born of a chronic poetic infection, an incurable destruction of their host by words. We feel the power of his images as though we were watching the 'negatives' of God's own creationist film clack and shudder onto the spools of pure space. Thus we witness image after image flash onto the retina of our mind's eye:

'Eternity's icy wave would devour man's golden image'

'I sing you wild fissure.'

'Light with magnetic scourge drives out the stony night.'

The translator Will Stone subtly and beautifully ushers us into those 'pure spaces' where the projection of Trakl's mind is forever being played out. Those interested in discovering such a major poet should, in this book at least, immediately isolate themselves from the arguments for and against translation. Stone has given us almost a bone-by-bone crib rather than a word-by-word one. Like a palaeontologist reconstructing the image of a creature from a distant past, Stone assembles this wonderful resurrection, always allowing Trakl's voice to be spoken through the two now assimilated minds.

In Trakl's poetry we have the 'image of man' continually disrupted, pared down, marginalised by the phantasmagoria of the world opening up inside his head. Trakl embodied a feeling of oncoming extinction by casting aside his own body-weight in words, as if dust thrown from the palm of his hand. As in the war poems of August Stramm, who died in

1915, a year after Trakl, we see a language stripped back to those flashpoints of the psyche that need no stylistic device or usage of language to render them as 'poetry'. And it is because of such 'flashpoints' that we feel his experiences so compressed into the moment, so undeflectable as mirrors of mortality. In this seminal book of translations, Stone has managed to put on and take off, from poem to poem, the masks of those faces which Trakl felt itching most beneath his flesh:

'But in dark caves a mankind more silent bleeds
from hard metals forms the redeeming head.'

To translate great poetry effectively, the translator must at times possess a sensibility as heart-rending and haunted as the poet whom he is translating. Stone, a supreme individualist himself, achieves this with translations that permanently affect the reader with their formidable knowledge of what is being accounted for. His experience in handling such European poets as Nerval, Baudelaire and Rodenbach lends these translations great vitality and resonance. Stone has tapped-in brilliantly to what Trakl really was: a visionary (a term nearly every purblind or myopic English poetry critic has for years been attempting to neologise into something more acceptable – vision as 'foresight' or 'temperament'.) We should treasure this collection for reintroducing to the English speaking world a poet who never quite allowed 'reality' to disrupt his slipstream of almost pure being:

'On to the grave goes space
And into dream this earthly passage,'

Traditionally German Romanticism focused on a myriad of interrelated themes, including nature, longing, the occult, night and death. In the poems of Trakl we receive all these in a work of almost supernatural power, with the evocation of the soul and the deliverance of man's image at a time when it had never been more in doubt, never closer to being demasked.

Will Stone's greatest accomplishment in this book is to arrive at Trakl's side as a living counter-force to the work, treating the original lines as one treats a wound. Stone, whose poetic glance never displaces the original sound or music of the poems, captures Trakl's precarious balance between obscurity and lucidity. Recognising the handicap of Trakl's relative unfamiliarity among English speakers, the translator's comprehensive introduction and biographical notes provide a valuable contribution to modern literature. Of course we discover the lurid facts regarding Trakl's mental instability, alcohol and drug addiction, the fiercely debated theory of his incestuous attraction to sister Grete. But the real achievement of this introduction is to inform us of a life lived firmly in the grip of suffering – not just the product of a schizoid personality, but of an imagination impatient for the potential of poetry to find a suitable match, to locate the most enduring mask for each persona, to name those unnameable beings who walked, crawled and (with great psychological effort) surfaced eventually up onto the pages of his poems. It is these 'unnameable beings' that catapult the reader's mind into the kind of compulsive concentration necessary to endure the boundless reaches of Trakl's mind.

This endurance takes us finally to those last great poems: 'Klage' and 'Grodek'. In the latter we witness 'red clouds, in which a wrathful God resides,' and a state of despair where 'all roads lead to black putrefaction'. These lines should not be so surprising given the horrors endured by Trakl as medical orderly in the Austrian Army in the early stages of WWI. I think Trakl's contemporary Gottfried Benn, noting the atrophy of the senses caused by that epoch, should have the last word: 'A people's or a race's degeneration always seemed to me to imply a decline in the number of men born with the potentialities and the secure source of inner values that enable them to give legitimate expression to the essential nature of that last, late phase of their own civilization and to carry on, in spite of all obstacles, toward an undefined goal.'

Two Chosen Broadsheet Poets:

Adam O'Riordan and Zoe Brigley

Adam O'Riordan was born in Manchester in 1982 and read English at Oxford University. He studied poetry under Andrew Motion at the University of London where he was awarded the inaugural Peters, Fraser and Dunlop poetry prize. He currently works part-time for the publisher Enitharmon, and as a tutor. In 2006, he was awarded an ACE writer's bursary, and this year he will begin a Ph.D on Michael Donaghy. A pamphlet, *Queen of the Cotton Cities*, of his poems is about to be published by Tall Lighthouse.

Small Adult Skull

The dome I hold is an empty cathedral
at the minim rest in an organist's rehearsal.

No clues here to a life
however the shadow-play
of my anglepoise might
attempt to aggregate a face,
feign grief, surprise, delight.

It waits like a glass box
in a bankrupt jeweller's.

This monotony of bone
is a snapshot of the moon.
I turn it through its cycle,
feel its pull: from swaddling
-cloth to specimen case.

I contemplate it for hours on end
but it gives up not the briefest song.

Blossom

This knuckle
           of blossom
twisted from the branch,
held like a match
to your sleeping face

so the next breath you take
           will draw you
from a private dark,
slow the carousel
of blood-bright shapes,

as ammonium carbonate
           or a burning feather
might revive a castaway;
naked, salt-bitten, sun-wrecked,
the wind at her heart.

The Hands Of An Apostle

The finger tips and palms come together
to case the prayer they hold inside them
and carry the words a little closer to heaven.
Dürer scratched this attitude of devotion
in lines fine as a banknote. Turned landscape
and it's one hand bent to break
the surface tension on a font of holy water,
a child's game of church and steeple,
the palms of strangers at a dance,
the convict's greeting through the glass.
The whorls turned away from other flesh
content themselves with the dull pulse
in the replica they rest against.

The Moth

landed between *paper tiger* and *paper weight*
on the open dictionary, just short of *Papillon.*
A natural under the spotlight,
which must have drawn it from the night's
hot lung towards its sixty watts of promise.
Perfect, the disciplined pulse of its wings;
two coffee-stained teeth and all the grace

of your grandmother in her wedding dress.
Which you will know from the message I left.
But I didn't mention the crane flies, the midges,
that I'd had to kill the lights and I'm sitting
on a bed too small to contain your absence,
listening to something the size of a small bird,
ricocheting off the walls, clicking like a stuck tape.

Anchor Work
For ACO'R on his 84th

I picture you on the rocker in your attic,
still buoyed by that menagerie of vice;
Panther cigars and Famous Grouse.

While under another summer's legacy of dust
your whetstone dreams of how it once
burnt the blunt edge off a scythe.

A lifetime away I thumb the seamanship manual
you sent to me, the dimmed-delicate colours of 1937
where a swastika is still marked *Merchant.*

The lists of distinguishing badges;
W inside the Star of David to signify Writer.
A coding and decoding which, at this late hour,

you may have begun to forget;
like the years of hoisting and hauling the colours
of ships in commission while the flag on the jackstaff

flutters and rumples in the harbour,
where perhaps we hear a six gun salute
startle the gulls into motion.

I set this down: a snick of lead hidden
in the grooves of a barrel made for blanks,
to cut at the jackstay, strike the topmast,

raise the frail rigging of your ribs into utterance,
set your tongue at the watertight doors of your lips,
renew your habit of affirmation through speech.

May these words be enough to maintain your soundings,
as when struck by a squall, a lace line is attached
to the throat of a sail on a splintering mast.

Zoe Brigley is a young Welsh writer whose poems appeared in Broadsheet 4. Her poems have been published in various magazines and journals, and she has appeared in anthologies such as *The Gift* and *Reactions 4*. She received an Eric Gregory award in 2003. She is currently working on her Ph.D thesis at the University of Warwick where she teaches creative writing and literature part time. The Ph.D thesis is on three contemporary women poets associated with Wales: Gwyneth Lewis, Pascale Petit and Deryn Rees-Jones.

Calendar

• • •

My gullet:
a snake pierced
by arrows.

• • • •

To lash by beast.
To slay by wind.
To strafe by flood.
To void by rain.

⁖

Besieged, hated are our towns
and compounds ringed by cactus.
They play the conch shell and drum
at gates all night; not even
their lights tempt us from haven:
the chrysalis bud: a wick
that bursts wingspans of flame.

Epithalamion

*These stars, the Pleiades, guard our spirit and seed; these are the
home for the Dakota's fathers.*

Infinity
Street lamps brighten, the sky fades orange;
stars are dull, become a clue to laws
of other times, relics: the stone walls
found under Antarctica, pyramids that spelled
the stars of Orion's belt, tunnels burrowed
in stone to gaze at planets;
regret is round as a circle and can be worn as a bracelet,
but is deeper than the lake in a brown-headed wood
where they dive at night not finding the bottom

Crown
When night-fall drapes the horizon
the singing begins; first in the stars,
the sniff of a feathery nose,
a hunt in night-beds and cells,
then in the erotic charge of one
the hungering desire of the North Star's orbit,
that outstretched love of moon for water;
for in the love of women, the love of men
each must gift the other's head with stars.

Meon Hill

Did you see a stranger with a long grey switch,
his iron shovel mining for a coin or trick?

I am broken ramparts, a nunnery tumbled;
for like the Ploughboy at Alveston, I see
the black dog and ride by tree-trunks
on intricacies of leaves: the sign
of the cross at my throat and ear.
Where I tend the slopes and hedges,
banks and cornfields near Meon,
my trouncing hook juts out an extra digit.

Herbs so hearty: Devil's Parsley.
Shepherd's Purse: Devil's Curse.

I am an apple bitter of rind: I fall
seedless. Yet I would be the Woodsman
stripping bark to bristling choke, or
piercing vegetable matter to a white eye.
At night I hear the owlish, hooting hounds,
the feathery sniffing of their noses,
the bright clink of claws in the lane:
the Ploughboy's red-eyed guardian mastiff.

Leaves in the lap: Devil's Nightcap.
Nightingale sing: Devil's Plaything.

Leaves that die on the boughs sound out
the sea on shingle; here the hound hangs
by its white eye, the fields dug with toads.
I feel the node of every pitchfork point
and lie beneath the dank brook-bed
binding the Devil to his own delight.
Such a long lesson in learning
how to wear my sex like a jewel.

On Meon Hill, the Devil dropped his load
by the lane that runs along the turnpike road.

Our Lady Of The Rock

And the angel of the Lord found her by a fountain of water in the wilderness, by the fountain in the way to Shur. And he said, Hagar, Sarah's maid, whence camest thou and whither wilt thou go?

— Genesis 16.7–8

It wakes Sarah – the same bright yellow dawn
                as on the boat that brought her
        and coaxed her, onto deck to watch
white cliffs, the horizon.

She opens windows wide over the street:
                these jostling roofs, the abbey:
        spiked towers on the hill, its shrieks
out-stripping the swallows.

To stretch above and reach to wry brook-beds,
                is watching close: a man's step
        (the bats squeal evening and night:
always the flapping wings).

The café where her sister sits; Hagar
                at table, her black hair tied
        round her head, coiled in feint of sleep,
proving her white bare neck.

Notice the flash of white cotton, the glare
                at the window and how these
        shutters close. The serene dun lulls,
gifts Sarah's head with coils.

                Then Sarah at table, still the cherub.
        Their mother watched her mouthing,
                jawing in the choir's front row.
                Hagar gets up to leave;

                turning her face to the hotel she finds
inside the room is clean and

bare – the book and window agape.
　　　Past the abbey, the grass,

　　　　　grows wild, long strands caught in cross-hatched breezes,
tips swirling: black and white dots
　　　between TV channels. Angels
　　　　climb ladders to the spire.

　　　Sitting cross-legged on the stone floor, dozing
like Jacob, cold was creeping
　　　through her dress. The last mural is
　　　　crumbling: a woman

　　　　　lifting dish to boy's mouth and the other
watching with bow and bright shaft.
　　　'Hagar and Sarah', he said in English
　　　　and the rhyme of steps followed her outside.

The Jewel-box

*Herr K. is to be put in place of your father just as he was in the matter
of standing beside your bed. He gave you a jewel-case; so you are to
give him your jewel-case.*
　　　　　　　　　　　　　　　　– Sigmund Freud, *Case Histories I*

I become a closed garden, collapsing castle. Yet hear that!
A knock at my crag: a buzzard's reach of nesting thatch,
brim of nails, bone or teeth. Remember the rivet grip and
the ram. My lover is a pauper to whom I gift my fingers
as music for speaking and silence; yet I am a soldier.
I do not beg for fleshly talk, a luxurious bed: muscling
in a square room, I bring love. Who is that there raveling in
the closed garden? The ram, who will have my purse, brings
a pearl and a boy knock-knocks at humming piano keys.
My love is the thrum of brown nightingale, for he sings
the bell of me and recalls begging entry. *Who shall enter?*
Remember the widow: she, of knitting or dam, spindles
at my door. But who will come in? My love knocks at pearl
and purse; yet I am a square room with such long lessons
in my fingers, tokens of paupers. But still a knock-knock
at eagle's defiance, at a buzzard's reach. Now will you not come in?
A pauper without, I tap at doorframes and windowpanes.

Notes for Broadsheet Poets 8

For number 8 of this ongoing series, two important manuals for poets young and old come immediately to mind. The first, which was already alluded to in **Notes for Broadsheet Poets 1**, is **Rilke**'s not enough known *Letters to a Young Poet* originally translated by M.D. Herter Norton (Norton, New York), and, more recently by **Stephen Cohn** (Carcanet, £9.95) who features in this issue. Quotations from this text in the ensuing pages are from Cohn. The second manual very well worth purchasing is the 'Afterword' and 'Appendix: Fourteen Notes on the Version' at the end of **Don Paterson's** *Orpheus: A Version of Rainer Maria Rilke* which has recently been published by Faber (£12.99 hardback) and will soon appear in paperback. Hannah Salt, who teaches at the University of Vienna, stated in her review of the latter book in *Magma 37* (Spring, 2007): 'Paterson's 'Afterword' is a permanent contribution to Rilkean studies and will, I suspect, be read long after his versions of the Sonnets'. Thanks, then, to Faber and to Carcanet for allowing us to quote from the two above texts here.

*   *   *

The ten letters which comprise the manual (interestingly the same in number as the *Duino Elegies*) are what the aspiring young poet, Franz Xavier Kappus, calls the ten 'important' letters saved from his correspondence with Rilke about his own poetic strivings. In them, as Kappus attests, 'a great and unique man' speaks. There is no doubt that Rilke was a purist and uncompromising in his approach to his role as a poet. He believed that one's personal life should be sacrificed for dedication to the art, and that a profound, questing approach to life was as important for the aspiring poet to have as inspiration and a grasp of craft and technique.

In Letter One, written from Paris, 17 February 1903, Rilke advises Kappus: 'There is only one way. *You must go inside yourself*. You must seek for whatever it is that obliges you to write. You must discover if its roots reach down to the very depths of your heart. You must confess to yourself whether you would truly die if writing were forbidden to you'. He continues to tell him to choose subjects which his daily experience offers him: his sorrows, hopes and preoccupations; the images in his dreams and the objects held in his memory. He adds: 'If your daily life seems mean to you – do not find fault with it; rather chide yourself that you are not poet enough to evoke its riches; if one is truly creative there is no such thing as poverty, and no place that is poor or meaningless'.

In Letter Three, written from Viareggio, near Pisa on 23 April 1903, Rilke gives more wisdom. 'To be an artist means that you cannot enumerate or calculate but must grow as the trees grow – letting the sap flow at its own pace, standing firm through the gales of spring, never fearing that there will be no summer. For there *will* be summer'. He continues to impress on the young poet the painful lesson he himself has to learn every day: '*patience* is everything!'

In this same letter, Rilke compares the experience of the artist to sexual experience: 'they are really only different manifestations of the same longing and of the same fulfilment.' The poetic force, he says, is 'strong as a primal urge'. Here Rilke is talking about 'sexual' 'in its largest and purest and most generous meaning' which means loving as 'a human creature', and not only as a male when love can become 'disfigured'.

In Letter Four, written at Worpswede bei Bremen on 16th July 1903, he recommends the young poet to stay close to Nature – 'to the small things which scarcely anyone notices and which can for that very reason invisibly lead to what is great, what is immeasurable'. He urges: 'What matters is to live everything. For just now, live the questions. Maybe you will little by little, almost without noticing, one distant day live your way into the answers'.

He asserts that 'the principle of motherhood is to be found in the male as well, corporeally as well as abstractly, for the act of begetting is a kind of giving birth, and surely, man also gives birth to whatever things he may create out of his inner riches'. His rumination here links back to what he said in the previous letter about the similarity between sex and composing a poem.

'And if what is close to you is distant', he urges, 'it means that your own distance reaches out beneath the stars and is very great...'

In Letter Six written in Rome, 23rd December 1903, he talks about the poet's necessity for the right kind of solitude. 'There is only *one* kind of loneliness, and it is great and is not easy to bear... What is required is this: solitariness, great inner solitariness... To be as lonely as we were when we were children'.

In Letter Seven, also written in Rome on 14 May 1904, interestingly, he writes about having copied out, in his own handwriting, one of Franz Xaver Kappus's best poems, a sonnet, and Rilke returns it to Franz as a present 'for I know that it is important and can be a new experience to rediscover a work of one's own in another's handwriting. You must read the poem as if it were a stranger to you: you will feel at the deepest level how very much it is your own'.This is something well worth trying for every poet, to read one's own poem as if it were somebody else's and in that way distance it from oneself, which enables one to appraise it more objectively.

In Letter Eight, written from Sweden on 12 August 1904, Rilke claims that it is our griefs which, if we properly let them into us, enable us to grow. Wrongly dealt with, 'we may die of them', but we can turn the negatives around, for Rilke believes 'that virtually all our griefs are moments of energy' – 'even sorrow is transitory; the new thing that has supervened has entered into our heart, has occupied its innermost chamber and is no longer even there – it has already entered our blood... We have been changed as a house changes when a guest enters it. We cannot say who has come, we shall perhaps never know. But there are many indications that it is the future that enters into us in this way, in order to be transformed within ourselves, long before it actually occurs. And that is why it is so essential to stay solitary and attentive when in the midst of sorrow'.

He then continues to ruminate upon our destiny. 'We must accept our destiny however far it may chance to take us: everything, including the inconceivable, must be acceptable within it. In the end this is the only valour that is asked of us: to be brave in the face of the most unheard-of, the most marvellous, the most inexplicable things that we may possibly encounter'... 'For if we can imagine each individual destiny as a greater or lesser space, we shall see that few people come to know more than a corner of their room – a window-seat, a strip of carpet to pace up and down. And this gives them security of a kind. And yet, a perilous uncertainty is so very much more human...'

In Letter Nine, also written from Sweden on 4 November 1904, he speaks of the impact of his letters not only on Franz Xaver Kappus but potentially, also, on us. He wonders whether his *letters* really have been of assistance. But he quickly adds: 'You must not answer: Yes, of course they are. Instead, receive them quietly and with not too many thanks, and let us, please, wait and see what may come of them'. He hopes that Franz 'may more and more come to have faith in whatever is hard and in your solitariness even among other people. And for the rest – you must let life have its way with you. Life is right in any event, believe me... As regards your emotions: every emotion that concentrates and exalts you is pure. What is impure is an emotion that takes hold of only one side of your nature, and will in consequence distort it... Whatever makes more of you than you have ever been before, even at your best times, is all that it should be. Every heightened moment is good if it suffuses all your blood, if it is not dark or drunken, if it is transparent and unclouded even in its depths'.

*   *   *

In the 'Appendix: Fourteen Notes on the Version' to his *Orpheus: A Version of Rainer Maria Rilke* (Faber, £12.99 hardback), **Don Paterson** talks very articulately and refreshingly about the difference between translations and versions. This Appendix is a highly interesting, inspiring manual for all would-be translators and version-makers. It analyses humbly, provocatively, originally and amusingly the whole process, with the complications involved, of attempting translations/versions. All translators/ version makers/poets are advised to buy this useful little book to keep for reference on their shelves. The following extracts are intended to whet your appetite for the complete piece in the original.

He speaks of the attempted fidelity to the original, its main aim being 'one of stylistic elegance (meaning, essentially, the smooth elimination of syntactic and idiomatic artefacts from the original tongue: a far more subtle project than it sounds)... It glosses the original but does not try to replace it'.

Versions, however, he claims, attempt to be poems in their own right. 'While they have the original to serve as detailed ground-plan and elevation, they are trying to build themselves a robust home in a new country, in its vernacular architecture, with local words for its brick and local music for its mortar'. Concomitant with this, he admits that they will have 'their *own* pattern of error and lyric felicity'.

Paterson reminds us that we must not forget the silences waiting to be translated behind every poem; indeed, Rilke's big claim was that he was trying to say the unsayable. He asserts that versions, in order to be real, 'must first reinhabit that extralinguistic silence the original poem once itself enjoyed – which is to say the poem must make a symbolic exit from language altogether. In this meditative space, its pattern of idea and image is reconsumed by its own strangeness, and when it re-emerges into language rediscovers itself in original speech'.

He advises that then allegiance must shift from the original source poem to your own subjective interpretation of them – to that 'wholly personal mandala of idea and image and spirit that floats free of the poem and resides, for a while, only in that symbolic mentalese that functions in an intercessory role in the line's reincarnation'.

An important point worth listening to is this: 'If you believe words to be indivisibly part-sound and part-sense, then lyric must also unite sense. Reciprocally, the words we choose to convey the most urgent sense automatically tend to exhibit a higher level of musical organisation. Lyric presents an additional strategy besides syntax to bind our words together'.

He continues: 'Poetry is just as interested in what words connote, however, and the overlap between their connotative haloes, their common feel, is often strongly manifest in shared features of their sounds'.

'Lyric unifies meaning as powerfully as does syntax. Indeed, since lyric is part-music, and music can draw sense from thin air, its use supplies the speech-meaning with precisely that additional music-sense'. He goes on to describe this 'music-sense' as 'intransitive', its meaning therefore 'utterly resistant to paraphrase', and concludes: 'Lyric unites the intransitive atmospheric and emotional sense of music with the transitive and paraphrasable senses of speech. Consequently, ... one can no more translate a poem than one can a piece of music'. This idea of translation being impossible is echoed (see Introduction to *'Translation as Metamorphosis'* issue of *Agenda*, Vol. 40, No. 4) in William Trask's words: 'Nothing is translateable. Therefore I translate'. Michael Hamburger also remarks in his book of essays, *Testimonies*, that translation is 'a heroic and a foolhardy act at the same time'.

Paterson adds to the above, perhaps, heroic approaches to getting on with the job, with his comment about trying to translate a poem which has no obvious plain sense, 'and its merits exist purely in its music, its "vibe" ... it cannot be translated other than through an act of faith. No one has agreed an exchange rate. The results might be terrific, but their "fidelity" is totally unverifiable'.

He proposes that 'fidelity' to a translation is as impossible as a translation itself. Trust is what is important, and versions can at least be 'trustworthy'.

He makes interesting points about rhyme and shows the pitfalls in clinging to a rhymed version or translation, particularly when the target language is poor in rhyme and has different rhyme patterns to the source language. As he avers, in an original poem, the form equals the content or subject matter, and vice versa, since 'form and content both are part of the same dynamic process'.

His warning is worth heeding: 'If the content tries to stay fixed, the rhymes will merely be *inflicted*, and will be a disaster. Rhyme is the insertion of a heavily foregrounded word at the end of the line which must usually be naturalised by everything that precedes it'.

In a version, that fluidity of sense implied by the rhyme 'has to be carefully negotiated. If rhymes are to be used ... *then some aspect of the content must change'*. Note the italics. Otherwise, he say, 'translationese' results and this is a recipe for failure. In other words, he bravely states (and many purist translators will disagree) that to imitate both form and content leads to disaster.

He cleverly puts in a nutshell: 'in translation, the integrity of the means justifies the end; in the version, the integrity of the end justifies the means'.

He concedes: 'the translation and the version can be thought of as separate parts of a linear sequence, the first expert operation, the second intuitive process – and they need not be carried out by the same organism'. Humbly, he adds – and I am sure most of us totally agree: 'the only incontrovertibly superior qualification is held by those who are both *genuinely* bilingual *and* gifted poets, but this skill-set is mere freakish coincidence' and examples of those with this 'superior qualification' are rare.

He concludes about the effect on a poet of writing versions: what it can both add to and subtract from the poet's own voice: 'Versioning allows a poet to disown their own voice and try on another. This voice might fit well, or might fit badly. When the poet returns to reclaim their old voice, it either no longer quite fits, or has altered, having apparently kept some strange company of its own in the meantime. Sometimes it has just disappeared. None of this is ever regretted'.

Biographies

Luis Benítez was born in Buenos Aires, Argentina in 1956. He is a very well-known, internationally established poet and has received numerous awards. His 9 books of poetry, 2 essays and 2 novels were published in Argentina, Chile, Mexico, Uruguay, USA and Venezuela. His latest book of poems is: *The Elephant's Afternoon and Other Poems* (Venezuela, 2006).

David Brooks, an Australian poet, fiction-writer and essayist, is also the editor of *Southerly*, the premier journal of Australian literature. His latest collections of poetry are *Walking to Point Clear* (2005, Brandl and Schlesinger) and *Urban Elegies* (2006, Island Press). He teaches at the University of Sydney and lives part of each year on the Slovenian coast, a short drive from Duino.

John Burnside's latest collection, *Gift Songs*, was published in March by Jonathan Cape, along with his novel *The Devil's Footprints*.

Elena Karina Byrne is a teacher, editor, Poetry Consultant and Moderator for *The Los Angeles Times* Festival of Books, and former 12-year Regional Director of the Poetry Society of America. She is now Literary Programs Director for the Ruskin Art Club and Museum of Contemporary Art. A ten-time Pushcart Prize nominee, her many recent publications include *Best American Poetry 2005*, *Yale Review*, *Paris Review*, *APR*, *Denver Quarterly*, *Ploughshares*, *Verse*, *Tri-Quarterly*, and *Poetry Daily Anthology*. Her books include: *The Flammable Bird* (Zoo, 2002, Tupelo); *Masque* ('07) and *The Fable Language* ('09) are forthcoming with Tupelo Press. Elena's work in progress includes *Voyeur Hour* and a collection of essays entitled *Insignificance*.

David Cooke was born in Cheshire. He graduated in English from London University and worked for a number of years for the Poetry Library in London. His poems have appeared in numerous poetry magazines including *Poetry Wales*, *Orbis*, *Stand* and *Babel*.

June English was born in Dover, Kent in 1936. Her first full-length collection, *The Sorcerer's Arc*, was published by Hearing Eye (London), in 2005. She is currently Poet in Residence to *Sing for Your Life Ltd*, an intergenerational scheme funded by the Sidney De Haan Research Centre for Arts and Health, Folkestone.

Angie Estes is the author of three collections of poetry, most recently *Chez Nous* (Oberlin College Press, 2005). Her second book, *Voice-Over* (2002) won the *FIELD* Poetry Prize and was also awarded the Alice Fay di Castagnola Prize from the Poetry Society of America. Her awards include a Pushcart Prize and a 2007 National Endowment for the Arts Fellowship in Poetry.

Antoinette Fawcett is half-Dutch. She has lived and worked in several different countries, including Holland, Norway and China but is now based in Cumbria. Her poems and translations have appeared in *Poetry Review*, *Poetry London*, *Acumen*, *Interpreter's House* and *Other Poetry* amongst others. She edits *Comet*, the newsletter of the Norman Nicholson Society, and was Creative Writing Tutor for the Norman Nicholson Project in 2005/6.

Roger Garfitt's *Selected Poems* are published by Carcanet. Lester Young is one of the *Presences of Jazz* he celebrates in performances with the John Williams Septet.

John Greening, born 1954, lives in Huntingdonshire. His most recent collection, *The Home Key*, was published by Shoestring. Another collection, *Iceland Spar*, is forthcoming. His studies of Yeats and Poets of the First World War were published by Greenwich Exchange. He is currently editing an anthology of poems about composers.

Paul Groves is the author of three full-length collections, most recently *Eros and Thanatos* (Seren, 1999). He has lectured in Creative Writing for over a decade, and lives near Monmouth.

Stuart Henson's most recent collections are *Ember Music* (Peterloo, 1994) and *A Place Apart* (Shoestring, 2004). A selection of his work also appeared in the *Oxford Poets 2002* Anthology.

Nicholas Jagger is a poet and artist living in Yorkshire. His work has appeared in *Agenda*, *HQ*, *Scintilla*, and *Stand*. He is currently working on a collection of poems based on Nietzsche's *Also Sprach Zarathustra*.

Judith Kazantzis has published ten collections of poetry including her *Selected Poems*, plus a novel, *Of Love And Terror*. Her latest collection is *Just After Midnight* (Enitharmon, 2004). She spent 2005–6 at Sussex University as Royal Literary Fund Fellow. See also www.writersartists.net

Edward Ragg is a poet and wine consultant. A selection of his poetry will shortly appear in Carcanet Press's *New Poetries IV* anthology. His poems have appeared in journals such as *PN Review*, *Agenda*, *Critical Quarterly* and *Aesthetica*. He is currently editing, with Bart Eeckhout, a book of essays on Wallace Stevens entitled *Wallace Stevens Across the Atlantic*. He lives in Bejing where he also teaches at Tsinghua University.

Stephen Shields is from Athenry, Ireland. A lover of dogs, he has worked as a lawyer and a boxing administrator. He began writing again with the Athenry Writers' Group and his prose and poetry has been published in various Irish magazines, including *The Cuirt Annual*, *West 47*, *Crannog* and *Markings*. He has been anthologised in *Turbulence: A Corrib Anthology and Splinters*. *Agenda* is his first assay into the world of British poetry.

Alexander Small comes from Strathaven (Stra`ven) in Lanarkshire, Scotland, and is a graduate of Edinburgh University, with Honours in English Language and Literature. He now lives in Orkney, where he works at one of its neolithic sites. Although he has been writing for some years, his work has appeared in only a few poetry magazines.

Paul Stubbs was born in 1970 and lives in Norwich. His first collection, *The Theological Museum*, was published by Flambard in 2005. He has translated Dante's *Paradiso* and works of Greek literature. His poems appear regularly in magazines, including *Poetry Review* and *The Shop* (Ireland).